THE ANGLO-ZULU WAR

New Perspectives

ZULULAND in 1879

Zululand in 1879

THE ANGLO-ZULU WAR

New Perspectives

Edited by
ANDREW DUMINY
CHARLES BALLARD

UNIVERSITY OF NATAL PRESS
Pietermaritzburg 1981

ISBN 0 86980 244 5

First published 1981
Reprinted, 1983, 1986, 1988

Typeset in the University of Natal Press
Printed by The Rapid Results College
Durban
South Africa

Contents

List of Maps

Cover picture: 'On the march to Ulundi', from *The Graphic*, with acknowledgements to the Killie Campbell Africana Library, Durban.

Glossary of Zulu Terms

All definitions of Zulu terms in this glossary are taken from C. de B. Webb and J. B. Wright (eds.), *The James Stuart Archive of Recorded Oral Evidence relating to the History of the Zulu and Neighbouring Peoples*, volume I (Pietermaritzburg, 1976), p.xxiii.

isAngoma (izAngoma)	diviner; one inspired or possessed by an ancestral spirit and employed to detect practitioners of witchcraft.
amaBele	sorghum; millet; grain.
inDuna (izinDuna)	civil or military official.
isiGodlo (iziGodlo)	king's or chief's private enclosure; women of the king's establishment.
iKhanda (amaKhanda)	major military centre.
iKhehla (amaKhehla)	man who has put on the headring; elderly man.
iKholwa (amaKholwa)	Christian.
ukuLobola	to formalize a marriage by the conveyance of cattle or other property from the man's family to the father or guardian of the woman.
iLobolo	cattle or goods handed over in a marriage transaction by the man's family to the father or guardian of the woman.

iMpi (iziMpi)	military unit or army; battle or war.
umNumzana (abaNumzana)	head of an *umuzi* or household.
ukuSisa	to place livestock in the care of a dependent, who then has certain rights of usufruct.
umuZi (imiZi)	homestead, collection of huts under one headman.

Note on Titles and Orthography

In opening the Centenary Conference on the Anglo-Zulu War at the University of Natal, Durban, in February 1979, the Chief Minister of KwaZulu, Chief Mangosuthu G. Buthelezi pointed out that most historians have depreciated the status of Zulu monarchs in comparison with titled or highly ranked Europeans. For example, 'King Cetshwayo' is usually referred to only as 'Cetshwayo' while 'Queen Victoria' remains 'Queen Victoria'. This seeming lack of sensitivity on the part of historians for Zulu reverence for royalty and etiquette may have been due to cultivated prejudice or neglect by some authors; but it is more likely the result of the recent trend in historical writing to streamline prose. The individual has been shorn of what may be called superfluous titles and Christian names except where necessary. Our editorial policy was to leave the question of titles to the individual contributors.

Various anomalies still exist with regard to Zulu orthography. Zulu linguists insist that 'Thukela' is the correct spelling, while 'Tugela' has passed into popular and widely accepted usage. The Chief of the Mandlakazi, 'Zibhebhu' is also spelled 'Zibephu' and 'Zibepu'. Linguists, however, all seem to agree that 'Isandhlwana' is incorrect and should be spelled 'Isandlwana'. Thus, Zulu orthography was in most cases left to the discretion of the contributors.

Contributors

Colin Webb
    King George V Professor of History, University of Cape Town

Norman Etherington
    Senior Lecturer in History, University of Adelaide, Australia

Bill Guest
    Senior Lecturer in History, University of Natal, Pietermaritzburg

Peter Colenbrander
    Lecturer in History, University of South Africa, Pretoria

Elaine Unterhalter
    Completing a doctorate at London University

Charles Ballard
    Lecturer in History, University of Natal, Durban

Jeff Guy
    Lecturer in History, National University of Lesotho, Roma

Andrew Duminy
    Associate Professor of History, University of Natal, Durban

ANDREW DUMINY
CHARLES BALLARD

Introduction

The Anglo-Zulu War of 1879 was inaugurated by a carefully stage-managed
meeting on the banks of the Tugela River on 11 December 1878 at which
King Cetshwayo of the Zulus was given an ultimatum which demanded
the dismantling of the Zulu 'military system'. The very foundations of
Zulu society rested upon this 'system', and for this reason alone the
harassed Zulu leaders could not be expected to comply. They found
themselves forced to prepare for a struggle for survival, in anticipation of
which the military preparations of Sir Bartle Frere, the British High
Commissioner, were already far advanced when the ultimatum was
delivered. In view of the concern which Cetshwayo and his advisors had
shown for maintaining good relations with the British High Commissioner
and with the 'white south', their puzzlement can be appreciated.

Given the disparity in military resources between the Zulus and the
British (assisted by Colonial volunteers and 'native levies'), the final
conquest of Zululand was a certainty, depending largely upon problems of
transport and supply being overcome. However, the invasion of Zululand
saw a series of military actions of unexpected severity. In January the
main advance from the west was temporarily checked when the Zulu
army inflicted a devastating defeat upon the British force at Isandlwana,
after which a now equally-famous attack was made upon the small military
post at Rorke's Drift. In the north, a detachment which had become
separated from the main army, was all but annihilated at Hlobane and,
in the south, the Zulus offered ferocious resistance. It was only after they
had lost the cream of their army among the 2 000 killed at Kambula and
after more than a thousand warriors lay dead before the 'wall of iron' at
Ulundi that they finally accepted defeat.

From one point of view, the Anglo-Zulu War was merely a chapter in the history of the South African frontier. The nineteenth century had seen almost continuous conflict on the Cape Colony's eastern frontier, where six major wars involving British troops had occurred since 1812, and the Orange Free State and Transvaal borders had also been notorious trouble spots. However, while it is true that the Anglo-Zulu War was but another episode in this continuing saga, there are grounds for arguing that it was quite distinct from these earlier conflicts, both in its causes and in its significance.

Earlier South African frontier wars were set against the background of land occupation and cattle theft. The basic cause of war was not the 'policy' of politicians or military strategists but the fact of inadequate governmental control over people who lived on the frontiers. Disputes thus multiplied to produce grievance and, eventually, conflict.

On the Cape's eastern frontier, the picture was greatly complicated by the activities of missionaries, who frequently championed the idea of extending the frontier in accordance with their 'civilizing' ambitions. A further complication was the presence of British settlers, whose numbers had been greatly increased as the result of the settlement of 1820. This community, which lived in very close proximity to the frontier, developed an understandable feeling of insecurity. Apart from being suspicious of the unfamiliar 'savage' and 'warlike' tribes which lived to the east, most of the settlers possessed a stern religious morality (most of them were Methodists) and were totally committed to the belief that 'progress' depended upon the genius of individuals, freely competing with each other. The British settler aimed to 'make good' in the country of his adoption and could see no justification for measures which impeded rather than applauded his flair for self-advancement. For many of them, the enclosure movement in Britain and the clearing of the Scottish Highlands was a recent (and for some a bitter) memory and they could see no reason why the frontier chiefdoms should be afforded special protection. To the British settler, in fact, the formal frontier appeared more and more as a barrier to progress. By the end of the 1830s, the experience of a frontier war, in which many of the settlers lost what they had laboriously built up over a period of fifteen years, shortened their tempers and sharpened their prejudices.

A third complication on the Cape's eastern frontier was the role of the British military. After the frontier war of 1812, an imperial garrison was based permanently in Graham's Town. Apart from patrolling the bush, the military soon assumed responsibility for the recovery of stolen cattle in place of commandos, composed of frontier farmers. While the motive behind this reform was to terminate the malpractices of the 'commando system', the new 'reprisals system' was a cause of as much, if not even greater unrest, for the military patrols could 'chastise' chieftains more effectively than had the commandos, which could only be summoned at times of exceptional and obvious need. The effect of military reprisals was, therefore, an increase in the rate at which the Xhosa and Thembu people were deprived of their cattle. In some cases, even in times of 'peace' (as for example occurred to Maqoma in 1829), offending chieftains were 'punished' by being expelled from the land which they occupied. Such activities contributed to land and food shortages and hence to open warfare, especially in times of drought. In addition to influencing the course of events in this day-to-day manner, the military understandably viewed the 'reprisals system' as no more than a stop-gap arrangement because the real cause of depredations seemed to lie across the frontier. Military men therefore readily fell in with plans to establish order by means of extending British rule eastwards and, thereafter, imposing controls by means of martial law.

Despite the influence of the missionary, the settler and the military, British policy on the Cape's eastern frontier — as formulated in the last resort by the Colonial Office, the British Treasury and ultimately the British Cabinet — remained that of limiting action and responsibility wherever possible. The story of the conquest of the Xhosa people is thus a lengthy piecemeal operation. While disunited chiefdoms sometimes settled down and attempted to adjust to what was for them a very rapidly changing world, more often there were periods of festering unrest which boiled up into major wars when they flung themselves at the advancing frontier. Committed to non-involvement as far as possible, the 'reluctant' British Empire saw itself as being *forced* into taking up arms by the 'perfidy' or the inherent war-lust of 'barbarous' Africans.

It is interesting that, during this period, the British government persisted in its reluctance to extend colonial frontiers in South Africa despite two other considerations, both of which affected the security of her southern African possessions. The first of these was the presence by 1840 of an increasing number of emigrant Boers, or trekkers, in the interior. It was obvious that their activities would create new areas of conflict and that the ramifications would be felt on the Cape's eastern frontier. The second was the presence *within* the colonial borders of a growing number of Nguni (especially Mfengu) people. In 1848 British Kaffraria was annexed and directly administered through the High Commissioner. This fact of 'native administration' obviously added a new dimension to the frontier problem, for it meant that the Colonial (and ultimately the British) government could not remain blind to the probability that happenings beyond the borders would affect the attitudes of blacks who fell under the colony's direct administration. In the interests of internal security, it seemed essential to destroy independent African polities which set white authority at defiance. As early as 1851, for example, in a letter to Richard Paver, Stockenström was arguing that the effect of the Colony's expansion across the Keiskamma (and her possible further expansion, at the conclusion of the war that was then raging, across the Kei), made it essential that the power of the Basutos and also the 'Zoolas' should be curbed. However, despite these pressing considerations, British involvement in Natal was half-hearted and, in 1853 when the Orange River Sovereignty was abandoned, commitment to action in the trekker-infested interior was dropped.

The Anglo-Zulu War of 1879 was obviously very different in origin from those earlier frontier wars. True, some of the ingredients were the same. There was, for example, a missionary presence in Zululand as there had been in Xhosaland. There was in Natal a vociferous British settler community with the same fears, prejudices, aggressions and economic vitality as the 1820 Cape community. Furthermore, there were in Natal large numbers of blacks under white administration and this, as in the Cape, caused anxious glances to be cast across the Tugela at the black society which lived there. But in one important respect there was a difference. This was that, whereas a complex system of inter-tribal relations operated amongst the Xhosa, there was in Zululand a system of relatively centralized control. This meant that, when frontier disputes between the Natal colony and Zululand arose, it was possible to negotiate directly with the Zulu King, and there was therefore no need, as in the eastern Cape, for the permanent presence of the British army.

Paradoxically, it was the existence of a stable and powerful government that contributed to the decision to conquer Zululand. By 1877 it seemed necessary, in the interests of a white-dominated British South African confederation, to destroy the Zulu 'military system'. In contrast to the other frontier wars, there was thus a *policy* decision to commence hostilities. This would not have been possible were it not that, by 1878, a perceptible change had taken place in Britain towards a more positive Southern African policy. Part of the explanation lies in the growing rivalry of the industrial powers in Europe. The investment of capital outside Europe also helped to stimulate imperialism because it created new pressures on governments to protect overseas investments. In southern Africa, the discovery of diamonds in Griqualand West sparked off a phase of industrial development, supported by foreign investment, and the later discovery of gold to the north in 1885 aroused visions of rapid expansion. From being the imperial poor relation, southern Africa could now be imagined as a region of immense economic potential. In this new industrial era, there arose a need to stabilize labour supplies and this seemed to require the destruction of independent African polities, together with their self-supporting economies.

At about the same time, significant breakthroughs occurred in armaments. In 1871 the British army officially adopted the breech-loading Martini-Henry rifle and also the Gatling machine gun. These weapons gave it a marked superiority in frontier warfare, even if in massed attacks spears and assegais were supplemented with now-outdated muzzle-loading guns.

While these developments, together with the personality of Lord Carnarvon at the Colonial Office, induced the British government to follow a policy of Confederation in South Africa, it may be doubted whether there would have been a translation of theory and ideal into positive action had it not been for the roles that were played by two individuals who were on the scene. The first, Sir Theophilius Shepstone, had himself hoisted the British flag in Pretoria in 1877. Despite his former expressions of sympathy for the Zulu people as Secretary for Native Affairs in Natal, he was to play a prominent part in the events which led to the ultimatum of December 1878. The other was Sir Bartle Frere who, after taking up the High Commissionership in March, 1877, supervised the conquest of the Transkei, following the outbreak of the last Cape frontier war. To Frere it seemed that the subjection of the Zulu was the logical sequel, both in the interests of white security in southern Africa generally and of restoring the rapidly-fading fortunes of confederation.

Given the new concern of the British government about southern African affairs and its endorsement of the move which Frere advocated (not always with honesty), it is not surprising that the Anglo-Zulu War made a greater impact on British party politics than had any of the previous southern African frontier wars. The cost to the British treasury far exceeded that of the earlier wars, and the loss of life suffered by Zulu and Briton was much higher than had been the case on the Cape's eastern frontier. The defeat and 'massacre' of British troops at Isandlwana came as a profound shock to the British public. The Anglo-Zulu War thus played its part in building up opposition in Britain to Disraeli's Conservative government and inaugurated a new phase in British political history, during which colonial events assumed greater prominence.

Indicative of this new public interest in Britain is the fact that the Anglo-Zulu War received far greater newspaper coverage than the earlier frontier Wars. To first-hand reports from professional reporters and part-time informants were added illustrations by war artists who were on the scene of battle. In addition, a steady stream of books on the subject began to appear almost before the last shots had been fired. A survey of the literature which has appeared during the last hundred years, shows that this public interest has not flagged. No less than 25 specialised studies dealing with the war as a whole or with aspects of it, have been published. In the earliest of these, British aggression in Zululand received rough treatment from the Colenso family. The Bishop condemned Imperial policy in a critique of the High Commissioner entitled *Bishop Colenso's Commentary on Frere's Policy in Zululand,* while Frances Colenso echoed her father's sentiments in her somewhat emotional *History of the Zulu War* and *The Ruin of Zululand.* The first contribution by a professional historian was Sir Reginald Coupland's *Zulu Battlepiece: Isandlwana* which appeared in 1948.

In 1965 Edgar Brookes and Colin Webb devoted three chapters of a *History of Natal* to the subject. A year later, Donald Morris's *Washing of the Spears* appeared. This book has become recognized as the definitive account of the war. It was followed in 1973 by two popular histories, unimaginatively entitled *The Zulu War*, one by Alan Lloyd and the other by David Clammer. Soldiers' letters formed the basis of Frank Emery's *The Red Soldier*, published in 1977. What was lacking was a Zulu perspective, until the recent publication of two works. One is the scholarly study of Jeff Guy, *The Destruction of the Zulu Kingdom.* The other work is that of the gifted author, Magema Fuze, who wrote *Abantu Abamnyama* over seventy years ago, the first book ever written by a Zulu in his own language. Fuze recalled his impressions of Zululand and so provides an alternative to the earlier accounts of the Zulu kingdom under King Cetshwayo's rule which had been written exclusively by whites. *Abantu Abamnyama* was published privately by Fuze in 1922. After being translated into English by the late Harry Lugg, as *The Black People*, and edited by Trevor Cope, it was published by the University of Natal Press in 1979. Interestingly, this work reveals that the Zulus, in viewing their own past, do not give the Anglo-Zulu War the same emphasis as do the 'conventional' histories, written by others.

The approach of the centenary of the Anglo-Zulu War in 1979 resulted in the appearance of more popular histories, biographies, centenary stamps, medallions and illustrations. The KwaZulu government and the Natal Provincial Administration sponsored commemorative ceremonies, honouring those on both sides who had fallen in battle. The intention was to promote a theme of reconciliation and mutual respect. These good intentions were to some extent marred by a tendency to adopt a 'popular' view, with an exaggerated emphasis on the 'glamour and the tragedy' of the war.

In view of the attention which so specialized a topic had already received, it could be doubted whether there was anything more to be said on the subject. However, with the aim of generating a more sober awareness among the public and the academic community, the Department of History at the University of Natal, Durban, convened a Conference in February 1979 entitled *The Anglo-Zulu War: A Centennial Reappraisal 1879–1979*. The response from the general public exceeded all expectations, with over two hundred and fifty delegates attending. Scholars with specialized knowledge of the various aspects of the period responded with no less enthusiasm than the public; sixteen historians, linguists and social anthropologists presented papers at what turned out to be one of the largest historical gatherings ever held in southern Africa. The papers reveal the extent to which the war remains the subject of debate. The collection of essays appearing in this volume is selected from the proceedings of the conference.

The current debate between the 'Liberal' and 'Radical' revisionist schools of southern African history has impinged itself squarely on interpretations of the Anglo-Zulu War period. Colin Webb analyses both schools for their flaws, strengths and different approaches with reference to examples from the war era. He issues a challenge to both 'Liberal' and 'Radical' to work to resolve their ideological dilemma. The alternative to co-operation, Webb warns, is a marked trend towards complete fragmentation in the ranks of historians.

Norman Etherington looks anew at Shepstone's 'coronation' of Cetshwayo KaMpande as King of Zululand in 1873. With the aid of missionary records and an exhaustive scrutiny of official sources, he charts the expansive drive of Shepstone to incorporate the Zulu Kingdom into the economic and political vortex of a south-eastern Africa which would be firmly under British Imperial and colonial rule. Peter Colenbrander surveys the political economy of the Zulu kingdom up to the eve of the war. This analysis of the Zulu resource base and the political control of resource distribution in the form of land, livestock and women suggests that, in the Zululand of the 1860s and 1870s, class tensions were heightened by an increasing shortage of the material means of life. Colenbrander's assessment tends to refute any suggestion that the pre-war structure of Zulu society and economy was static and rigid.

Across the Tugela River on the southern boundary of Zululand lay the British colony of Natal. In 1879 it had a white settler population of 23 000 and an African population that numbered between 200 000 and 250 000 inhabitants. The colonial response to the war is examined by Bill Guest. This small settler society was prone to view the Zulu Kingdom as a threat to its security. Through a content analysis of settler opinion reflected in the colonists' newspapers, letters and papers, Guest concludes that the Natal settlers lacked any real enthusiasm or ardour for a war with the Zulu kingdom. The orchestrations for war emanated from Frere, the Crown's agent, with settler sentiment for war following in the High Commissioner's wake. Guest illustrates the fear and panic generated among the settlers by the disastrous defeat at Isandlwana. Only when the lives and property of whites appeared to be directly threatened by an expected Zulu invasion of Natal did the settler community throw its energies into the war effort.

A most original case-study of the impact of the 1879 British invasion on a particular district in Zululand is contributed by Elaine Unterhalter. The Nquthu district in south-western Zululand was devastated by Imperial and Colonial troops. The people of Nquthu saw their cattle confiscated, their crops and kraals looted and burned. The catalogue of atrocities perpetrated by the British forces reminds us that war is an ugly and inhumane exercise with much tragedy but little 'glamour'. More importantly, Unterhalter shows how the political and economic structure of Zulu society in the Nquthu district was disrupted by pillage and conquest, and how the resilient Zulu social system survived in the immediate post-war period and blunted the challenges posed by the appointed Chief, the alien Hlubi.

The post-war settlement of Zululand is examined from two distinct aspects. First, Charles Ballard delves into the prejudices and personalities of Sir Garnet Wolseley and the white frontiersman, Chief John Dunn, and relates them to the metropolitan policy and to colonial settler and missionary attitudes toward a defeated Zululand. What emerges is a scenario of Wolseley's scheme to rule Zululand indirectly through appointed puppet chiefs, amenable to the will of the British government. Dunn's pervasive influence over Wolseley is illustrated in the terms of the Ulundi treaty — namely, the permanent exile of King Cetshwayo and the exclusion of white settlers and missionaries. The second study focuses on the activities of Natal colonial officials in post-war Zululand. These are documented and analysed by Jeff Guy. Much of the internecine strife that emerged between the royalist Usutu and the opposing factions of Zibhebhu and Hamu was the result of the manipulations of Natal officials opposed to Cetshwayo's restoration.

The historian's most challenging task is to portray history in convincingly relevant terms. By linking the past one hundred years of Zulu history with the present, a greater appreciation of one's own historical and cultural heritage may be realized. The growing cultural consciousness of the Zulu people was demonstrated by Chief Mangosutho G. Buthelezi, the Chief Minister of KwaZulu, who opened the Conference. A direct descendant of Chief Mnyamana Buthelezi, a commander-in-chief of the Zulu army during the Anglo-Zulu War, he is also descended on his mother's side from King Cetshwayo himself. Chief Buthelezi pleaded for a 'Zulu approach' to Zulu history, arguing that much that has been written is the result of the attempt to 'dramatise and justify the rape of Zululand', and is based upon the observations of biased foreign observers. To restore the balance and to arrive at a more accurate picture, attention should be paid to oral tradition and to black perspectives. Relating the Zulu experience to the present, he said:

'We went through our dark days of despair, we experienced hope-lessness but we arrived to believe in a new South Africa.... An important difference between a black and white perspective of South African history is that a white perspective looks at yesterday as it leads to today. In the black perspective, we see yesterday and today leading to tomorrow.'

COLIN WEBB

The Origins of the Anglo-Zulu War: Problems of Interpretation

During and after the war of 1879, Cetshwayo protested that he did not understand why the British had attacked his kingdom. A century later, there are reasons for doubting whether we have yet found the answer, though our uncertainties are very different from those which filled the Zulu king's mind. He lacked information; we possess it in great abundance – such abundance that it appears to support confusingly discrepant interpretations.

Thirty or forty years ago the position was simpler. Asked to explain why Britain attacked the Zulu, most South African historians (though even at that stage not all)[1] would have spoken with one voice. The fundamental issue, they would have said, was the incompatibility of a barbarous and warlike kingdom with civilized and peace-loving neighbouring states. True, the final impetus to war came not from the Zulu, but from the High Commissioner in South Africa, Sir Bartle Frere. True, too, his ultimatum was a response, not to any specific Zulu threat, but rather to a series of essentially trivial Zulu 'offences'. Nevertheless, paltry though the offences were, they were indicative of the larger problem. They reflected the overbearing, innately aggressive attitude of the Zulu to the civilized states now ringing them round. Had Frere not forced on the war when he did, the struggle in the end would almost certainly have been fought, not on Zulu soil, but 'among the homesteads of Natal and the Cape Colony'; for the problem, at root, was 'whether the rule of law or the rule of the assegai was to prevail . . . . If Africa was to be civilized, war with the Zulus at some stage was . . . inevitable.'[2]

Scholarly orthodoxies once established die hard! The origins of the one just summarised are to be found in the historiography of the late nineteenth century, from which beginnings it endured for more than the allotted three score years and ten.[3]

In the 1960s, however, a markedly different assessment of the origins of the war began to gain ground with a spate of new literature on Natal and Zulu history, and a major new work on British policy in South Africa in the 1870s.[4] Its exponents were historians who would probably now (with the current fashion for categorisation) be labelled members of the 'liberal school'. Sceptical about determinist explanatory formulae, deferring instead to a philosophy of free will and individual moral responsibility, they questioned the view that the war of 1879 was to be explained in terms of the 'unavoidable' clash of 'barbarism' with 'civilization'. The incontrovertible fact, in their judgment, was not that 'barbarism' and 'civilization' were incompatible. (The very words were too subjective to be serviceable tools.) The incontrovertible fact was that war between the British and the Zulu started at a specific moment in this country's history, and having started then brought with it a train of consequences which would not have been reduplicated had it occurred under different conditions at some other time.

What was needed, therefore, was a much closer examination than had hitherto been made of the specific circumstances that gave rise to the war.

The results of these investigations included some disconcerting findings. For one thing, it appeared that the Zulu were far less of a threat to their colonial neighbours than had commonly been supposed. If they wore an aggressive look after Cetshwayo's accession in 1872, this was largely because of an unresolved border dispute with the neighbouring Transvaal. But this was an issue that was capable of resolution without a British attack on the Zulu kingdom: indeed, the dispute was only indirectly of the Zulu's own making. When, in the first half of 1878, the matter was investigated by a boundary commission, the Transvaal's case was found to rest on dubious evidence. The confirmation of Zulu rights over most of the disputed territory was therefore recommended, and the way lay open for the removal of the most important cause of tension and anxiety underlying the Zulu's apparently hostile stance.

The argument that war was unavoidable because of the innate aggressiveness of the Zulu was thus, on investigation, shown to be untenable. The threat to the peace of south east Africa came, in the first instance, not from the Zulu kingdom, but from the Transvaal; and if British power had been used to restore Zulu territorial rights the way would have been open for a return to the conditions of peaceful co-existence which had characterised the Zulu kingdom's relations with its neighbours through most of the preceding half century.

As a matter of historical fact, however, that was not how British power had been used. On the contrary, it had been used to destroy the Zulu kingdom. And for the revisionist historians this, in turn, was an aspect of the situation requiring most careful scrutiny.

What was required was a shifting of the spotlight sharply on to Frere. His role in precipitating the war had long been known: the decision to attack the Zulu kingdom had not been taken by the British government; it had been taken by Frere in defiance of the British government's expressed desire to avoid war in South Africa at that moment. His motives for acting as he did had not, however, been adequately probed by historians of the old orthodoxy. Accepting the thesis that the Zulu kingdom was a standing menace to its white neighbours, they had argued that Frere, with his feet firmly planted on South African soil, was far more vividly aware than his superiors in London of the imminence of the Zulu threat. Perceiving the British government's failure to comprehend the danger, and being advised of its unwillingness to authorise military operations, he had no option in the end but to go it alone; and in doing so launched a war which, while unwanted in London, was nevertheless essential for the security of South Africa.

With the research undertaken by the revisionists, this feature of the old orthodoxy crumbled too. Evidence emerged indicating a strong measure of disingenuity in Frere's protestations of concern about the *imminence* of the Zulu menace. His real concerns, it appeared, were focussed elsewhere, and were the product of developments across a broad front in the months after his assumption of the South African High Commissionership.[6]

Basic to this reassessment was the fact that Frere's appointment was no run-of-the-mill Colonial Office posting. On the contrary, he had been carefully selected because the Secretary of State for the Colonies, Lord Carnarvon, was seeking a man with the experience and ability − the qualities of statesmanship − to bring into being a great new British dominion in the form of a federation of the South African states and colonies.[7] For Frere, the challenge was immense. He was facing the crowning moment of his career: an opportunity to secure a place in history as one of the great constructive proconsuls of empire; and (important, too, seeing that the smallness of his private fortune was a worry to him) an opportunity to win the honours and rewards that would assure him a comfortable and respectable position in society after retirement.[8]

His assumption of the South African High Commissionership had in it, thus, a large investment of personal interest. Yet almost from the start his mission was blighted.

Within a couple of weeks of his arrival in South Africa, Britain annexed the Transvaal, believing that the extinction of the independence of a troublesome Afrikaner republic would ease the way forward to federation. In fact, the annexation was a blunder — one of the major blunders committed by Britain in South Africa during the nineteenth century.[9] The Boers proved fractious, recalcitrant, potentially rebellious subjects. Elsewhere in South Africa there was sympathy for their cause and, commensurately, antipathy to a federation policy which, it now seemed, was to be forced through by high-handed acts of power politics. In the Cape, this antipathy was reinforced by other considerations, most notably by reluctance to link up with the states of the interior until their domestic and frontier problems had been resolved. And in the Free State the mood was even more unsympathetic; for there, two earlier acts of British interventionism (the annexation of Basutoland in 1868 and the annexation of the Diamond Fields in 1871) had turned opinion sharply against collaboration with the imperial power.[10]

The task facing Frere was, thus, as delicate as it was difficult. Before a start could be made with inter-state discussions of the spiny constitutional problems which federation would entail, white opinion across the length and breadth of South Africa had to be wooed. For that, patient endeavour was needed. But Frere, from the start, found himself distracted by a succession of wars and disturbances along South Africa's unsettled frontiers.

To make matters worse, he began to lose the strong backing he needed in London. In January 1878, Carnarvon, the grand designer of the federation scheme, resigned from office, and was replaced by Sir Michael Hicks Beach, an earnest and well-intentioned man, but a man new to colonial affairs and lacking Carnarvon's forceful devotion to the federation cause.[11] At the same time, problems in the international field began adversely to affect Frere's position and prospects. Britain had been drawn into two major international crises — one in the Balkans, the other in Afghanistan. Both aroused intense public concern and, as the international outlook darkened so, inevitably, South African affairs (federation included) were pushed lower and lower down the scale of imperial priorities.[12]

In effect, therefore, Frere found himself increasingly on his own — committed to a great task of colonial reconstruction, but without the strong and enthusiastic headquarters' support that he had been able to count on when he took up the job.

Then came the biggest blow of all. In the first half of July 1878, there arrived on his desk the report of the commissioners appointed to investigate the Transvaal-Zulu border dispute, and at one turn he found himself being pushed on to a path which was bound to lead to the ruin of the great enterprise to which he had committed the last years of his official career. Basic to the success of the whole endeavour was the task of convincing the white communities of the beneficence of the British paramountcy under which they would be embraced if they agreed to federate. But now, lying before him, was a boundary recommendation — in favour of the Zulu and against the Boers — which, if implemented, would define Britain in exactly the opposite role: not as benefactor of settler interests, but as patron of black rights. Throughout South Africa, white opinion would be alienated; in the Transvaal, there would probably be armed revolt. One way or the other, federation would be consigned to the grave; and his own career, instead of moving to a success-laden finale, would write itself out in derelict failure.[13]

Not surprisingly, therefore, a switch in emphasis is discernible in Frere's correspondence after July 1878. Previously, he had adverted to the Zulu relatively infrequently — mainly in connection with his conviction (fed and fattened by exchanges with the Administrator of the Transvaal, Sir Theophilus Shepstone) that a conspiracy was afoot among the African chiefs and that 'peace and freedom from aggressive wars' would be unattainable until British supremacy had been established throughout southern Africa.[14] Now, after receipt of the report of the boundary commission, the Zulu kingdom moved obsessively to the very forefront of his mind. At the same time, his consultations with Shepstone became closer. It was a fateful combination of intelligences. Shepstone, uneasy about the over-crowding of the Natal locations, had long advocated the acquisition of Zululand as a dumping-ground for the colony's 'surplus' Africans.[15] Now he, like Frere, had an additional reason for desiring the extinction of Zulu independence; for the ratification of Zulu territorial rights in the disputed area would infinitely complicate his already difficult assignment as Administrator of the Transvaal.[16]

Two men, whose careers were threatened with failure thus moved into harness together, and Frere's reports to London about future relations with the Zulu kingdom suddenly took on a much more bellicose tone.[17] He himself never accounted for this switch — perhaps because no one ever challenged him to do so. But there can be little doubt where the explanation lies. He needed a war with the Zulu — and he needed it quickly — if the dangerous boundary award was to be rendered irrelevant. Once the Zulu kingdom had been defeated and demolished in war, its territorial rights would cease to be an issue. What would be at issue would be a completely new settlement in south-east Africa. If that were carefully managed to serve white interests, then at last there might be some prospect of winning the loyalty of the Transvaal Boers, and converting the rest of white South Africa to a more favourable view of confederation.

That, in outline, is the explanation of the origins of the war developed by the revisionist historians. Unlike the older orthodoxy, it is based on detailed scrutiny of evidence; and it has a further very obvious advantage in that it accounts for Frere's insubordination in forcing on hostilities against the wishes of the British government.[18] Try as they might, this was a feature of the situation which the earlier historians had been unable to explain. Granted that war with the Zulu was, in their opinion, unavoidable — that it was bound to be fought sooner or later — that still did not enable them to explain Frere's determination to precipitate hostilities in the summer of 1878-9 regardless of the wishes of the men in London. To that problem there was now an answer: he could not defer to their wishes once he had received the report of the boundary commission — not unless he himself was to preside over the death-agonies of the confederation scheme.

The picture, thus, is a highly individualised one of a man committed to a great project of constructive statemanship, then finding himself trapped by circumstances and deciding to cut through to a solution by the drastic expedient of a resort to arms.

The very fact that the revisionist version is so personalised, however, has produced a reaction. It dates from 1974, the centenary of Carnarvon's assumption of control at the Colonial Office, but does not involve any serious disagreement with the detailed findings of the revisionists about the roles played by Carnarvon and his underlings, Frere and Shepstone. On the whole these are accepted. What is demanded, however, is a *radical* alteration of view-point.[19] For events of the magnitude of the Anglo-Zulu war are not, in the opinion of the new 'radical' critics, to be explained by 'the personal preoccupations' of individual men. Such preoccupations may explain 'the precipitating causes of conflict', but they ignore the 'underlying structure' which shaped the intentions of these men. The fault with the revisionists was that they concentrated on the performance of the actors, without pausing to investigate what the play itself was all about. As a result, they got things badly wrong. Taking the name of the play — 'Confederation' — at face value, they failed to perceive that the political plot rested on a much more important economic sub-plot, to be summarised for convenience as 'the advance of capitalist production in southern Africa'.

With the sub-plot recognised, the whole picture changes. It becomes clear that the truly critical moment for the Zulu was not Carnarvon's appointment to the Colonial Office, nor Frere's selection for the post of High Commissioner, nor even the arrival on Frere's desk of the findings of the boundary commission. The truly critical moment was the discovery of diamonds in South Africa in the late 1860s. From that moment forward, there was in Griqualand West a burgeoning capitalist industry, which as it developed generated a host of new problems that could best be handled by inter-state agencies. Moreover, the very existence of that industry had two other effects: it exposed the weaknesses of the South African economic infrastructure, and it held out promise of great new wealth — wealth which, if centrally deployed, could be used to strengthen the infrastructure and generate a phase of unprecedented growth.

Thus, when Frere was appointed to South Africa, his assignment was not that which the liberal revisionists had supposed. True, he was to create a new political order. But, in concrete terms, the objective was an order appropriate to the needs of *developing capitalism*, and as soon as the Zulu kingdom proved an obstacle to the achievement of that end, its destruction became the obsessive object of his policy.

Judged from the position of the revisionists, the wheel it seems has turned full circle — or almost so. Once again the explanation of the war is being sought in a conflict of systems rather than in the unique particularity of Frere's personality and the circumstances that faced him in 1878. The very phrases of the historians of the old orthodoxy can, it seems, be picked up and, with appropriate verbal modifications, be used again: '... fundamentally the problem was whether capitalist enterprise was to prevail ... If Africa was to be furnished with an industrial economy, war with the Zulu at some stage was ... inevitable.'

What then are the implications? Is a new gulf opening up, as wide and unbridgeable as that which separated the revisionists from their predecessors? The answer hopefully is 'No', though much will depend on the precision with which the two sides phrase their arguments in future. To date, all that is available from the pens of the 'radicals' is a couple of essays challenging the 'liberal' interpretation of the origins of the war and outlining their own alternative view-point; but embedded in those essays are ambiguities of formulation which leave open the question how wide the divide will eventually be.

If the authors are saying (as they seem to be in certain passages)[20] that the *motives of the men* who initiated the war must be seen within the framework of an attempt to construct a federal South Africa in which capitalist production would be facilitated, the gap will probably narrow to the point of eventually closing; for the revisionists (though they expressed themselves badly, too) held a broadly similar view. Naively, no doubt, they formulated their statements about the framework of action in simple political terms. But implicit in those formulations was an unexpressed economic assumption: that Carnarvon and Frere, when they talked of creating a powerful new dominion in South Africa, had in mind a state supported by a strong economy — and a strong economy, in the context of the times, was bound to be conceived in capitalist terms. The difference thus lies in emphasis and expression rather than philosophical position.

But the path to agreement may, in the end, be a lot more difficult than that; for the radicals, at certain moments, seem to be moving on a different track. They seem to be saying that capitalism caused the war — in the sense that it was the *needs* of developing capitalism that pushed Carnarvon and Frere on to the course that ended in conflict with the Zulu.[21] The distinction, at first glance, may seem casuistical. On closer scrutiny, it is not. The dictum 'capitalism caused the war' asserts the primacy of the impersonal forces of the system over individual will and intelligence. Carnarvon and Frere bending to the demands of the developing capitalist system are different creatures from Carnarvon and Frere, operating within the economic framework of their times and judging it to be for the 'good' to construct a South African federation in which capitalist enterprise could flourish.

Two worlds are before us: one a world of individual judgment and will; the other a world of economic imperatives. If it is the latter which the radicals occupy, the prospects of agreement are slim.

Although liberals recognise that men may, from time to time, bend to economic necessity, they argue that this is not always so. As often as not, the reverse is true: men bend the economic system to their own ends, exploiting the opportunities which it provides to pursue goals which they regard as 'good'. Each case has to be individually examined. Thus, before there can be any acceptance of the dictum 'capitalism caused the war', the radicals must (if that dictum expresses their views) produce the empirical data: they must identify, with supporting evidence, the economic imperatives that were at work in the 1870s; and they must demonstrate the transmission system through which those imperatives were personalised in the wills of Carnarvon and Frere. In plain terms, they must show that Carnarvon and Frere were responding to specific pressure emanating from within the capitalist system.

To judge from the most authoritative study of confederation to date, these demands will be difficult to meet. One of the more notable features of the evidence relating to Carnarvon's career is that it points to a negative conclusion: he arrived at his decision to federate South Africa *without* any significant pressures from definable interest groups.[22] With continuing research, the picture may, of course, change. New evidence may emerge indicating economic needs or pressures that have not so far been identified. But, if that should happen, the demands of the liberals will remain essentially unchanged. They will argue that there can be no simple ascription of the war to the capitalist system unless the newly identified economic pressures can be shown to have been *more* influential in shaping the purposes and actions of Carnarvon and Frere than the political and personal interests already identified; and they will ask for a precise evaluation of the operation of these forces.

How this challenge will be handled remains for the moment, an open question. What is clear, however, from similar historical debates in other fields, is that an inability to meet the demands of the liberals will not necessarily destroy the radical position. Its defenders may admit the ambiguity (perhaps even the inaccuracy) of phraseology suggesting that the war resulted from the *needs* of developing capitalism; but, having admitted that, they may nevertheless argue that 'capitalism caused the war'. Properly understood, they may say, that expression does not mean that Carnarvon and Frere were acting under pressures emanating from the economic system. Properly understood, it means that their actions were informed by purposes, apparently freely devised, but in fact shaped by the *values* inherent in the prevailing capitalist order; and of that, they may add, there could be no clearer proof than the assumption, held by both men, that the greatest good was to be served, not by respecting the rights of either Boers or Zulu, but by creating a new South Africa in which the forces of capitalist enterprise would have freer play.

At that point further consideration of the war of 1879 as an event in itself ceases to be possible: discussion has moved into the realm of general theories about the nature of man in society. Nevertheless, it is here that the liberal and radical positions become firmly defined.

The view that men's values are shaped by the societies of which they are part causes no dispute. Where disagreement does arise is on the question whether or not it is possible to identify the factors that shape a society's values, and more particularly, whether or not a hierarchy of influences can be established, with primacy of place going to the productive forces. Claims that this is so have, over many years, been strongly disputed by liberals — on the grounds, once again, of inadequate evidence. Today the position is different. Some liberals, acting on 'hunch' rather than the persuasiveness of the evidence, are willing to concede primacy of place in the shaping of societal values to the underlying system of production.

Nevertheless, having moved to this position, liberals would still hold back from endorsing statements suggesting that capitalism caused the war; for such statements, in their judgment, would be a distortion of reality, over-emphasizing the role of the capitalist value system and doing so to no good end. An event such as the war of 1879 — the conquest and subordination of a militarily weaker society by a militarily stronger one — is not a phenomenon unique to a capitalist order. Similar events have occurred throughout history wherever economic power is structured politically, and inequalities of power exist. Why, then, emphasize capitalism as the cause of war? The causes of war lie only remotely in the values associated with a particular economic order; conflict emanates directly from the wills and purposes, the predicaments, problems and ambitions, of men wielding the instruments of structured power. Gazing fixedly at the former (the value system) reveals little more than we already know: that men's actions are informed by the values of their times. Looking closely at the latter (individual wills and purposes) may yield a little more wisdom than we presently possess by extending awareness of the manifold ends to which power may be turned.

As with the problem of the hedgehog and the fox, so here, the liberals would argue, the issue is whether we wish to know one big thing, which in the end may tell us very little, or whether we wish to know many little things, which in the end may tell us very much. Granted the primacy of the productive forces in shaping societal values; granted further that men formulate their purposes in terms of the values of the society to which they belong: nevertheless, those purposes remain too subtle and complex to be subsumed under labels and formulae expressing predominantly economic ends. To employ such labels is to simplify to the point of parody. Unquestionably, it is right to set historical events in context by taking cognizance of prevailing values and assumptions. Thus, in the case under consideration, it is correct to point out that Carnarvon and Frere would have assumed without question that a federated South Africa would be supported by capitalist enterprise which would take advantage of the country's cheap and abundant black labour supply. That was part of the context of thought in which they operated. But to elevate context to the position of prime cause of any event is to place explanation on a level of such generality that it ceases to be informative. Arguing that capitalism (in the form of the capitalist value system) caused the Anglo-Zulu war is as unedifying as arguing that feudalism (in the form of the feudal value system) caused the Norman conquest of England. Particular events cannot be explained by general conditions. Particular events require particular explanations, and particular explanations can only be constructed by detailed examination of the evidence relating to the intentions and purposes of the participants.

A retreat into general theories about the nature of man in society thus fails to eliminate disagreement between radical and liberal. On the contrary, it demonstrates more positively than ever that the debate turns on the question of hard, intellectually persuasive data.

NOTES

1   The most notable exception was C.W. de Kiewiet. See his *The Imperial Factor in South Africa* (Cambridge, 1937), ch. X.

2   C. Headlam, 'The Failure of Confederation' in *Cambridge History of the British Empire*, vol. VIII (London, 1963), pp.485–6.

3   An early example of the incorporation of the orthodoxy into the textbook literature is Robert Russell, *Natal: the Land and its Story* (Pietermaritzburg, 1896), pp.220–4. A late example is A.N. Boyce, *A History for South African Schools* (Cape Town and Johannesburg), p.405. Probably influential in perpetuating this view-point was George McCall Theal's *History of South Africa from 1873 to 1884*, vol.1 (London, 1919), ch. XIII.

4   Representative examples of the work of the revisionists are: C.T. Binns, *The Last Zulu King* (London, 1963); E.H. Brookes and C.de B. Webb, *A History of Natal* (Pietermaritzburg, 1965), ch.XIII; Donald R. Morris, *The Washing of*

the Spears (London, 1966), pp.266–91; and C.F. Goodfellow, *Great Britain and South African Confederation. 1870–1881* (Cape Town, 1966).

5   For a full discussion of the report of the boundary commission see R. L. Cope, 'Shepstone and Cetshwayo, 1873–79' (University of Natal, unpublished M. A. thesis, 1967), ch. 13.

6   For a discussion of these developments, see C. F. Goodfellow, *Great Britain and South African Confederation. 1870–1881* (Cape Town, 1966), chs. 7, 8, and 9; and De Kiewiet, op.cit., chs. vi, vii, viii.

7   J. Martineau, *Life of Sir Bartle Frere*, vol. II (London, 1895), pp. 161–2.

8   Martineau, op.cit., pp.162–3 and 392–3; see also Goodfellow, op.cit., p.123.

9   For Frere's views on the annexation see Martineau, op.cit., pp. 183–4 and 186.

10 See Headlam, op.cit., in *Cambridge History of the British Empire*, vol. VIII, pp.479–82; Goodfellow, op.cit., chs. 5, 6 and 8; De Kiewiet, op.cit., ch. vi.

11 For Frere's reaction to the news of Carnarvon's resignation see Martineau, op.cit., p.219.

12 Lady Victoria Hicks Beach, *Life of Sir Michael Hicks Beach*, vol.I (London, 1932), pp.97–104.

13 Frere's response to the report of the boundary commission is fully discussed in Cope, op.cit., pp.330–42.

14 Martineau, op.cit., pp.223–35, and Cope, op.cit., pp.319–24.

15 Cope, op.cit., pp.15–16.

16 Natal Archives, Shepstone Papers, Case 7, Letterbook 3, pp.130–1: Shepstone to Frere, 12.10.78.

17 The change of tone can be traced in the correspondence published in British Parliamentary Papers C.2220, December 1878, and C.2222, February 1879.

18 For a discussion of Frere's insubordination see Brookes and Webb, op.cit., pp.130–1; and C.de B. Webb, 'Lines of Power – the High Commissioner, the Telegraph and the War of 1879', *Natalia*, 8 (December 1978), pp.31–7.

19 A. Atmore and S. Marks, 'The Imperial Factor in South Africa in the Nineteenth Century: Towards a Reassessment', *Journal of Imperial and Commonwealth History*, vol.III, 1 (October 1974), pp.120–7.

20 See, e.g. *Reality*, January 1979, pp.8–9, where in an article entitled 'The British Invasion of Zululand: Some Thoughts for the Centenary Year' Jeff Guy writes: 'In its most fundamental terms the Zulu kingdom was invaded to facilitate the advance of capitalist production in southern Africa; it is within this framework that we have to understand the individual motives and actions of the men who initiated the war . . . . By his confederation scheme Carnarvon hoped to break down the political divisions between the British colonies, Boer republics, and independent African states and communities. Once this was done, and the people of southern Africa brought under centralised control, it would be possible to build the infrastructure needed for more effective exploitation of southern Africa's wealth.'

21 Ibid., p.12, where the following appears: 'As I have stated above, the framework in which the war must be seen is the *needs* of developing capitalism in southern Africa. This *required* a single political and administrative system which allowed greater control, more efficient communication, and the free flow of labour on the sub-continent.' (Italics mine).

22 C.F. Goodfellow, op.cit., pp.210–11, 216 and passim.

NORMAN ETHERINGTON

Anglo-Zulu Relations 1856 - 1878

The Anglo-Zulu War has long been a war buff's favorite because it seems to lack so many of the features which make war hateful to the rest of us. There were no flagrant attacks on non-combatants, no concentration camps, very little rape and pillage, only a little annexation of territory. On the other hand there is a great deal to gladden martial spirits: incredible bravery against overwhelming odds shown by soldiers on both sides; cunning generalship, regimental loyalty, manly comradeship and self-sacrifice. The war's general popularity has been boosted by an apparent absence of a crassly materialistic *casus belli*. Some still blame the war on the inability of the magnificently anachronistic Zulu monarchy to live in peace with nineteenth-century progress. But for most historians it is more appropriate to lay the blame on Sir Bartle Frere, Britain's High Commissioner and a perfect scapegoat. When a bully with a black hat and moustache is caught with a smoking gun in his hand, posses and juries don't ask very penetrating questions. Neither, it is embarrassing to admit, do historians.

Frere was the sort of villain cinema audiences love to hate, a sanctimonious, pig-headed, officious, self-righteous, ambitious city slicker from out of town. In his treatment of the Zulu-Transvaal boundary dispute Frere resembles nothing quite so much as the sinister banker of western movies who uses legal technicalities to bamboozle honest ranchers out of water holes or oil wells. After a panel of upright local citizens pronounced in favor of the Zulu claim, Frere first suppressed their report and then released it with outrageous conditions attached. The Zulus, he said, could keep the title and the Transvaalers could keep the land. He went on to lay down the conditions on which Cetshwayo would be allowed to save his own land from foreclosure by British troops. No black-hatted banker ever laid down more impossible conditions or set a shorter deadline for compliance.

One hundred years after the event there is no reason to revise this estimate of Frere and award him a retrospective white hat and a shave. But there are excellent reasons for establishing the Anglo-Zulu war in a much broader context. It was no more Frere's war than the Boer War was Milner's war or World War I was Kaiser Bill's war. The objects for which the war was fought were of vital importance to the creation of modern South Africa. Frere, like the black-hatted banker he resembles, acted on behalf of a syndicate. Because he cited Shepstone's coronation of Cetshwayo in 1873 as a partial justification of his ultimatum to the Zulu people, it is worthwhile to look again at the long course of Anglo-Zulu relations which produced the coronation and its aftermath.

Frere recognised that in the final accounting his right to invade Zululand was grounded only on an elemental 'right of self-preservation'.[1] He undertook what modern practitioners of war would call a 'pre-emptive first strike'. But lacking any convincing evidence of Cetshwayo's supposed aggressive designs, Frere offered as secondary justifications the king's breaking of 'laws' allegedly proclaimed by Shepstone at the coronation, namely:

1st   That indiscriminate shedding of blood should cease in the land.
2nd   That no Zulu shall be condemned without open trial and the public examination of witnesses for and against, and that he shall have a right of appeal to the King.
3rd   That no Zulu's life shall be taken without the previous knowledge and consent of the king, after such trial has taken place, and the right of appeal has been allowed to be exercised.
4th   That for minor crimes the loss of property, all or a portion, shall be substituted for the punishment of death.[2]

To prove that Cetshwayo had failed in enforcing these conditions, Frere relied on the evidence of the 'the English and Norwegian missionaries who left Zululand to avoid expulsion'.[3] His ultimatum of 1878 demanded that their rights be guaranteed along with the rights of other Europeans, that certain civil liberties and internal peace be given to the Zulu people, that the status of disputed territory along the Transvaal border be settled and that the Zulu military machine be dismantled.[4] This account will, therefore, be looking carefully at missionaries, the internal condition of the kingdom, and the question of the disputed territory. The evidence supporting the account comes mostly from religious and official sources which are tainted by various special interests, but in most cases these interests can be precisely identified and appropriate allowances made. Witnesses from the Zulu side are, as always, sparse and inevitably mediated by white reporters, translators or transcribers.

Background to the Coronation

The deep background to the coronation was the Zulu 'civil war' of 1856 which emphasised anew the most fundamental defect in the constitution of the kingdom: the lack of a settled principle of succession. To a great extent the Zulu monarchy was grounded on an analogy with the Nguni homestead — the king was the family head writ large. The theoretical monopoly of women and cattle claimed by household patriarchs conferred enormous power which, when transferred to the level of a kingdom, could be of incalculable benefit to a clever monarch. It was notorious, however, that the price of this power in every household was an incessant rivalry between fathers and sons. Nguni fathers commonly brought peace in the Oedipal war by delaying as long as possible to designate their heirs thereby pitting siblings against each other. These conflicts had existed from time immemorial and were a cause of the perpetual fragmentation which characterised Nguni political life prior to the time of Dingiswayo. Age-set regiments created powerful centripetal forces to bind the kingdom together but buried deep in the bosom of the state were the explosive internecine rivalries of the family. Shaka, as is well known, tried to avoid the problem by not fathering children. His death at the hands of his brothers showed plainly the futility of this non-solution to the problem of securing an orderly succession. Fratricidal war continued until Mpande — Claudius of the Zulu royal house — stood alone for a time. Then, as his own children matured, the old drama began again. As in the courts of Britain's Hanoverian kings antagonistic parties of fortune seekers attached themselves to the king, to the Prince of Wales and to anyone else who might one day be king, so in Zululand factions grew up around Mpande's elder sons. When the factions of Mbulazi and Cetshwayo resorted to war in 1856, Mbulazi and many of his backers perished.

In Shaka's day the Zulu monarchy constituted the whole political universe and a man in Cetshwayo's position might have acted at once to confine all other potential rivals. But in the changed circumstances of Mpande's era the Transvaal Republic and Natal existed as possible sancturies for political refugees. One of Mpande's sons, Mkungu, escaped with his mother to Natal where he was eagerly seized upon by Shepstone as a hostage against the uncertain future of Zululand. Bishop Colenso, who at that time had barely begun missionary operations and was Shepstone's more than willing aide in schemes for imperial expansion, enrolled the boy in his school. For some time thereafter Colenso spoke and wrote without much discretion about having 'the future king (most probably)' under his 'own roof'.

> If ever the British Government interferes, as, I imagine, some day it must, in the affairs of Zululand, a youth like this, civilized, and (may God in His mercy grant it) Christianised, would surely be the person whose claims would be most likely to receive our support, more especially as he is even now regarded, both by friends and foes, as the rightful successor to Panda's authority.[5]

The existence in Natal of one openly spoken of as rightful heir to the throne was to be a constant irritant to Cetshwayo. By the same token it seems to have been a boon to Mpande in the Oedipal sweepstakes because it left the succession still uncertain in a practical sense. However much power had passed to Cetshwayo (that is still very much a matter for conjecture) Mpande would not be Lear so long as there was someone else on whom he might bestow his realm. Affecting messages purporting to be from Mpande arrived at Shepstone's office lamenting Cetshwayo's unfilial behavior and encouraging a belief that another son would one day be king. Mkungu in Natal was Mpande's hostage as much as he was Shepstone's.

Missionaries benefited greatly from Mpande's changed position. Since 1851 the Norwegian mission led by Hans Schreuder had held a monopoly of preaching rights in Zululand but had been prevented from making much of their situation by the severe restrictions imposed by a suspicious monarch.[6] After the civil war, Schreuder reported joyfully that Mpande was 'a different person to talk and preach to':

> You cannot at all imagine his change of attitude, which I observe and feel when we are together . . . . The King is very favourable towards the missionaries, and under the present conditions we need not fear that the king will try to make obstacles for our work.[7]

Lacking sufficient Norwegians to exploit his new possibilities, Schreuder invited fellow Lutherans from the German Hermannsburg mission in Natal to share his good fortune. Sensing an opportunity, Bishop Colenso made an exploratory expedition to Zululand in 1859, aided and abetted by Shepstone who still lacked first hand knowledge of the country. Schreuder was understandably enraged by this blatant attempt to muscle in on his territory but, more than that, he feared that Colenso's association with Mkungu would make all missionaries suspect. In his irate conversations with the Anglican evangelists Schreuder made revealing comments on the balance of power in Zululand.[8] Shepstone, he contended, had made a cardinal error by continually sending political messages directly to Mpande rather than through Cetshwayo. The error had been compounded by Colenso who not only harbored Mkungu but had foolishly sent two letters from the boy to his father (on Schreuder's advice Mpande returned them unopened). Thanks to the Zulus' 'complete system of espionage', the movements of Colenso and Shepstone were almost instantly known to Cetshwayo.[9] Colenso's expedition of 1859 was widely thought to be the opening gambit in a plot to challenge Cetshwayo's right of succession. In short, Shepstone had thus far blundered badly in his relations with the Zulu court and was regarded with a mixture of scorn and suspicion by most notables. That Mpande was able, despite his limited right of direct rule and Schreuder's disapproval, to admit Colenso's missionaries and grant them land indicated that the king still possessed significant power.

Early in 1861 Shepstone was forced to try to repair some of his blunders by a crisis in Natal-Zulu relations which was largely his own fault. Shepstone had long cherished the dream of setting up a black kingdom with a white administration where, freed from interference from bigoted settlers, he could prove his theory that the enlightenment of Africa could be financed by taxing the Africans who were to be enlightened. Sir George Grey had scotched Shepstone's plan for a black kingdom south of Natal in the mid-1850s, but by 1860 he was an eager partner in a scheme to take a slice of northwestern Zululand for the same purpose. The scheme promised to kill two birds with one stone: part of the alleged 'surplus' black population of Natal would be removed; at the same time a British buffer would be erected against Transvaal aspirations to reach the sea via Zululand. Before any steps had been taken to consult Cetshwayo about the proposal, rumors began to circulate in Natal. According to Schreuder, early in 1860,

Natal kafirs when over for their friends (in Zululand) . . . declared that preparations were being made in Natal for the invasion and conquest of Zululand. They told the ships which brought the troops, the number of the Regiments, the location of the soldiers for crossing the various drifts of the Tugela at one time, and the number of field pieces which were to accompany the expedition.[10]

The rumors also spread to the Transvaal and laid the foundations for an ambitious plot. Schreuder's account of the plot and its outcome is of exceptional interest:

A few months since (i.e., a few months before July 1861) one of Panda's Captains who had escaped to the Boers came from them to Ketchwayo to fetch him to the Boers telling him that the English were about to invade his Country, kill him and put the boy who is with the Bishop on the throne. He also brought a promise from the Boers of protection if he would flee to them. He refused to go to the Boers, but as a consequence of their message confirming as he supposed the statements of the Natal Kafirs he sent orders to kill all the family of which the boy at the Bishop's is a member. One of Panda's wives and one son were killed but the Captain in charge of the other two escaped to the Boers. They then sent down three of their number to persuade Ketchwayo to go to them and they promised to give up the princes. He started but was afterwards persuaded to return and send some of his Captains in his place. The result of their negotiations was the promise to deliver up the princes, on condition that their lives and the life of the Captain who brought them should be spared, that the Zulus should wear clothes and only punish by due course of law. They also promised at another time to come and put Ketchwayo in the Royal Hut. They desired Ketchwayo to come alone for the boys, and that they might take him without risk when thus in their power, they made the men they had with them drunk and put them in a wagon disarmed and bound them; Ketchwayo however disappointed them by taking a small army with him and so escaped.[11]

Here are powerful reverberations of past and future events. In the cynical pursuit of land and power the Afrikaners were attempting to repeat a tactic which had served them well in 1839 and would serve them again in the 1880s, i.e. they tried to capitalise on divisions in the Zulu state and exploit the willingness of members of the royal house to mortgage part of Shaka's patrimony in return for present help in gaining the elusive prize of an uncontested title to the throne. Just as striking is the foreshadowing of Shepstone's own subsequent Zulu policy. The Transvaal adventurers offered to guarantee Cetshwayo's succession and later to crown him, in return for land in what became the disputed territory and for vague promises of internal 'civilizing' reforms which could later be useful in claiming the status of protecting power.

Whether or not Shepstone consciously set out to imitate the Afrikaners after their plan came unstuck is not known, but he certainly acted with uncharacteristic speed when word of the episode reached him in March, 1861.[12] Of course it would not do to admit in official memoranda that he had bungled badly and stood in imminent danger of seeing his proposed black kingdom annexed to the Transvaal. Instead, he pretended to respond to urgent requests from both Mpande and Cetshwayo, despite the fact that the only urgent request he had received from Cetshwayo was a demand to know 'whether a report which had reached him and pervaded the Zulu country, were true, namely, that Mr. Shepstone was going there to negotiate the cession of a portion of it, and that in the event of failing, it had been determined to take it by force of arms'.[13] Cetshwayo's suggestion that Shepstone should stop the rumor mill by ceasing to keep Mkungu in Natal was twisted by Shepstone into a request for British ratification of Cetshwayo's status as heir apparent. He would seize this fortuitous opportunity, he explained, to negotiate the cession of some land to Natal. By all accounts — Colenso's, Schreuder's and Shepstone's — he returned absolutely empty-handed from his first fearful venture into Zululand. Shepstone would later claim that he had been officially hailed with a mighty 'Bayete' as befitted one who stood in Shaka's place as arbiter of the kingdom and that it was this royal salute that caused him to be invited back to crown Cetshwayo in 1873. This is mostly nonsense. Alice Mackenzie (whose account of the 1861 trip Colenso pronounced to be 'authentic') was told by Shepstone himself that he went to Zululand on his own initiative in the hope that 'his influence might be of service in settling things there'.[14] Privately Mpande lamented his lost children but did nothing to support Shepstone when Cetshwayo demanded Mkungu's return. There was a ferocious row over Shepstone's counter proposal that Mkungu's near kin should join him in Natal. As a half-hearted apology an elephant tusk was presented to Shepstone just before his departure.

In Schreuder's narrative Shepstone comes off even worse:

> On Thursday Ketchwayo asked Mr. S. what he had come for? He said to acknowledge him as successor. Ketchwayo replied, we do not thank you for that, the Zulus can settle that for ourselves and we have settled it. 'What have you come for, you had some great thing to say what is it?' Mr. S. said 'I think that is a great

thing that Panda has acknowledged you in my presence as his successor.' 'No Mr. S. that is not a great thing he has done so three times before and it is just as uncertain as ever as far as he is concerned. What have you come for Mr. S.?' He (Cetshwayo) then became very angry and said many things he ought not to have said, his Captains interfered to quiet him and the meeting broke up in great excitment. The next morning Ketchwayo sent to Mr. S. to say they had been very angry the day before and as he did not wish to part so asked him to see him again. Mr. S. replied, 'You killed me yesterday and I cannot see you again.' .... Ketchwayo also demanded the return of the prince with the Bishop and told him that he was the cause of all the slaughter among them and that they should never leave off killing one another till they had all the Royal Family in the land.[15]

Just how inconclusive the proceedings had been was demonstrated less than two months later when Natal was swept by a great Zulu invasion scare. Rumors flew in all directions that Cetshwayo had swept into Natal bent on grabbing Mkungu away from Colenso. Shepstone 'took a strong view of the danger', advised the bishop to evacuate his family to Pietermaritzburg and rode off toward the border with a force of several thousand Africans in battle dress. Methodist missionaries returning from a conference with Schreuder gave convincing proof that the fears were groundless but by this time Zululand was gripped by its own English invasion scare.[16] Cetshwayo sent anxiously through the Norwegian missionary O.C. Oftebro asking why Natal troops had gathered on the border.[17] Serious mistrust evidently lingered on both sides of the Tugela.

If anyone had gained from the confrontation of 1861 it had been Cetshwayo. Without moving a muscle, without conceding a point he had been recognised as heir-apparent by the government of Natal. That would certainly discomfit internal enemies who had previously been able to point to Shepstone's protection of Mkungu as proof that the future of the kingdom was still in doubt. Similar recognition had come from the Transvaal and it remained to be seen how far their new claims to Zulu territory could be enforced. Between 1856 and 1861 the basic groundwork of political relations between Zululand and her white-ruled neighbors had been laid down. Political power continued to be divided in Zululand with Mpande continuing to hint coyly that the succession was not quite finally settled.[18] Cetshwayo consequently still worried most about his own security even as he worked to nullify the Transvaal land claims which had arisen from his nervous action in 1861. These tensions and problems were becoming better known to the outside world thanks to the reports of the numerous missionaries whom Mpande had admitted in his hour of danger. Most of these missionaries were Lutherans who tended to look to the Norwegian leaders Schreuder and Oftebro for advice. That meant that they tended to be identified with Mpande even though the canny Norwegian pioneers carefully refrained from doing anything to antagonise the future king. The new Anglican missionary Robert Robertson adopted a deliberate policy of favoring Cetshwayo but was hampered in this respect by having a former Lutheran, S.M. Samuelson, as a colleague, as well as by his association with Colenso, notwithstanding that Mkungu had been quietly moved away from the bishop's station late in 1861 and that Robertson adhered to the anti-Colenso faction in the Anglican schism of the 1860s. Having reason to suspect all missionaries, Cetshwayo relied on their services less and less while making greater use of white traders who offered secular and diplomatic services which were apparently free from subversive implications.[19]

For Shepstone the Zulu-Transvaal boundary dispute was a godsend which promised one day to enable him to undo the humiliation suffered at Cetshwayo's hands in 1861. Year by year Afrikaners encroached on Zulu land; for reasons that are still far from clear, the Zulu let them alone. Now a British annexation of part of the disputed territory, which had been regarded as a threat in 1860, seemed attractive. Shepstone began to receive a series of messages asking for a buffer strip to be taken by Natal.[20] Because the Colonial Office continued to stand by its rejection of Grey's annexation plan, Shepstone could not accommodate the Zulus. He maintained, however, a continuous propaganda campaign on behalf of his scheme both in Natal and London, and encouraged Zulu authorities to believe that some action would soon be taken to curb Transvaal aggression. Eventually he succeeded in convincing a Colonial Secretary of the wisdom of his plan, but that was due to the working of new forces — forces generated far beyond the little triangle of disputed territory which would be instrumental in bringing about Shepstone's coronation expedition and the Anglo-Zulu War.

Natal's Expanding Imperial Frontier

Because Britain's eventual route to African empire lay along the 'missionary road' and because Rhodes and the Cape played flamboyant

parts in empire building, it is usually forgotten that Natal once aspired
to be the gateway to Central Africa. To recapture the possibilities which
seemed to lie open a century ago, draw one line from Durban to Mombasa
and another line from Durban to Kinshasha. These lines enclose an arc
of roughly forty-five degrees containing vast human and material resources.
Visionaries in Shepstone's day perceived that triangle both as a wedge of
pie to be gradually eaten up and as a funnel directing the wealth of Africa
to the port of Natal. Thomas Baines' 1874 map of 'The Gold Fields of
South Eastern Africa' captures the Natal perspective perfectly. Durban
sits just right of centre on the line of the map with Cape Town nowhere
to be seen. From Durban gold-colored circles representing probable
mineral deposits rise like gas filled balloons towards the intoxicating
atmosphere of Central Africa. As they rise to regions labelled 'Supposed
Realm of Queen of Sheba' and 'Monomotapa of Medieval Geographers',
they also expand.

Natal's expansive vision was part of her Nguni inheritance. The *mfecane*
which followed the rise of the Zulu monarchy sent ribbons of migration
into the far interior. These ribbons laid down long-distance lines of communication. Many of the black trekkers of the *mfecane* left relatives
behind in Zululand and Natal. That meant that they also left claims
and obligations concerning women, children and cattle which time and
distance could only gradually obliterate. As Secretary for Native Affairs,
Shepstone was inevitably drawn into these distant relationships. His
border agents were charged to record the movements and check the
credentials of all Africans who passed the frontier. His magistrates had to
resolve vexedly complicated *lobola* cases which came to them on appeal
from chiefly courts. His own incorrigibly suspicious mind made him
quiz all messengers from faraway chiefs in order to uncover any treasonable
communications or rebellious intentions. Thus Shepstone was making more
than an empty boast when he sent the following message to Lobengula the
Ndebele king in 1871:

> The Lieutenant Governor of Natal thanks Lobengula ... for his
> friendly message ... he also accepts the tusk of ivory ....
> The Government of Natal is the largest Native power in South
> Eastern Africa, and its territory is the resort of refugees of all ranks
> from surrounding Tribes. The Lieut. Governor of Natal is looked
> upon as the Father of all, and hears what all have to say. He is
> therefore intimately acquainted with the domestic circumstances
> of surrounding populations, he does not seek for this information,

it comes to him.[21]

After the discovery of diamonds in Griqualand West in 1867 reports of mineral deposits like those indicated by the gold balloons on Baines' map were treated as more than just hot air. Exploring parties seized gratefully on Natal's established lines of communication to the interior. Shepstone willingly put his official resources at the disposal of promising expeditions. In 1870, for instance, he sent his official messenger Elijah Kambule and Captain Frederic Elton to aid A.L. Levert of the London and Limpopo Mining Co. in his successful bid to win a mining concession in Matabeleland.[22] The leader of another exploring party hailed Shepstone's name as 'a host itself among the Native tribes of Central Africa'.[23] Natalians with sufficient imagination to picture themselves at the portal of a golden road to the north did not share in the carping criticisms perennially aimed at Shepstone by the bumpkins of the 'up-country party'. To the visionary, Shepstone was 'the one-day-to-be Governor General of all the native tribes residing between the Cape and the Zambezi'.[24]

Mineral discoveries which fired the minds of some colonists provoked headache in others. Diamond digging at Kimberley drastically upset the South African labor market by pushing wages far above anything which had ever before been offered to unskilled African workers in Natal and the Cape. Almost overnight large streams of labor were diverted from existing channels. Small white employers whose knowledge of the labor market extended no farther than the bounds of their own farms or kitchens pressed Shepstone to adopt their old quack remedy of a land squeeze on local Africans. Big employers on the other hand knew that the black population of Natal with or without reserves could not support itself and at the same time provide the steady labor force required for plantation agriculture. They turned instinctively to Shepstone who had a long standing reputation as an 'unfailing source of labor'. As early as 1855 Shepstone had noticed that 'many, if not the majority of our laborers, do not belong to the tribes of our immediate neighborhood; they come from a distance, numbers from beyond the Drakensburg [sic], and some from latitudes far north of Delagoa Bay'.[25] It may well be that the first information about employment opportunities in Natal reached distant peoples through the lines of communication resulting from the *mfecane*. Whether this were so can probably never be certainly known because until the labor crisis of the early seventies, the movements of migrant workers were not the subject of systematic scrutiny. Magistrates sent in only very rough approximations such as Melmoth Osborn's 1866 report from Newcastle that over 1000 'Basuto' workers had passed into Natal through his district in the course of the year.[26] Now that the flow of workers had become a net out-migration Shepstone and his principal allies, the coastal planters, set out to study labor migration.

A Select Committee of the Legislative Council was established in 1872 to report on the 'Introduction of Native Laborers from beyond the Border of the Colony' and obtained most of its information from Shepstone and his border agent, the same indefatigable Frederic Elton who had helped open the way for mining in Lobengula's kingdom.[27] The Committee's report reached conclusions similar to those being reached by colonial officials in Griqualand West at the same time.[28] The great labor catchment area of southern Africa appeared to be a coastal strip 150-300 miles wide extending from the borders of Natal northwards to the Zambezi. Excepting only 'the military Zulu tribes, who as a rule are disinclined to manual labor', the catchment was said to contain a pool of several million potentially willing workers. Because the Natal government was believed to be known and respected throughout this huge area, the Committee did not think it necessary to advertise in order to 'create a desire in this immense mass of foreign native population to seek service in Natal'. What was required was a government agent stationed near Lydenburg in the eastern Transvaal from whom job seekers could obtain information about wages and routes to Natal. Depots offering food and shelter should be set up along each of the three main paths of migration. One of these paths ran through rough inhospitable terrain in the Transvaal, striking the Natal border about eighty miles west of the lower end of the Newcastle division. Another ran from coastal Mozambique directly through Zululand where there were frequent reports of passing workers being robbed and harried. The third path ran roughly midway between the others, straight through the territory in dispute between Zululand and the Transvaal.

This suggested a powerful new argument in favor of Shepstone's old black kingdom proposal. As early as 1870 a private entrepreneur, Percy Whitehead, had unsuccessfully sought Colonial Office permission to purchase 1,5 million acres from the Zulus in the territory, to settle the land with white farmers under the laws of Natal and in this way to make a permanent corridor for the passage of migrant labor.[29] Each passing month brought new evidence that Transvaal and Zulu interlopers were deliberately interfering with labor supply routes, so Shepstone had the full support of Lt. Governor Musgrave in stepping up the campaign on behalf of his own scheme in 1872.[30] Until a safe corridor did exist, Natalians would have to make what deals they could with neighboring authorities. A Labor League, composed mostly of planters, sprang up to coordinate activities. In 1871, John Dunn — by this time well established as the most powerful of the white men gathered around Cetshwayo — offered to guarantee safe passages through Zululand for an annual fee of £100 plus a levy of 5 shillings on each worker.[31] The Labor League took up the offer and dealt exclusively with Dunn until they found that he was making other labor contracts on the side.[32]

One way of circumventing difficulties in Zululand was to move labor by sea from the Mozambique coast, but this in turn entailed tedious negotiations with the Portuguese. David Leslie, a private trader attempting to build up a labor supply business at Delagoa Bay in 1871, complained to Shepstone that every possible obstacle was being thrown in his way by Portuguese officialdom.[33] Shepstone sent Frederic Elton to investigate and threw his weight behind attempts to revive Natal's old claims to Inhaca and Elephant islands.[34] These negotiations came to nothing as did the attempt of St. Vincent Erskine (son of Natal's Colonial Secretary) to get Portuguese cooperation for his plan to make a labor supply deal with the Shangane chief Mzila. Erskine explained that 'the fact of the matter is that a considerable revenue is derived from direct traffic (in migrant labor) with Natal (from Delagoa Bay) and the authorities are alarmed at the possibility of its being diverted to another channel'.[35]

The news that Britain would force an anti-slave trade treaty on the Sultan of Zanzibar in 1873 was greeted with jubilation in Natal because it promised to diminish Portuguese influence and open an alternative source of labor. When, in the wake of this news, William Mackinnon announced that his shipping company would inaugurate a packet service on the east African coast via the recently opened Suez canal, the editor of the *Natal Mercury* predicted that the Sultan would soon learn that shipping free labor to Natal was infinitely more profitable than sending slaves to Persia or Arabia.[36] Freed slaves carried to Natal on Mackinnon's ships would find a 'natural home' in Natal and British interventions in East Africa would

> open up trade all along the coast, and place Natal in a better position for pressing on the Imperial Government the necessity of buying the Portuguese Government out of the country south of the Zambezi . . . . Natal must consequently carry out a Monroe doctrine of its own,

and insist that the Anglo-Saxon race shall hold undisputed sway
from Capetown to the Zambezi. Besides, we wish to obtain a supply
of labor for our coast planters from these localities and this we
will never be able to do satisfactorily until we have control of the
various ports.[37]

To follow up these possibilities the government of Natal sent the
ubiquitous Captain Elton up the coast in March 1873 to confer with
Portuguese officials on labor migration from Delagoa Bay and to meet
with Sir Bartle Frere who had been given the task of negotiating the
anti-slaving treaty. Frere took an immediate liking to Elton and appointed
him assistant political agent and vice-consul at Zanzibar.[38] The expansive
energies of Natal now reached half way up the coast and had made their
first impact on the man who was to start the Anglo-Zulu War.

In the midst of all this exciting activity, word came to Shepstone that
Mpande lived no more.

The Coronation Expedition

Though the king died sometime in late September or early October,
1872, it was not until the 26th of February, 1873, that messengers from
'the Zulu Nation' arrived at Shepstone's office lamenting that 'the nation
wanders' and asking that Shepstone come to 'establish what is wanting
among the Zulu people'.[39] As we have seen, Shepstone's explanation
for this 'invitation' was that he had been hailed as Shaka's successor in
1861 and was therefore required to place Cetshwayo on the throne. In
view of what others have said about the fiasco of 1861, this is improbable
to say the least. Though there is no certain evidence to go on, by considering
the general configuration of forces in Zululand, Natal and southern Africa
as a whole, it is possible to make sensible guesses about why the coronation
invitation was issued and accepted.

In Zululand Cetshwayo faced three major problems at the time of his
father's death. First there were his royal siblings in Natal. In 1871 Natal
magistrates could count five sons of Mpande in the colony, at least two
of whom seemed to be engaged in active intrigues with a view to seizing
power in Zululand.[40] After leaving Colenso, Mkungu had purchased a
farm in Weenen County where he proceeded to gather large numbers
of 1857 refugees until Shepstone intervened to stop him in June, 1872.[41]
Mtonga who had first arrived in Natal in 1865 had accumulated a considerable following by the time that he applied to move from Pietermaritzburg

County to the Newcastle division five years later.[42] Though Melmoth Osborn and Shepstone agreed that he should be forbidden to settle so near the sensitive disputed territory, Mtonga went stealthily ahead with his plans. When Shepstone's messenger delivered a peremptory eviction order in August 1872, Mtonga pulled a gun and spurred his horse across the Buffalo River to asylum in the Transvaal. This deeply embarrassed Shepstone who had promised Cetshwayo that Mtonga would be kept strictly under the surveillance of Chief Zatshuke. Now that the young man was evidently implicated in 'some revolutionary scheme in the northern part of the Zulu country' Shepstone thought it 'but fair to acquaint Cetshwayo with what has taken place in order that he may guard against any consequences'.[43] Whether or not Cetshwayo received that warning he must have known through other channels that brothers were plotting as father lay dying. He would welcome a reiteration of Natal's support of his own rights. John Shepstone asserted later that Cetshwayo's overwhelming object at the time of the coronation was 'to annihilate the ambitions, aspirations as he believed, of one or more of his own royal brothers'.[44]

Cetshwayo's second big problem was the disputed territory. Each passing year had brought fresh encroachments. At this very moment a potentially dangerous sibling was again in the hands of Afrikaners who would not be bought off a second time by empty promises. There was the distinct danger that the Boers would use Mtonga as they had once used Mpande. Why Cetshwayo did not cut the Gordian knot by attacking his enemies is a puzzle still awaiting solution. There is precious little evidence to support Shepstone's boast that he held the Zulus back. It may be that Shepstone's obviously genuine desire to acquire a buffer zone offered a safe, even a profitable alternative to a war which might repeat the debacle of Blood River. The message which Shepstone reported in February 1873 urged again 'what has already been urged so frequently, that the Government of Natal be extended so as to intervene between the Zulu and the territory of the Trans Vaal Republic'. On the other hand, it may be that some internal Zulu problem made war seem risky.

By all reports the internal condition of the kingdom was badly unsettled in 1873; that was Cetshwayo's third big problem. Missionaries reported that from the time of Mpande's death the Zulus were 'more or less in a state of excitment' because of fears that 'the succession would be disputed and a civil war ensue'.[45] In January, 1873 the Resident Magistrate for Newcastle received a spate of reports that fearful slaughter

was taking place across the border as Cetshwayo sought systematically
to eliminate dissident elements.[46] While the Zulu kingdom refrained until
shortly before the war from making money through the sale of Zulu labor,
entrepreneurs such as Dunn were using the country's strategic position
astride labor migration routes to skim profits. As Dunn was an integral
part of the local economy, the profits he skimmed — and those skimmed
by numerous other white traders in the land — must have been partly
distributed to the comparative advantage of some and the consequent
disadvantage of others. One might expect this to have shown up in the
distribution of cattle through the working of *lobola* and other exchanges.
The monarch's power to intervene in the *lobola* system by fixing the
date for age-set regimental marriages was an important tool of government
but one which evidently required sensitive treatment. Whether or not
Cetshwayo utilized it with tact and skill is still an open question as is
the effect of the firearms trade. An Anglican missionary was astounded
to find in 1860 a very large number of rifles in the land; he estimated
that there was at least one at every homestead in the land.[47] In later
years credible reports of a large trade in firearms proliferate and yet
the Anglo-Zulu War was to provide devastating evidence that the rifles
were not operationally integrated into Zulu military technology.[48] Were
the guns instead a means of coping with the distribution problem which
appeared along with new wealth in the kingdom? Whoever gained from
the new wealth, Cetshwayo was clearly not a loser for he maintained close
and cordial relations with traders.

He appears to have shared the traders' general distrust and dislike
of missionaries. Traders disliked missionaries not so much because of
their gospel but because mission stations were competing centres of
trade. It was frequently charged that missionaries themselves were heavily
involved in trade but in fact it was the mission residents — almost
entirely immigrants from Natal — who were doing the trading. Because
the mission station residents were carefully excluded from the ordinary
life of the kingdom and were generally regarded with comtempt, the
opportunity to turn a profit was one of very few inducements that
missionaries could use to attract Africans from Natal.[49] In addition
to sharing the traders' dislike of independent commercial operations,
Cetshwayo had a strong distaste for Christian teachings. F.B. Fynney
summed up the general situation pretty well in a memorandum written
for Governor Bulwer in 1877:

during the reign of the late king Umpande, the missionaries were considered almost as a necessity in Zululand, not from the fact that they came there as servants of God . . . but as people who (being learned whitemen) knew everything, and would be ready to do anything required by the king . . . Bishop Schreuder especially enjoyed the friendship of Umpande, for many years and had great influence over him.

That state of things now has entirely altered. Cetshwayo's disposition differs greatly from that of his Father. He is more self-reliant, arrogant, and conservative. If he wants anything, he can find many traders ready and willing to supply his wants, and he — together with his Chief izindunas can see no good in either the missionaries or their work. He does not believe in their doctrines, and looks on any Zulu who professes so to do as a Zulu spoiled. He feels that each mission station is a separate power, set up in his land, which to a great extent is calculated to rob him of his influence over the people he governs, and forms a place of refuge for all the Abatakati (witches) and those who wish to throw off their allegiance to him.

This is no new idea on his part, as from the first, he wished to get rid of the missionaries.

I have good reason for believing that some of the missionaries have very unwisely interfered in Zulu politics . . . .[50]

According to Colenso, Cetshwayo had wanted to expel all missionaries in 1869 but was stopped from doing so by Dunn who advised him that his country would then be speedily annexed to Natal.[51] It was one of the new king's objects to settle the status of missionaries once and for all in 1873. He acted against the Lutherans before sending his coronation invitation to Shepstone. When reports of Mpande's death appeared in Natal papers before any official announcement was made, Cetshwayo blamed Schreuder and threatened to ban him from the kingdom. The *Natal Colonist* attributed this false accusation to a section among Cetshwayo's advisers who were violently opposed to the Norwegians.[52]

It seems very likely that Schreuder politicked actively to bring Shepstone to Zululand and thereby retrieve Lutheran fortunes which were sunk to a very low point in 1873. The Hermannsburg society had been in trouble since 1869 when two of their missionaries turned to Shepstone for help after a gang of rowdies had damaged their station. For appealing to Natal Cetshwayo peremptorily ordered both men out of the kingdom.[53] When their benefactor Mpande died the Hermannsburgers seriously considered withdrawing *en masse*.[54] They had made almost no converts during fourteen years of work and must have known that the extension of their missions to the Utrecht district of the Transvaal would maintain Zulu hostility. Meanwhile, Schreuder's abrasive personality had created a split in the Norwegian ranks which became a permanent schism in 1874.[55] Whatever his reasons, Schreuder, who had once been the unbending foe of British imperialism, huddled in conference with Shepstone and Colenso at Maritzburg's Victoria Club a few weeks before the coronation invitation arrived.[56] Afterwards Schreuder did all he could to ensure that the government of Natal took up the invitation. He asked the Norwegain consul

> to communicate to Mr. Shepstone, that from a confidential conversation with the prince, when no natives were present, I do positively infer, that both the Prince himself and the Zulus think it of vital importance for his kingship, that the English in a formal official way partake in his installation as King: some old Zulus of rank are very anxious just on this point.[57]

Schreuder's reward for these services was an unofficial status as Shepstone's adviser on Zulu affairs throughout the coronation expedition, a role which was widely remarked and not a little resented.[58]

But Shepstone, who had shown little inclination to support missionaries in Zululand since getting his fingers burned with Colenso and Mkungu, had more important things to discuss with Cetshwayo than troublesome preachers. He wanted the disputed territory as a secure corridor for labor migration and northward expansion. He wanted guarantees for the passage of migrant workers through Zululand. He wanted to undo the damage done to his prestige in 1861 and to acquire 'a good deal of additional influence and real power, not only over the Zulus, but over all other native powers of South Eastern Africa, for the power to control the Zulus includes that of controlling all the rest'.[59] Fear of a general African rising against white colonialism was a constant axiom in Shepstone's thinking. It was generated deep within his own complex psyche and kept alive by abundant evidence that African networks of communication did exist extending right up to the Zambezi. When Shepstone wrote that the power to control the Zulus was the power to control the rest, he really meant that control of Africans was in essence a question of prestige and that if the Zulus were seen to be getting the better of white men, other kingdoms would attempt the same feat. Now that peace and supremacy were required throughout southern Africa to facilitate mining, agriculture and labor migration, control of the Zulu kingdom was vital.

It may seem surprising that Shepstone had almost total support from the white population of Natal in his coronation expedition. His local 'native policy' was regularly attacked in the Legislative Council and only a fraction of the population cared about his expansive visions of empire. Counterbalancing these considerations, however, were the perennial fears of Zulu invasion, the thirst of colonial militiamen to swagger before the foe and, above all, a desire to do something about the current labor shortage. Natal newspapers played up the labor supply aspects of the expedition,[60] particularly after Lt. Governor Pine told a group of planters who petitioned him for more labor that Shepstone was currently in Zululand for precisely that reason.[61]

How well, then, did Shepstone and Cetshwayo succeed in achieving their respective goals in their second great confrontation? Shepstone was handicapped at the start by Colonial Office refusal to sanction in advance any annexation of territory on the disputed frontier. At the same time the 'official mind' gave distinct indications of bending in Shepstone's direction. The annexation of Griqualand West had effected a basic change in official thinking by bringing into sharp focus the problems of migrant labor in a politically fragmented subcontinent. Before the annexation Knatchbull-Hugessen at the Colonial Office adhered to the established wisdom of twenty years' standing: 'we do not wish to extend our South African possessions'.[62] After the annexation, when the Afrikaner republics began to interfere with labor supply to the diamond fields, he changed his tune:

> These Boers must be taught to respect British subjects. Every day shows in a stronger light the mistake that was made in abandoning the Orange River territory − these people are worse neighbors than the Kafirs.[63]

In the course of 1873 Lord Kimberley came round to accepting that assessment as well as the proposition that the destiny of the Transkei was 'consolidation under British rule' and that 'a little war' in Zululand would soon lead to the same result.[64] For the moment, however, Shepstone was denied both the power to negotiate any annexations and an escort of regular troops. (Barkly remarked with unintended irony that Shepstone had shown he could do without troops in 1861.)[65] The task of overawing Cetshwayo and his legions was left to Natal's unruly Volunteers whose preparatory maneouvres at Estcourt accidentally terrified the nearby chief Langalibalele.[66]

Before Cetshwayo could be overawed he had first to be found. Shepstone's forces set out from Natal late in July 1873 and by August 12th they were at Eshowe only two or three miles from the king's head-quarters. For the next sixteen days Cetshwayo kept Shepstone waiting with one maddening excuse after another. George Cato tried to put a charitable construction on the delay in a letter to William Shepstone which nicely conveys the atmosphere of the occasion:

> Ketchwayo is like a man going to have his tooth out, the nearer he gets to the Doctor the more funky he gets, but don't like to show it. He therefore keeps on sending kind messages, and we have to outwit the cunning of the savage. I shall propose to your Dad that he sends Fat Parson Robertson to the Prince, with the Bible in one hand, and Olive branch in the other.

Less charitable observers interpreted the delay as a mark of calculated disrespect and it was only by threatening to return to Natal that Shepstone managed to stage his ceremony on 1 September. By that time it had become common knowledge that the Zulus had pre-empted him by holding their own ceremony a month earlier. According to one version of the event, this prior ceremony was a deliberate political act carried out with impressive solemnity:

> Many of the old Isinduna . . . were jealous of British sanction being supposed to be necessary to the ceremony, and accordingly Ketchwayo was proclaimed by Masipula, the Zulu Warwick, or King-maker, at a place about twelve miles from Magwaza (Robertson's mission station). All the chief men of the nation made speeches on the occasion, which were for the most part panegyrics of the new monarch, and expressions of their own fidelity. That of Prince Uhama, who had been more than suspected of designs on the crown, was specially applauded. It seems it is a custom . . . when rival princes engage in mortal combat, that the victor should disfigure his slain enemy, by making a scar with an asseghai over his forehead, and across his nose and mouth. So Uhama stood forward and said, 'It has long been foretold that I should be gashed here, and here, and here' . . . but you behold me, and see that I am still without a scar, and I assure you most positively that I mean to remain so'. Thus he managed to convey an idea of his own fidelity and of his sense of his brother's superiority.[68]

The death of Masipula a few days after Shepstone's arrival in Zululand ensured that the British ceremony would appear in quite a different light. As an example of British control of the Zulus, useful for intimidating other kingdoms, the coronation expedition was a laughable failure.

Shepstone did not do much better in achieving his other objectives. On the question of labor supply his conversations with Cetshwayo led to nothing much beyond a new agency for John Dunn who was to supervise the passage of 'Amatonga' workers for an annual salary of £300.[69] On the question of missionary rights Cetshwayo seized the initiative with a suggestion that most of the missions should be closed. After extensive negotiations Shepstone managed to win only an extension of the *status quo*: 'an understanding that those who were already in the country should not be interfered with, and that, if any of them committed an offense for which the offender might be considered deserving of expulsion, the case should be submitted to the Government of Natal, and its assent be received before the sentence should be carried out'.[70]

The celebrated 'laws', whose proclamation Rider Haggard would immortalise in *King Solomon's Mines* and whose 'breaking' Frere would use as an excuse for war, were not the result of discussions between Shepstone and the king. Their wording is ambiguous and can arguably be interpreted as not referring to Cetshwayo but to his subordinates and the people at large. At any rate Shepstone did not pretend that they amounted to anything more than a kind of 'ordination sermon or Bishop's charge' which was 'but sowing the seed which will still take many years to grow and mature'.[71] All things considered, there is no reason to dispute the contemporary judgments of the Anglican missionary Robertson who called the whole coronation expedition 'a farce', and of the Natal politician John Akerman who claimed that 'the tin pot coronation of Cetwayo (sic) is laughed at everywhere, except where the farce has been used to make capital of'.[72] The Zulu king had won two of his three objectives: British renunciation of claims to the throne through Mpande's younger sons, and a strict limitation on missionary activity. His third objective — a curb on Transvaal aggression — was not in Shepstone's power to give. In contrast, Shepstone secured only an understanding on migrant labor which cost Cetshwayo nothing. On a number of later occasions the king would vehemently deny that he had accepted any laws from Natal. 'Did I ever tell Mr. Shepstone I would not kill?', he asked in 1876. 'Did he tell the white people I made such an agreement because if he did, he has deceived them . . . . Why does the Governor of Natal speak to me about my laws? Do I come to Natal and dictate to him about his laws?'[73]

The Aftermath of the Coronation in Whitehall

No one at the Colonial Office ever wrote or acted as though the coronation created any enforceable rights for Britain or British subjects in Zululand. Frere's bluster of 1878 about 'conditions' laid down at the coronation made it that much easier to make him the scapegoat when the war turned out to be inopportune and unpopular. The published correspondence between Hicks Beach and Frere gives the impression that the Colonial Office had done nothing to bring on a conflict and wished to avoid one at all costs. It is to that extent quite misleading. Within eighteen months of Shepstone's return from the coronation his view of South African affairs had been swallowed by the Colonial Office hook, line and sinker. From that time forward war was accounted an overwhelming probability.

Lord Kimberley faced the prospect of eventual British interference in Zululand with equanimity. He wrote somewhat flippantly across a newspaper account of the coronation expedition, 'fine practice for the Volunteers'.[74] He was nevertheless relieved that no incidents or annexations marred the occasion, and he took no further interest in Zulu affairs until turfed out of office by the election of 1874. Thanks to Langalibalele's panic at the manoeuvres of the militia and his subsequent flight from Natal, Kimberley's Tory successor Lord Carnarvon had an opportunity to hear Shepstone's opinions at first hand. Sent to London to explain his government's mishandling of the sordid Langalibalele affair, Shepstone arrived just about the time that Carnarvon was writing in exasperation that 'these South African questions are a terrible labyrinth of which it is hard to find the clue'.[75] A few weeks later, after several conversations with Shepstone, Carnarvon announced to his staff that he had decided what to do about Native Policy in South Africa.[76]

Notwithstanding historians' frequent complaints about Shepstone's reticence, there is enough material in his memoranda and Carnarvon's notes with which to reconstruct the substance of the advice he offered in September 1874.[77] He blamed the mistakes and atrocities of the Langalibalele affair on hot-headed settlers of the up-country party and on foolish old Lt. Governor Pine; a new constitution with increased representation for either officials or coastal districts would set things straight. For the orderly administration of Africans in Natal Shepstone recommended a paradoxical combination of immigration and emigration. Three years earlier he had drawn attention to the problems posed by a burgeoning migrant labor force for whom his methods of indirect rule through chiefs were inappropriate.[78] A force of black police under white supervision was needed to supervise their movements and to prevent their misbehavior. At the same time something must be done with the 'surplus' of resident Africans who would soon overpopulate Natal's reserves and be crowded off Crown lands. Shepstone's solution was, of course, the black kingdom to be planted in the disputed territory.[79] Through this one simple annexation unhappy Africans in Natal would find happier homes, a vital labor migration route would be permanently secured against interference from Afrikaners and Zulus, the Boer republics would be shut off from the sea, and a road would be opened to the north which was capable of infinite extension if governed by Shepstonian methods:

> That ultimately this (strip of territory) will also be occupied by Europeans cannot be doubted, but if the land can be acquired, and put to the purpose I have suggested, the present tension in Natal will be relieved, and time be gained to admit of the intro-duction of a larger proportion of white colonists . . . . But it will be a mistake to suppose that the relief afforded by this measure would be but temporary or that the difficulty it is proposed to abate could ever again reach its present dimensions; because the outlet being to the North, the abatement admits of permanent extension towards a climate unsuited to Europeans but not so to natives . . . .[80]

Here was a truly breathtaking vision of empire which Shepstone could rationally defend by pointing to his success in making African administration pay its own way through taxes and import duties. So long as African administration was kept physically and legally away from white settlers, Shepstone was confident that his methods would suit 'any class, country or nation' of Africans south of the Zambezi.[81] Moreover Shepstone held that without some such plan, the economic development of southern Africa would produce and be engulfed in frightful chaos.

There is no certain evidence that Carnarvon adopted Shepstone's vision in its entirety, but the honours and special commissions heaped upon him later suggest that Carnarvon was very impressed, as do the outlines of his plans for South African confederation. Carnarvon's aim was once thought to be simply a consolidating, money-saving federation limited to South Africa. With one telling quotation Clement Goodfellow demolished that interpretation:

> We cannot admit rivals in the east or even the central part of Africa, and I do not see why, looking to the experience that we now have of English life within the tropics — the Zambezi should be considered without the range of our colonisation. To a considerable extent, if not entirely, we must be prepared to apply a sort of Munro [sic] doctrine to much of Africa.[82]

Goodfellow ascribed this outburst to Carnarvon's own ebullient personality temporarily intoxicated by confederation euphoria. It may be more soberly explained by Carnarvon's adoption of the Natal perspective. Once he accepted the Nguni inheritance, understood the logic of the developing economy, saw Durban as the bottom of an imperial funnel, it was easy enough for him to see why autonomous republics and independent kingdoms which threatened vital supply lines could no longer be tolerated.

Proving that Shepstone had more to do with shaping Carnarvon's vision of confederation than, for example, J.A. Froude, is a task beyond the scope of this paper.[83] It is enough to notice that for a little space of time during the 1870s, Natal was seen by the Colonial Office as Britain's imperial frontier in Africa. After assisting Bartle Frere at Zanzibar, Frederic Elton became Britain's first full-time consul in Mozambique where he continued to do what he could to divert labor southwards.[84] His reports to the Foreign Office recommending the purchase of Delagoa Bay and the extinction of Portuguese sovereignty in East Africa were forwarded to the Colonial Office to be filed under 'Natal'.[85] When the editor of the *Northern Echo* sent Carnarvon his leading article suggesting that a 'Central African Trading Company' be floated to exploit Lt. Cameron's discoveries in the upper Zambezi and Congo river basins, it was filed under 'Natal'.[87] So was John Kirk's report on the plans of William Mackinnon and Sir Fowell Buxton to lease the mainland territories of the Sultan of Zanzibar.[86] From the Tugela River to Mombasa, from the Drakensberg to the lower Congo, Colonial Office filing clerks at least saw Africa as an extension of Natal.

Remembering that from this perspective Zululand looks more like a roadblock than a detour, it is not hard to see why Carnarvon and the agents he chose to do the work of confederation all agreed that sometime soon Zululand must become British. Elton, who had accompanied the coronation expedition on part of its way and who now had an alarming backdoor view from Mozambique of the arms trade to Zululand, expected British intervention.[89] Sir Garnet Wolseley, who was sent out to implement the constitutional reforms Shepstone had recommended and who was Carnarvon's first choice to be High Commissioner after Barkly's recall, made a strong plea for annexation of the disputed territory shortly after his arrival in Natal.[90] A few weeks later he asked for a wholesale annexation of Zululand on the excuse that Cetshwayo had broken Shepstone's 'laws'.[91] If, he wrote, the Transvaal-Zulu tug of war were allowed to continue much longer it would be 'destructive to all our trade and agriculture'.[92] Robert Herbert, Carnarvon's cousin and Permanent Under-secretary at the Colonial Office expected a war with the Zulus to be imminent from 1873 onwards. So did Carnarvon, only for various reasons he kept hoping that it would be put off — rather like St. Augustine praying to the Lord to make him pure, but not yet. Take, for example, this dithering reaction to reports of turmoil in the Zulu kingdom during April 1877:

> I hope it does not mean we shall have a great pressure put on us to annex Zululand. This must and ought to come eventually, but not just now. There are however signs of this tendency.[93]

Of all Carnarvon's hand-picked men only Henry Bulwer really believed that war could be delayed very long. The thesis that the Colonial Office opposed a Zulu war can only be defended by reading the files of 1878, it must founder on the files of 1873-77. When Bartle Frere put the gun to Cetshwayo's head he was no maverick assassin acting alone. He was very much part of a conspiracy.

The Aftermath of the Coronation in Zululand

Against this background of official fatalism firmly grounded in a shrewd appreciation of the great changes overtaking south and east Africa, the activities of people within the Zulu kingdom could have little effect upon the ultimate course of events. Inside Zululand the imperial perspective was obscured by a forest of parochial problems. Missionaries and the Zulu court played out a drama of their own with no very clear idea of its larger significance.

After the coronation, the situation of European missionaries deteriorated rapidly. Deprived of Mpande's protection, tired of preaching to tiny bands of outcasts and divided among themselves by Schreuder's pig-headedness, the Norwegians were thoroughly demoralised. So were the Hermannsburg missionaries who had never really recovered from their setback in 1869. Only Robert Robertson of the Anglicans remained briefly optimistic after Cetshwayo became king. From the beginning of his Zulu mission Robertson had made the heir-apparent the focus of his attention, hoping that 'by being much with Cetywayo — by gaining his confidence, by really shewing that Christianity among his people increases rather than diminishes his strength — a good measure of success may be the result'.[94] In 1870 the policy had seemed to be on the verge of paying dividends when Cetshwayo promised to let Robertson educate his son Dinuzulu as soon as the boy was old enough.[95] A few months after the coronation Robertson wrote this illuminating appreciation of the new king:

> I have long had a high opinion of Ketshwayo's mental powers, but I certainly did not give him credit for so much strength of character and so much political sagacity as he is now displaying. Acting entirely on his own judgment, he is undermining the power of the great Zulu chiefs, which has long been a menace to the throne. Before the days of Chaka, this country was covered with small independent tribes, but in the commotions which followed Chaka's death, these tribes or the fragments of them, clustered round certain chiefs who thus became powerful and eventually dangerous. The original heads of these tribes, or rather their descendents, who are well-known by their patronymics, have been sought out by the king and desired to rebuild the houses of their ancestors. Many great men will thus become inferior to some who are at present their dependents. I have hopes, indeed I may say more than hopes, that this is not the only matter which the king will take into his own hands and deal with successfully.[96]

This passage gives real meaning to the observation frequently made in the mid-1870s that Cetshwayo was a 'conservative' bent on 'reviving Shaka's policy'. Far from implying, as has been generally supposed, that Cetshwayo meant to consolidate power through a policy of indiscriminate terror, Robertson portrays the king as most discriminating in pursuit of a redistribution of power in the land. Unfortunately there were to be no more such telling reports from Robertson for he and Cetshwayo drifted rapidly apart.

    To some extent the estrangement was due to Cetshwayo's preoccupation with matters of state. Reforming the kingdom proved to be a bigger task than he or Robertson had anticipated. By March 1874 the Anglican missionary S.M. Samuelson noticed a marked increase in the number of state executions taking place in his vicinity. This he attributed partly to increased accusations of witchcraft and partly to Cetshwayo's punishment of men who failed to spend enough time at court.[97] There were, however, also personal reasons for Robertson to turn against the king. In 1864 he had lost his first wife in a wagon accident; his second wife died at Durban in June 1874 after a long wasting illness. His life then entered a downhill run of heavy drinking and lovemaking with young girls on his station.[98] When a fellow missionary arrived unexpectedly to find him gloriously drunk in 1876, Robertson escaped summary dismissal only because of the embarrassment his church would have suffered through the disgrace of its most famous Zulu missionary. Robertson blamed his troubles on Cetshwayo and the heart of darkness.

> When you pass judgment upon me in that comfortable room at Whately try and fancy yourself in the King's kraal in the heart of the Umfolozi Bush with thousands of wild Zulus around you who, whatever else they have learned from the white man have learned the name of the Evil one and call themselves 'the boys of Satan'. You have heard of course of the *new* line of action which has lately been adopted toward the missionaries by the King and his advisors. Three Christians have been killed and it was intended to kill others.[99]

With a fierce determination born of despair Robertson now tried to redeem himself by bringing down the king. He became the anonymous Zulu correspondent of the *Natal Mercury* and wrote voluminously to anyone who would listen to his tales of Cetshwayo's tyranny. This dramatic reversal meant that for the first time in decades Christian missionaries could present a united front on Zulu affairs. They were putty in the hands of a clever man like Shepstone who knew how to manipulate them.

It is well known that Shepstone reversed his opinions on the Transvaal-Zulu border dispute as soon as he raised the British flag in Pretoria. The standard explanation of his shift is that before the annexation Shepstone supported the Zulu cause as a way of keeping the Transvaal away from the sea; afterwards he tried to win popularity among the Afrikaners by taking their side, only to have Frere pull the rug from beneath his feet by eliminating the black menace which had hitherto kept the Krugerites in check. This explanation errs by narrowly concentrating on the rivalries between Boer and Briton. It neglects the geo-political basis of Carnarvon's confederation strategy which Shepstone summed up shortly after the

Transvaal annexation.

> I dare say it would have been possible to get the President and Raad
> themselves to propose the annexation of the country if the pressure
> of surrounding circumstances had not been so great; but the tension
> was so extreme that one accidental shot might, and most probably
> would, have annihilated the Republic and cost England millions
> to gain the position she now holds, and may firmly hold, with ease
> over the native races of South Africa.
>   The Transvaal commands South Africa as regards position and
> soon will do so otherwise.[100]

From Shepstone's point of view the object of the mission was not the
capture of Afrikanerdom but the taking of a strategic position which
happened to be in the hands of Afrikaners. The Transvaal lay across or
adjacent to all the principal labor migration routes as well as all the easy
roads to the beckoning north. The armed black nations who were best
able to threaten movement along these roads, and who themselves supplied
little or no labor, were situated in a horseshoe configuration around the
Transvaal: Lobengula's Ndebele, Mzila's Shangane, the Swazi, the Zulu,
the Sotho. Shepstone for whom the combination of these peoples was
a recurrent nightmare did not imagine that he was merely playing 'the
Zulu card' in order to deal with the Afrikaners. He played 'the Transvaal
card' in order to deal better with the Zulus and those whom he imagined
to be the Zulu allies. Employers throughout South Africa shared his point
of view. In September 1876 there were loud complaints from the diamond
fields about the labor shortage caused by the Transvaal-Pedi war.[101] The
Port Elizabeth Chamber of Commerce hailed Shepstone's annexation of
the Transvaal because it strengthened the weak link in the chain of defense
against a 'Native Combination'. The Chamber noted that

> the long unsettled condition and warlike desires of the natives have
> seriously retarded the advancement of public works, drained the
> labor market in every way, greatly increased the rise in wages, the
> cost of living, and the public expenditure for internal protection
> and frontier defense.[102]

It was only natural that Shepstone's whole attitude toward the Zulus
should alter once he was established in Pretoria. Before, he had required
Zulu cooperation in order to annex a corridor through the disputed

territory. Now he had only to uphold the Transvaal claims in order to secure the corridor free of charge. The only possible threat to its security was the Zulu kingdom. In his first comments on the invitation to crown Cetshwayo, Shepstone had written that 'the power to control the Zulus includes that of controlling all the rest'. After the annexation of the Transvaal he wrote to Carnarvon suggesting that this axiom was to be the basis of his entire defense policy.

> We might as well surrender at once as do anything that would confirm all these populations in their suspicions that we fear the Zulus. Nor do I think it would be a very difficult thing to break up the Zulu power, and when that is done, you may calculate more certainly upon peace in South Africa. Cetywayo is the secret hope of every . . . independent chief, hundreds of miles from him, who feels a desire that his colour should prevail, and it will not be until this power is destroyed, that they will make up their minds to submit to the rule of civilization . . . the sooner the root of the evil (of black restlessness in South Africa) which I consider to be the Zulu power and military organization is dealt with the easier our task will be.[103]

Frere entirely agreed with Shepstone that a pre-emptive strike against the Zulus was an essential preliminary to the subsequent development of southern Africa.

> I have seen enough to feel sure that Shepstone is quite right as to the influence of any Kaffir disturbance, and still more of any Kaffir success, on the Kaffir population everywhere.
> It may be quite impossible to combine different tribes, long hostile to each other, against us − but no one tribe can be disturbed without others joining in the excitement . . . .[104]

In the light of all the pressing reasons for an immediate annexation of Zululand, Frere confessed to Carnarvon frankly that 'how any such result can be deferred to a more convenient season, when you have less on hand, is a more difficult question?'[105]

Frere and Shepstone seized eagerly on the missionaries to justify aggression which was really undertaken solely for reasons of state. The missionaries did not know this but did realise clearly enough that vague accusations of 'widespread killing' and 'indiscriminate bloodshed' would not be enough to sanctify British intervention. Some concrete instances of injustice or cruelty were required. The incident everyone had been waiting for occurred on 4 March 1877 when a Hermannsburg convert was accused of witchcraft, seized, and killed by one of Cetshwayo's impis. Even though the king sent an immediate message to the missionary in charge assuring him that the action had been aimed only at an evil individual and not Christians in general, the missionaries immediately raised the cry of pogrom. They forgot old rivalries and organised a theatrical withdrawal from Zululand. The only alternative, Oftebro wrote to Robertson, was to continue to wait and wait as they had for so many years.[106] Robertson in turn suggested sending a memorial of grievances to Natal and consulting Shepstone as soon as possible. The memorial of 18 May 1877 claimed that 'in 1873 the Zulu nation entered into a solemn compact with the English government . . . . According to the Zulu ideas it made Natal and Zululand "one country" '. Because Shepstone's 'laws' had been repeatedly broken the missionaries asked 'that the powerful Christian Government which your Excellency represents may be inclined to extend to us the help and protection we so much need'.[107] While awaiting an answer, two of the Norwegians went off to see Shepstone who recommended strongly that all the missionaries should immediately leave the country as Britain was about to break up the Zulu military machine.[108]

Most missionaries then obediently packed and left. Just as the exodus was getting into full swing they were chagrined to learn that Zululand was not to be annexed after all. Bulwer vehemently denied that Britain was poised to intervene and castigated the missionaries for threatening Cetshwayo with the mass withdrawal.[109] With the exception of the Hermannsburgers whom the king positively forbade to return, the missionaries shamefacedly made their various ways back to Zululand to await further developments. They had no way of knowing that the bellicosity of Frere and Shepstone had been thwarted by the humanity of Bulwer and the desire of Carnarvon not to arouse hostile opinion in Britain by another annexation so soon after the taking of the Transvaal.[110] Bereft of support from Shepstone, Robertson entered into negotiations with Cetshwayo. The king wanted all missionaries to leave except for the veterans Robertson Samuelson, Schreuder, Oftebro, Gundersen and Larsen. Robertson offered to stay on the condition that no station residents be seized without trial.[111] His letter to his colleague Shildrick makes it plain that his inflammatory letters to the *Mercury* and government officials had been calculated lies:

I quite agree with you that the King is not so bad as he is painted etc. He wished to save the life of Ungambaza but could not.

In writing this and my previous letter I am of course taking it for granted that the present regime is to continue. Both Mr. Samuelson and yourself look forward to a time when this land will belong to the white man. I look forward with perfect certainty to that day coming *unless the Zulus become Christians*. But that is what we are here for . . . . I confess when I see what a hell of a place Natal is becoming I shall be very sorry to see the Native policy of Natal introduced into Zululand.[112]

Robertson's sanguine state of mind seems to have been based on the expectation that Cetshwayo would after all outwit Shepstone in their current struggle over the disputed territory. On 3 October, 1877, Robertson wrote to his bishop that all sorts of rumors were abroad in Zululand concerning British intentions and that a special emissary had just been sent to Shepstone. Robertson continued with the astonishing assertion that

Regarding the King you have nothing to fear *if you do not interfere* with him. I am looking forward with great interest to the result of the present tussle between him and Sir T.S. Twice before, in 1861 and 1873 they have tried their strength, and on each occasion Cetywayo had the better of it. The mission of 61 was an utter failure and the coronation was a farce. Lately the King said to me, 'I love the English. I am not Umpande's son. I am the child of Queen Victoria. But I am also a King in my own country and must be treated as such. Somseu [*sic*] (Sir T.S.) must speak gently to me. I shall not hear dictation'. (and he added with great emphasis) 'I shall perish first.'[113]

Only three weeks later, Robertson revived his anti-Cetshwayo campaign with unprecendented vehemence.[114] It may be that late in October Shepstone advised Robertson that annexation was again imminent. The two were in close and frequent communication at this time,[115] and Robertson must have known that Shepstone had been enraged by Cetshwayo's refusal to discuss a compromise on the boundary issue.[116] He may well have encouraged Robertson to renew his propaganda campaign in favor of annexation. At any rate Robertson did renew that campaign with the support of other missionaries.

He opened a correspondence with Sir Bartle Frere.[117] He wrote to

Bulwer that Cetshwayo was 'ready for war, and a mere trifle may bring it about'.[118] Furthermore, provided that no taxation was imposed on them, most of the Zulu people 'would hail the English rule tomorrow'. Whatever Bulwer might think, Robertson assured him that war was inevitable, and tragic as it would be 'there are worse things than war sometimes'.[119] Other missionaries wrote to non-official luminaries with similar tales. Samuelson told his missionary society that 'half the Zulu nation would welcome Shepstone as their deliverer'.[120] Robertson urged Bishop Macrorie to pass his slanderous stories along to well-placed officials.[121] From Robertson, Macrorie now heard that 'the state of things in Zululand is as bad as it is possible to imagine' and that under no circumstances should the British trust the king's promises. Robertson's continued articles for the *Mercury* also beat the drum of Christian persecution. One of his articles which described dissension in Cetshwayo's regiments created a crisis for the Norwegian missionaries. The king blamed them for the report and ordered them out of the country.[122]

The Norwegians were glad enough of the order and refused to let Robertson exonerate them.[123] They used the incident as another excuse to seek British intervention, informing Bulwer that since 1873 they had regarded themselves as under Queen Victoria's protection.[124] Bulwer refused support but Oftebro continued to intrigue with Shepstone. Early in March, 1878, Oftebro returned from consultations in the Transvaal and again provoked a mass withdrawal of missionaries.[125] Again Robertson joined enthusiastically in the movement. He too had been receiving hints of British intervention and resolved to hurry the event. He wrote to Macrorie at the end of March

> By the last post, in addition to what your Lordship knows, I received the following mysterious communication 'The horses are coming in May. You understand?' Yes; I understand very well. All I hope for is, that there may be plenty of them.[126]

Within a few months the missionaries were out of Zululand. But the final declaration of war had nothing to do with their action. Like bad actors who miss their cues and bungle their speeches, the missionaries stumbled on and off stage during 1877 and 1878 little realising that their parts were dispensable.

Conclusion

It has been necessary to go through the evidence in some detail in order to emphasise that the Anglo-Zulu War was far more than just Frere's war and that the part played by missionaries and Zulus in bringing the war on was negligible. When it was convenient, evidence of missionary unhappiness and internal turmoil in Zululand could be trotted out in justification of British intervention. Both the unhappiness and the turmoil were real enough but they had nothing to do with Frere's ultimatum.

The Coronation of Cetshwayo in 1873 serves as a convenient mile post in the course of Anglo-Zulu relations. Before 1861 the two governments knew little about each other. The interests of both were parochial. In 1861 Cetshwayo's anxiety over his right of succession caused him to make promises which laid the groundwork for the long struggle over the disputed territory. Shepstone tried to get a footing in Zululand by recognising Cetshwayo's status as heir apparent. He tried to get a strip of land in the disputed territory to be used both as a laboratory for experiments in African administration and as a buffer against Transvaal expansion. But in this first face-to-face meeting Cetshwayo gave nothing away.

By 1873 the world had changed vastly for Shepstone but not so much for the Zulus. Economic development at the diamond fields and on Natal's plantations had created a network of migrant labor which reached out to places as remote as Shonaland and Zanzibar. More mineral discoveries seemed imminent but their development would depend on the smooth flow of men and materials unimpeded by local disturbances, robbery or extortionate customs levies. Now Shepstone went to Zululand with new objectives: to regularise arrangements for the passage of laborers through the kingdom; to negotiate the cession of part of the disputed territory which would not only provide room for experiments in administration but also a permanent bridge to the north; and to demonstrate with appropriate pomp and circumstance that the Zulu nation accepted British supremacy. Cetshwayo, on the other hand, still sought only to solve the old problem of his succession, to secure his northwestern frontier and to maintain his visible independence. To be sure, his land was changing; he rode out to meet Shepstone in a carriage pulled by four prancing horses. There were more missionaries, guns, trade goods in the kingdom. But his young men were still soldiers rather than migrant workers and he could reasonably attribute the tensions in the country to fifteen years of uncertainty about the locus of power.

Shepstone emerged a definite loser in his second contest with Cetshwayo but managed to conceal his failure in a self-congratulatory report printed for parliament. The Langalibalele affair gave him the opportunity to recoup his losses on a grand scale by convincing the Colonial Office that he had discovered the philosopher's stone of 'native policy' in southern Africa. What South Africa needed, he argued, was what he had been trying to achieve all along in Natal. Tough measures had to be taken to prevent ignorant and rapacious white settlers from digging their own graves by squeezing African farmers into destitution. Extensive reserved lands must be set aside and administered by English gentlemen using the techniques of indirect rule he had perfected. Outside the reserves a cheap black police force under white officers was needed to preserve law and order. So were curfews, pass laws, and wage regulations like the ones he had drawn up for municipalities in Natal. He further argued that an essential preliminary to achieving these large designs was a convincing demonstration that no African military force could hope to challenge British power. Once this was done the very real danger of a general anti-European conspiracy would disappear. Shepstone also argued that African administration in any territory south of the Zambezi could be made to pay its own way so long as there were enough arable land to support the population. He pointed to Natal's government accounts as proof of his theory. On his plan the British empire could be extended far into the tropics without undue expense to the British taxpayer.

Carnarvon accepted the greater part of Shepstone's argument and built his own version of confederation upon it. The agents Carnarvon chose to make confederation work believed in Shepstone at least as much as he did. Most gratifying of all for Shepstone, he received the Transvaal to govern. Once seated in Pretoria he did not need a black kingdom for administrative experiments. Nor did he need a strip of territory as a bridge to the north. He now required only one thing of the Zulu king and that was that he should visibly bend his knee before British might.

By 1877 Cetshwayo had discovered that an undisputed crown was not enough to order his kingdom. Meddlesome missionaries whom he had always distrusted were making things worse by telling the world that the king's attempt to settle the country amounted to nothing more than a bloody and capricious tyranny. Whether Cetshwayo could eventually have succeeded in overcoming his internal problems can never be known because war intervened. Shepstone and Frere were agreed that the Zulu military machine must be seen to be broken and did not much care when the job was done. All available military advice seconded their judgment. They were as ready to move in July and December of 1877 as they were in December 1878. What was really going on in Zululand did not concern them. In the third great confrontation between Shepstone and Cetshwayo the king was no more willing than before to give up Zulu autonomy. From that moment in 1877 war was put off only by Bulwer's humanity and the Colonial Office's jittery insistence that the time was not yet ripe.

There were certainly personal factors involved in the decision to go to war, but the objects sought by Frere and Shepstone — the end of political fragmentation in southern Africa, the subjection of African peoples to a form of indirect rule, the organisation of orderly labor migration and the efficient development of new mineral discoveries — these were not just quirky idiosyncrasies. They would become the dominant features of twentieth-century South Africa. It was to advance these ends that brave men lay dead in the whispering grass at Isandlwana one hundred years ago.

NOTES

The following abbreviations are used in these notes:

APS	Aborigines Protection Society Papers, Rhodes House, Oxford
BPP	British Parliamentary Papers
CO	Colonial Office Papers, Public Record Office, London
COL	Colenso Papers, Killie Campbell Africana Library of the University of Natal
CP	Carnarvon Papers, Public Record Office, London
FO	Foreign Office Papers, Public Record Office, London
GH	Government House Papers, Natal Archives
HER	Hermannsburg Missionary Society Archives, Hermannsburg, West Germany
KCAL	Killie Campbell Africana Library of the University of Natal
Net	*The Net Cast in Many Waters*, an Anglican missionary periodical edited by A. Mackenzie in London
SNA	Secretary for Native Affairs Papers, Natal Archives
SPG	United Society for the Propagation of the Gospel Archives, London
WMP	Wesleyan Methodist Missionary Papers, Natal Archives
WES	Methodist Missionary Society Archives, London

1   BPP LII of 1878–9, C.2222: Frere to Hicks Beach, 2 Dec. 1878.

2   BPP LII of 1878–9, C. 2222: Frere, various memoranda accompanying com-
    mission report on the Zulu-Transvaal border dispute forwarded to Hicks
    Beach, 16 Nov. 1878; LIII of 1875, C. 1137: *Report of the Expedition . . . to
    install Cetywayo.*

3   BPP LII of 1878–9, C. 2220: Frere to Hicks Beach, 30 Sept. 1878.

4   BPP LII of 1878–9, C. 2222: Frere to Hicks Beach, 2 Dec. 1878.

5   COL, folio X: Colenso to Bunyon, 9 May 1859; SPG, folio D8: Colenso to
    S.P.G. Secretaries, 8 Aug. 1857.

6   N. Etherington, *Preachers, Peasants and Politics in Southeast Africa, 1835–1880*
    (London, The Royal Historical Society, 1978), pp. 75–82.

7   Halfdan E. Sommerfelt, *Den Norske Zulumission* (Christiania, 1865), p. 286.

8   SPG, folio E7: Robertson to Colenso, 6 Dec. 1860; WMP 2/3/1: Blencowe
    to Pearse, 27 July 1861.

9   Soon after establishing his mission in Zululand, Robertson wrote to Colenso
    that 'Natal politics are known and discussed here to an extent I could not
    have supposed possible'. See SPG, folio E7: Robertson to Colenso, 30 Oct.
    1860.

10 WMP 2/3/1: interview between Schreuder and the Methodist missionary
    George Blencowe as transcribed by Blencowe and enclosed in Blencowe to
    Pearse, 27 July 1861. This recital is not in conflict with Colenso's versions
    of the same events. See SPG, folio D25: Colenso to Bullock, 4 May 1861.

11 Ibid.

12 SPG, folio D25: Colenso to Bullock, 4 May 1861.

13 SNA 1/7/5: Shepstone Memorandum, 30 March 1861; SNA 1/8/7: Shepstone
    to Scott, *confidential*, 22 June 1861.

14 SPG, folio D8: A. Mackenzie, unaddressed letter, 28 May 1861 enclosed in
    Colenso to Bullock, 30 June 1861.

15 WMP 2/3/1: Blencowe to Pearse, 27 July 1861.

16 SPG, folio D25: Colenso, unaddressed letter, July 1861 and Robertson to
    Colenso, 22 July 1861.

17 SNA 1/7/4: Oftebro to Walmsley, 23 July 1861.

18 Missionaries favourable to Cetshwayo often emphasised the limits to his
    power in the 1860s. Robert Robertson warned his missionary society that
    'it would be wrong to blame Cetywayo for all the butcheries which almost
    weekly take place; it is an evil system which he has inherited, and I doubt
    if he could alter it if he would' (SPG, folio E17: Robertson to Hawkins,
    17 April 1865).

19 GH, folio 1397: F.B. Fynney, memorandum, 5 Aug. 1877.

20 See, for example: SNA 1/1/15: Schreuder to Shepstone, 11 Jan. 1865; SNA
    1/4/1: Statement of Sidindi, Umrabelana and Komeweba, messengers from
    Zululand, 5 June 1869; and WES: Blencowe to Boyce, 15 Sept. 1870.

21 CO 179/102: enclosed in Keate to Kimberley, 6 June 1871. The subject
    of these negotiations was the presence in Natal of a young man alleged to
    be Mzilikazi's long lost son Kuruman, rightful heir to the throne Lobengula
    had just claimed as his own. That the supposed Kuruman was in Natal
    emphasises the point made above about the links between Natal and Central
    Africa. Shepstone at first supported the pseudo-Kuruman but dropped all
    support when Lobengula provided willing cooperation with mineral pros-
    pectors from Natal. T.J. Couzens has speculated in an unpublished seminar

paper (Institute of Commonwealth Studies, London, January 1974) that Shepstone revived the claims of Kuruman at the time of the ill-fated Patterson expedition of 1879.

22   SNA 1/3/21: Lucas to Shepstone, 24 July 1871; CO 179/99: Keate to Kimberley, 23 Sept. 1870; SNA 1/1/20: Levert to Shepstone, 30 May 1870; *Natal Witness*, 29 July 1870.

23   *Natal Witness*, 2 March 1869.

24   *Natal Witness*, 12 May 1868.

25   CO 879/1: 'Natal, despatches, Reports, etc. Relative to the Management of the Natives', Confidential Print, p.5. For the reference to Shepstone's reputation as a source of labour see *Mercury*, 19 Dec. 1872.

26   SNA, 1/3/7: Newcastle Annual Report, 1866.

27   Natal Legislative Council, 3rd session, 6th Council, L.C. No.12; CO 179/111: Musgrave to Kimberley, 6 Jan. 1873.

28   Cape Archives, Griqualand West papers, folio 71: Monthly Returns of African Labour.

29   CO 179/100: Murdoch to Rogers, 5 July 1870. The request was refused on advice from the Emigration Board that there was plenty of land still available for white settlement in Natal and that the colony should stay out of the Zulu-Transvaal dispute.

30   CO 48/462: Barkly to Kimberley, 29 Nov. 1872.

31   *Natal Witness*, 9 May 1871.

32   *Natal Colonist*, 18 April 1873.

33   CO 179/102: Keate to Kimberley, 12 Sept. 1871. Leslie also complained that Cetshwayo was causing difficulty through backdoor dealings with the Portuguese (CO 179/106: Keate to Kimberley, 17 Jan. 1872).

34   CO 179/102: Keate to Kimberley, 12 Sept. 1871.

35   Ibid.; see also CO 179/107: Musgrave to Kimberley, 8 Aug. 1872; FO 84/1386: Joao de Andrade Corvo to Murray, 8 July 1872; *Mercury*, 24 July 1873.

36   *Mercury*, 25 March 1873.

37   *Mercury*, 24 June 1873.

38   FO 84/1389: Frere to Granville, n.d.; CO 179/112: F. Elton, 'Slave Trade, etc. Report on East Coast, Portuguese possessions', 20 March 1873, enclosed in Musgrave to Kimberley, 25 April 1873.

39   SNA 1/7/6: Message from the Zulu Nation to the Lt. Governor, 26 Feb. 1873; *Net*, vol. VIII (1873), p.67, gives Mrs S.M. Samuelson's account of Mpande's death and burial.

40   SNA 1/3/21: Mesham to Shepstone, 1 Feb. 1871 and Dillon to Shepstone, 19 March 1871. The magistrates listed 'Umkungu', 'Umtonga', 'Usikota', 'Umcutshendu' and 'Ungatsha'.

41   SNA 1/3/22: Acting Resident Magistrate, Umvoti, to Shepstone, 4 June 1872 with Shepstone minute of 5 June 1872.

42   SNA 1/3/15: Hardwick to Shepstone, 11 Jan. 1865; SNA 1/3/20: Osborn to Shepstone, 27 Dec. 1870, with minute by J.W. Shepstone, 4 Jan. 1871; APS, C131/91: Colenso to Chesson, 12 Dec. 1875.

43   SNA 1/3/22: J. Scoble, A.R.M., Newcastle, to Shepstone, 27 Aug. 1872 with Shepstone minute 2 Sept. 1872; Colenso letter, *Natal Witness*, 29 July 1873.

50

NORMAN ETHERINGTON

44 SNA 1/7/11: J.W. Shepstone, confidential memorandum on 'the ability of the Government of Natal to prevent the King of the Zulus from murdering Natives attending Mission Stations in his country', 1877.

45 *Net*, vol.IX (1874), p.101.

46 SNA 1/3/23: Osborn to Shepstone, 30 Jan. 1873.

47 SPG, folio E7: Robertson to Colenso, 30 Nov. 1860.

48 Jeff Guy, 'A Note on Firearms in the Anglo-Zulu War', *Journal of African History*, vol.XI (1970), pp.561–563.

49 Etherington, pp.80–84.

50 GH, folio 1397: Fynney, minute paper, 5 Aug. 1877.

51 COL, folio N: Colenso to Shepstone, 20 Jan. 1869. The source of the bishop's information was a letter from Dunn. John Dunn's personal antipathy to missions, particularly when they served as trading centres, shows up clearly in the restrictions he placed on missionaries in his own 'chiefdom' after the Zulu War. See Charles S. Shields 'The Life of John Dunn with Special Reference to Zululand 1879–1897' (unpublished M.A. thesis, University of South Africa, 1939), 56–57.

52 *Colonist*, 14 Feb. 1873.

53 SNA 1/1/19: Hohls to Keate, 21 June 1869.

54 HER: Report of the meeting to consider the request of Dedekind to move, 21 April 1873.

55 SNA 1/1/24: Committee to the Directors of the Norwegian Missionary Society to Shepstone, 12 Dec. 1874.

56 COL, folio N: Colenso to Shepstone, 29 Jan. 1873. It is possible that in addition to discussing Zulu politics, the three men considered some version of the old black kingdom proposal. Colenso accepted Shepstone's thesis that African administration could pay its own way and leave a surplus with which to finance 'free Missionary operations . . . *unfettered by anything or anybody on earth*': he considered such an operation as an attractive alternative to struggling on in the essentially untenable situation produced by the Anglican schism (COL, folio M: Colenso to Shepstone, 5 March 1863). Schreuder now faced a similar problem.

57 SNA 1/1/23: Schreuder to Cato, 11 March 1873. Bishop Schreuder also reported that although Cetshwayo no longer accused him of having written the offensive letter about Mpande's death, he remained very hostile to all the newer missionaries in Zululand.

58 SNA 1/7/7: Shepstone, Report of the Expedition to Install Cetshwayo, August 1873; KCAL, Cato Papers: G. Cato to W. Shepstone, 20 Aug. 1873; C. Barter, *Stray Memories of Natal and Zululand: a Poem* (Pietermaritzburg, 1897).

59 SNA 1/7/6: Shepstone, memorandum, 3 March 1873.

60 *Witness*, 24 Oct. 1873.

61 *Mercury*, 23 Aug. 1873.

62 CO 48/454: minute on Barkly to Kimberley, 1 Feb. 1871.

63 CO 48/465: minute on Barkly to Kimberley, 4 April 1873.

64 CO 179/106: minute on Keate to Kimberley, 17 Jan. 1872; CO 48/462: minutes on Barkly to Kimberley, 23 Aug. 1872; CO 179/116: Bisset, memorandum, 5 June 1874.

65   CO 48/465: Barkly to Kimberley, 25 March 1873 and 25 June 1873.

66   N. Etherington, 'Why Langalibalele Ran Away', *Journal of Natal and Zulu History*, vol.I (1978), pp.1–25.

67   KCAL, Cato Papers: Cato to W. Shepstone, 20 Aug. 1873.

68   *Net*, vol. IX (1874), pp.24–25.

69   P.T. de Vos, *The Dunns of Zululand: Confidential Report to the Social and Economic Planning Council* (Durban, 1946), pp.4–6.

70   *Report of the Expedition*, 19–20.

71   Ibid., 16–19.

72   SPG, Wigram Papers: Robertson to Macrorie, 23 Oct. 1877; APS, C123/80: Akerman to J.E. Carlyle, 5 Oct. 1876.

73   SNA 1/7/13: Statement of Bayeni and Mauthonza, Messengers, 2 Nov. 1876. The authenticity of the message has sometimes been suspected but I believe it to be valid because its language so closely resembles Robertson's report of an interview with Cetshwayo in the same month:

      I spoke my mind very plainly to him regarding the great amount of bloodshed that has lately taken place, and warned him plainly that such unrighteous deeds would bring down a judgment upon him and his country . . . . He got into a great rage; some of the things he said were not wanting in cleverness. Regarding the killing, he told me to go and preach that doctrine to the Dutch . . . he said he killed none to speak of. It had been their custom to do so, and he was not going to change.

      (Robertson to A. Mackenzie, 4 Nov. 1876, reprinted in *Net*, vol.XII (1877), p.18.)

75   CO 48/469: minute of 27 Aug. 1874 on Barkly to Carnarvon, 25 July 1874.

76   CO 179/115–16: minutes on Lucas memorandum, 9 Aug. 1874 and Pine to Carnarvon, 24 Sept. 1874.

77   CP, PRO 30/6/4: 'Notes of Conversations with Shepstone', 1874.

78   CO 179/104: Shepstone memorandum, 18 Dec. 1871, enclosed in Keate to Kimberley, 20 Dec. 1871.

79   CO 179/116: Minutes of 9, 12, 16 and 18 Sept. on Lucas to Carnarvon. 9 Aug. 1874.

80   CO 179/116: Shepstone to Herbert, 30 Nov. 1874.

81   R.E. Gordon, *Shepstone: the Role of the Family in the History of South Africa, 1820–1900* (Cape Town, 1968), pp.192–93.

82   CP, PRO 30/6/4: Carnarvon to Frere, 12 Dec. 1876, quoted in C.F. Goodfellow, *Great Britain and South African Confederation* (Cape Town, 1966), p.117.

83   I have attempted it elsewhere in 'Labour Supply and Genesis of South African Confederation in the 1870s', *Journal of African History*, vol.XX, 1 (1979), pp.235–253.

84   *Mercury*, 26 Feb. 1874; CO 179/117: Wolseley to Carnarvon, 24 June 1875; CO 179/121: Bulwer to Carnarvon, 28 Aug. 1876; FO 84/1479: Elton to Frere, 5 Feb. 1877.

85   CO 179/119: F.O. to C.O., 31 July 1875.

86   CO 179/122: Editor of *Northern Echo* to Carnarvon, 25 April 1876.

87   CO 179/125: F.O. to C.O., 19 April 1877.

88   CO 179/125: F.O. to C.O., 23 June 1877.

89   CO 179/119: F.O. to C.O., 3 Dec. 1875.

90   CP, PRO 30/6/38: Wolseley to Carnarvon, 16 May 1875.

91   CP, PRO 30/6/38: Wolseley to Carnarvon, 8 July 1875.

92   CO 179/118: Wolseley, comments of 21 Jan. 1876 on Bulwer to Carnarvon, 26 Oct. 1875.

93   CO 179/123: minute on Bulwer to Carnarvon, 27 April 1877.

94   SPG, folio D25: Robertson to Colenso, 25 Jan. 1863.

95   *Net*, vol. VI (1871), pp.173–74.

96   *Net*, vol IX (1874), p.50.

97   SPG, folio E29: Samuelson, quarterly report, March 1874.

98   Etherington, *Preachers, Peasants and Politics*, p.45.

99   SPG, folio D46: Robertson to Moore, 2 July 1877.

100 CP, PRO 30/6/23: Shepstone to Carnarvon, 23 July 1877.

101 CP, PRO 30/6/36: Lanyon to Carnarvon, 14 Sept. 1876.

102 CP, PRO 30/6/33: Petition from the Port Elizabeth Chamber of Commerce, n.d.

103 CP, PRO 30/6/23: Shepstone to Carnarvon, 11 Dec. 1877.

104 CP, PRO 30/6/33: Frere to Carnarvon, 19 July 1877.

105 Ibid.

106 GH, folio 1397: Oftebro to Robertson, 17 March 1877, copy.

107 GH, folio 1397: Memorial to Bulwer, 18 May 1877.

108 O.G. Myklebust, *Det Norske Misjonsselskaps Historie i Hundre Ar*, vol. III (Stavanger, 1949), pp.43–45.

109 GH, folio 1397: Bulwer to Robertson, 26 July 1877.

110 CP, PRO 30/6/33: Carnarvon to Frere, 7 June 1877.

111 SPG, Wigram Papers: Robertson to Macrorie, 25 Sept. 1877.

112 SPG, Wigram Papers: Robertson to Shildrick, 15 Oct. 1877.

113 SPG, Wigram Papers, Robertson to Macrorie, 23 Oct. 1877.

114 GH, folio 1397: Robertson to Bulwer, 16 Nov. 1877.

115 GH, folio 1398: Frere to Bulwer, 1 Oct. 1877.

116 SPG, Wigram Papers: Robertson to Macrorie, 6 Feb. 1878.

117 Frere welcomed Robertson's information, but told him that all news should be sent through Bulwer (GH, folio 1397: Bulwer to Robertson, 11 Nov. 1877).

118 GH, folio 1397: Robertson to Bulwer, 16 Nov. 1877.

119 GH, folio 1397: Robertson to Bulwer, 1 Dec. 1877.

120 SPG, folio E32: Samuelson to the Secretaries, 31 Dec. 1877.

121 SPG, Wigram Papers: Robertson to Macrorie, 7 Jan. 1878.

122 SPG, Wigram Papers: Robertson to Macrorie, 6 Feb. 1878; SPG, folio E33: Samuelson, Quarterly report, March 1878.

123 SPG, Wigram Papers: Robertson to Macrorie, 6 Feb. 1878.

124 BPP LVI of 1878, C.2100: Bulwer to Carnarvon, 6 March 1878.

125 SNA 1/4/1: John Shepstone to Bulwer, 28 April 1878.

126 SPG, Wigram Papers: Robertson to Macrorie, 30 March 1878.

BILL GUEST

The War, Natal and Confederation

> The position of this Colony, having regard to the circumstances
> on either side of it and within it, is peculiar at this moment and
> cannot be judged from one standpoint of view alone.[1]

The decade 1870 to 1880 witnessed a series of attempts to create a
confederation in southern Africa. The failure of those efforts is a chapter
in British imperial history which has already been exhaustively studied,
both from the point of view of the metropolitan power from whence the
policy of confederation originated and from that of the Cape Colony,
which was intended to be the senior partner upon which such a confederal
association was to rest.[2] The relationship between Britain's confederation
proposals and the motivation of the Anglo-Zulu War of 1879 has been
similarly analysed in painstaking detail, both by other contributors to
this conference and in earlier published works.[3]

The purpose of this paper is to examine the response of Natal's white
colonists to the war-crisis of 1879, their role in its initiation and their
reaction to its outcome, with particular reference to the notion of a
confederation conference, in which they had previously been so willing
to participate.[4] The history of white societies in southern Africa may be
dismissed, in some quarters, as an unfashionable and irrelevant avenue of
research.[5] Yet the Anglo-Zulu War was, in part, officially prosecuted in
the name of Natal's colonists and the accusation that they had actively
'urged it on,' in order to serve their own selfish interests, gained such wide
currency in Britain that both Bishop Colenso and Lieutenant-Governor
Bulwer found it necessary to come to their defence.[6]

Such a study is unavoidably confronted with the problem of assessing
white public opinion in the colony, a difficult task in an historical context

which offers only fragmentary and sometimes contradictory evidence on the subject. At a superficial level, it seems feasible to assume that there was a readily identifiable consensus of settler opinion on the subject of war against the Zulu kingdom. After all, the overwhelming majority of Natal's white inhabitants appear to have shared a common British background in respect of language, culture, social attitudes and mid-Victorian Christian *mores*. Moreover, all the colonists apparently anticipated a common fate in the event of a Zulu invasion of Natal and it might be argued that, in relation to the colony's own black population, they shared a common class interest which was sufficiently strong to generate a united demand for more land and labour.[7]

Yet, on closer examination, it appears that such a convenient consensus of settler opinion may be, at least partially, an illusion. The occupational differences which existed among the Natal colonists might conceivably have made it difficult for them to recognize and articulate a common class interest. Those in northern Natal were predominantly pastoralists (and were partly Dutch-speaking), the inhabitants of the coastal regions were engaged primarily either in sugar farming or in commerce, while the economic interests of the farming community of the midlands could not and would not be readily identified with either of the other two districts.[8] In addition, there is perhaps an important distinction to be drawn between urban and rural whites, whose economic needs, political outlook and predisposition to panic at the prospect of invasion were not necessarily identical. For this reason, it may be erroneous to regard the views expressed at vocal public meetings in the urban centres, by urban-based political leaders and by newspapers published in the towns as being fully representative of the white community as a whole. It is also debatable to what extent, if at all, public opinion was manufactured by editorials written by individuals who were themselves active figures in the political life of the colony, or produced by local journals which had been successfully engaged to promote official policy.[9]

On these grounds it seems dangerous to assume that, by the late 1870s, all sectors of the colonial economy were in similar need of more land and labour, or that rural and urban whites were uniformly living in mortal fear of being murdered in their beds by Zulu raiders and that, for such reasons, they were bound to be overwhelmingly in favour of destroying Cetshwayo's kingdom. Much basic research, beyond the scope of this paper, has still to be done on the nature of public opinion and of politics in colonial Natal. What follows is therefore no more than a tentative and somewhat speculative study of the behaviour of the settlers during the war-crisis of 1879.

The outbreak of war in 1879 appears to have been accepted, if not welcomed, by many of the white colonists of Natal as the culmination of a longstanding restlessness among the black peoples of southern Africa which was popularly attributed to Zulu instigation. For some time rumour had been rife in the colony that the recent disturbances on the Cape's eastern frontier, in Griqualand West and also those involving the Pedi in the north-eastern Transvaal, were all part of a Zulu-inspired conspiracy against white settlement throughout the subcontinent.[10] The mere suggestion of such a 'hostile purpose on the part of the natives generally' would have been of understandable concern to white Natalians who, as the *Natal Witness* observed, had little interest in 'what Europe, Asia, America, and Australia, are doing while we have a Native Question to discuss . . . . It is a standing dish on our political bill of fare.'[11]

'On the eastern side of the continent the Colony of Natal formed the outpost of British territory'.[12] Its contacts with the white settlements of the interior were hampered by the Drakensberg mountains and, for the rest, it was virtually surrounded by indigenous societies. These included the tribes who inhabited the region to the southwest between Natal and the Cape Colony proper, the Sotho beyond the southern Drakensberg, who had already demonstrated their strength in confrontations with the Orange Free State Republic and, not least, the Zulu kingdom itself, the suspected storm-centre of south-east Africa, in uncomfortably close proximity across the Thukela river — which was often no more than a trickle of water.[13]

Within Natal's own borders the white colonists were widely scattered over the best areas of farmland with dense concentrations of blacks interspersed among them. Durban and Pietermaritzburg were the only towns of any significant size and, at the time of the Anglo-Zulu War, were still a whole day's journey by horse-drawn omnibus apart.[14] There were few other roads to facilitate communications among the various regions of the colony. That between Pietermaritzburg and Greytown was characterized by 'several nasty crossings and spruits' and involved another full day's journey.[15] As late as 1881, the roads of northern Natal were described as being little more than 'mud-hole tracks . . . a serious drawback to the success of our arms.'[16] The isolated farmers of the colony could draw little consolation from the railway for, although Natal had boasted the first stretch of line in southern Africa, from the Point to Durban, railway construction proper was still in its infancy in the colony, the first sod of the Natal Government Railways having only been turned in January 1876. Thereafter, progress had been depressingly slow. The inland line did not reach the colonial capital until 1880, having advanced no further than Botha's Hill by March 1879.[17]

It had often been suggested that it was 'only by inducing an influx of white settlers into the Colony that the evils which now retard its progress, and affect its peace, can be overcome.'[18] Indeed, the *Graham's Town Journal's* description of Natal as 'a British colony, so-called, but in truth a native territory scantily occupied by Europeans'[19] was, for its white inhabitants, embarrassingly accurate. By 1871 Natal's black population was already approaching 300,000, compared to a white community of about 17,000 and not more than 18,000 at most.[20] Under the circumstances, it was not surprising that the British government could not seriously consider the suggestion made in 1870 that the colonists of Natal be entrusted with powers of self-government.[21] By the same token it was equally understandable that the Cape Colony, with nearly 237,000 white and approximately 484,000 black inhabitants by 1875,[22] should have been so consistently unwilling during the 1870s to assume any responsibility for her troublesome and seemingly insecure neighbour, within or without a confederal association.

The inadequacy of existing postal and telegraphic communications in southern Africa could well have contributed to a sense of isolation among white Natalians. This shortcoming soon attracted the attention of the new High Commissioner for South Africa, Sir Bartle Frere, who observed that 'the inefficiency of our postal arrangements is one great source of our weakness in S. Africa. We should certainly not hold India many years with such defective postal arrangements.'[23]

Frere expressed his determination to improve upon the 'weekly' post between the Cape and Natal with a daily service, whilst the colonists of Natal hoped in vain for an east coast mail service to Britain, via Zanzibar and Suez, which would obviate the long delay involved in the west coast service via the Cape. But such schemes came to nought and Natal continued throughout the 1870s to receive its mail from the Cape, at the average rate of three deliveries a month, through the service provided by the Union and Castle Companies.[24] Under Frere's direction, the last 200 miles of telegraph line between the Cape and Natal was completed and the inauguration of the service between the two colonies in April 1878 was hopefully hailed in Durban as 'the prelude to fuller and closer union in

the future.'[25] By September 1879 Natal was also in telegraphic communication with Pretoria. But it was not until December of that year that
Durban's mayor was able to telegraph his respects to Queen Victoria,
following the completion of the underwater cable between the Umgeni
river-mouth and Aden, which at last linked Natal and the rest of southern
Africa telegraphically to Britain via the London-Aden-Bombay line.[26]
Consequently, throughout the war crisis of 1879 Natalians continued
to find themselves entirely dependent upon their slow and sometimes
uncertain system of communications with the Cape and via Cape Town
and Maderia to London.

The effect of Natal's geopolitical circumstances and of its tenuous
internal and external lines of communication was to induce an apparently
genuine sense of insecruity among at least some of its white inhabitants.
This attitude, fed by periodic scares of domestic uprising or Zulu invasion,
made the Natal government particularly alert to any threat, real or
imaginary, which challenged the colony's stability. The incidents involving
chief Fodo in 1847, chief uSidoi in 1857 and chief Matshana in 1858 had
demonstrated early on that the colonial government regarded any apparent
challenge on the part of the indigenous population to its authority in a
very serious light and as demanding a firm response on its part.[27] In
northern Natal the Weenen massacres of 1838 had not yet been forgotten,
while many colonists still had vivid recollections of the bloody Zulu
civil war of 1856 between the factions of Mpande's sons, Cetshwayo and
Mbulazi, and of the Zulu invasion scare of July 1861, when houses in
Pietermaritzburg were barricaded and troops were rushed to the Thukela
frontier in response to reports that major Zulu inroads were imminent.
The panic proved to be quite unjustified, yet it stands as another instance
of that pathological sense of insecurity which some of the colonists
displayed, from time to time, with regard to their black neighbours.[28]

The subsequent coronation of Cetshwayo on 1 September 1873 at the
hands of Theophilus Shepstone was apparently regarded in some quarters
as a source of considerable if only momentary relief, the *Natal Mercury*
describing the event as being:

> of high historical significance in the annals of South East Africa
> ... an assertion of peaceful supremacy as opposed to the dominance
> of brute force .... The name of 'Cetywayo' is no longer a bug-bear
> to frighten weak nerves, while the terrors of a Zulu invasion will
> cease to operate.[29]

Yet immediately thereafter, Natal found itself embroiled in the Langalibalele episode, a crisis-situation which was largely of the colonial government's own making. Once again some of the Natal settlers and their government revealed a deep-seated feeling of vulnerability to attack and a tendency to over-react at times of apparent danger. The refusal of Langalibalele's tribesmen to register certain firearms in their possession, in accordance with the recently revised Gun Law of 1872, and the subsequent failure of the chief to present himself at the office of the Secretary for Native Affairs in Pietermaritzburg when summoned to do so, were readily interpreted as acts of deliberate provocation which constituted an open challenge to governmental authority and to the continued well-being of the Shepstone system of administration, through which the colony's black population was controlled. Immediate credence was given to the rumours that Langalibalele's disobedience was accompanied by disturbing signs of preparation for military action on the part of the Hlubi and neighbouring Ngwe people and, further, that the chief was attempting to solicit the co-operation of other tribes both within and beyond the colony's borders. Emergency meetings were held in Estcourt, farming operations in the district were suspended, women and children were sent to places of safety in Pietermaritzburg and Mooi River and some Boer families departed with their stock to the Orange Free State. Indications of alleged black unrest were detected throughout the colony and, in several areas, local chiefs and indunas dutifully reported to magisterial offices to hear the message of the Secretary for Native Affairs instructing them to remain calm and continue to cultivate their lands.[30] As rumour swept the colony, the *Natal Mercury* took it upon itself to refute the assertion that the chiefs of the Inanda and Umvoti locations were in open rebellion.[31] The colonial government even found it necessary to pass a Bill 'To Prevent the Spreading of False and Alarming Reports' which were 'calculated to cause fear or alarm to the public tranquility.'[32]

In the new wave of panic, none of the colonists appear to have stopped to question those of their number who chose to sow alarm and despondency among them. Nor, apparently, did it occur to any of them that their own nervous reaction to the crisis might be interpreted by the Hlubi chief and his followers as a preparation for war against them, or that Langalibalele's alleged efforts to solicit the rebellious co-operation of other tribes was really no more than a precautionary measure on his part to find safe refuge for his followers and livestock in the event of a hasty departure from the colony, necessitated by a military attack on his location.[33] The colonists and their government were understandably sensitive to the actions of a chief so widely and influentially connected as Langalibalele, for he was renowned throughout the subcontinent as a raindoctor and he enjoyed extensive family connections with numerous other tribes, by virtue of the earlier wide dispersal of the Hlubi people and through the eighty-odd wives and more than one hundred children with whom he had favoured himself by 1873.[34]

On these grounds his ability to organize a widespread uprising appears to have been accepted without question by the colonists though, arguably, the large number of messengers passing between him and a variety of other chiefs during the latter half of 1873 was not exceptional for such an eminent personality as Langalibalele. The theory of a Hlubi-inspired black conspiracy against the settlers soon found its place in colonial folklore, while Langalibalele, his followers, and the neighbouring Ngwe, were punished with excessive severity.[35] The colony's rekindled sense of insecurity found expression in the formation of the Durban Mounted Rifles in November 1873[36] and of the Natal Mounted Police in March 1874.[37] Some re-assurance was also found in the active concern which the crisis in Natal had elicited from the various other white communities of southern Africa. The colony's government issued formal expressions of gratitude for the assistance which had been proffered during the emergency,[38] whilst the Natal press attempted to underline the significance of the whole episode for the future in terms of its 'lasting moral effect on the native mind throughout South Africa, by making evident the unity — the oneness — of the British power in these territories.'[39] Much was made of the vein of sympathy for Langalibalele which appeared to run through the tribal societies of the subcontinent yet, inexplicably, the Natal government did not institute any enquiry into the extent of other tribes' complicity in the Hlubi chief's actions, even though he stood accused at his trial of 'holding treasonable communication with other Chiefs' — a charge which was subsequently dropped.[40] Natal's newspapers stressed the importance of the crisis in demonstrating 'the value of a federal alliance' and 'a common cause' as 'the best possible ground for union.'[41] Before long, there was even talk of outright annexation by the Cape, a suggestion which was not encouraged from that quarter.[42]

By 1878, when Natal again found itself at the centre of widespread disturbances, the identity of interest which the Langalibalele crisis had briefly revealed among the white-controlled states of southern Africa had long-since been forgotten. Indeed, there was a notable absence of any such overt indication of common cause, as was demonstrated by the failure to achieve a uniform control of the trade in munitions.[43] As one prominent Natalian observed, in this connection:

> There is a fearful and lamentable want in South Africa of inter-colonial sympathy and interchange of ideas — If confederation is soon to come, it will be like a Turkish marriage; neither of the parties will have seen each others faces till they get into the bridal chamber itself — It's to be hoped they won't be disappointed.[44]

By 1878 Bishop Colenso, who did not subscribe to any theory of hostile black coalitions, whether Zulu-inspired or not, conceded privately that 'We seem in Natal to be in the very centre of a circular storm as regards the natives', though he insisted that the appearance of the situation belied its reality.[45] Even Lieutenant-Governor Sir Henry Bulwer, whose correspondence during that period of crisis reveals his restraint and sober judgement, confided to Theophilus Shepstone:

> I shall be obliged to keep an eye on each side of me. Here we are in the centre, and if anything happens on the Zulu side, we have a large frontier which will require all the resources that can be spared . . . . I am afraid the horizon looks very dark on all sides of us. From the Cape the news is bad enough . . . . It threatens, however, to be a . . . war I think such as has never been seen . . . . There are not wanting signs of the present crisis developing itself into a great contest of the black and white races in South Africa . . . the indications of such a danger have never been so strong as they are now.[46]

Under these circumstances it was hardly surprising that Sir Bartle Frere found many supporters among the white inhabitants of Natal when, in September 1878, he moved his headquarters from Kingwilliamstown to Pietermaritzburg and, having already placated the Cape's eastern frontier, gave his undivided attention to engineering and prosecuting the war against Cetshwayo's Zulu kingdom.[47] The possibility of such a war, in the cause of confederation and the conditions of stability which confederal proposals required to succeed, had long been recognized in the colony. Following Shepstone's annexation of the Transvaal in 1877, it was suggested in Natal that 'public opinion points unmistakably to Zululand as a probable theatre for the next scene in the act.'[48] And further:

Hitherto we have lived in a species of phantasmagoria of Zulu scares. We have been all our lifetime subject to bondage, our Colonists may well say, by reason of this black shadow across the Tugela . . . . The Zulu question is the keystone of the arch of South African politics . . . . There is a strong feeling both in Natal and the Transvaal, that it would be well were the Zulus shown, by strong measures, that the British Government is supreme in South Africa, and means to remain so. It is believed that an effective demonstration of British power will be required before the Zulu power shall cease to be a disquieting and disturbing element in South-East Africa . . . . Such a nation must of necessity form a constant menace to the peaceable European communities beyond their borders . . . . Civilization cannot co-exist with such a condition of things upon its outskirts.[49]

By late 1878 the assumption appears to have been widely established that Natal faced a very real threat of invasion from Zululand, 'more imminent now than it has been for many years past.'[50] Some of the colonists had always been convinced that the accession of a new king and the steady acquisition of guns 'combine to render an outbreak of the Zulus all but inevitable.'[51] The presence of the High Commissioner himself in their midst and the augmentation of Her Majesty's forces in Natal[52] helped to increase excitement among the colonists, while the numerous fortifications which had been built along the Zululand frontier during the 1860s and 1870s bore mute testimony to their insecurity but did little to assuage it.[53] For some, like G.C. Cato, a prominent colonist who had already served as Durban's first mayor, the situation demanded decisive action on the part of the imperial authorities:

You ask the question is the British Lion to commence roaring, — oh yes, in the usual way — Roar until he gets his stern kicked, and then he may turn round and bite . . . . You are right — there is a Big fight on the cards and I don't know who will live to see the end.[54]

Such attitudes promoted a colonial climate of opinion which Frere was able to exploit, in his determination to force a crisis with the Zulu kingdom. Magistrates in the outlying areas of Natal were advised to 'exercise the greatest vigilance and to take immediate measures for the defence of the defensive posts in your district', while the colony as a whole was subdivided into seven defence zones, each under its own local commander.[55] As the tension mounted, Frere was better able to convince himself that:

> If we make a speedy and satisfactory settlement with Cetywayo,
> we shall have comparatively little trouble with any one else . . . . No
> risk we can incur in drawing the monster's teeth and claws seems to
> me so great as that of leaving him able to spring on us whenever
> he pleases. Our own safety and the good government of Zululand
> seem to me inseparably connected. We can be safe only if we can
> compel Cetywayo to perform his Coronation promises to his own
> people — or, if he refuses to do so, we must assist his people to
> replace him, with some form of government which will do what
> we promised them Cetywayo should do, and enable them, as well
> as our Natal and Transvaal subjects, to sleep in peace, and enjoy
> the fruits of their own labours.[56]

Later, Frere was to plead, in defence of his armed invasion of Zululand:

> The great object seemed to me to be to avert Zulu inroads from
> Natal, and if Cetywayo decided for war to make his country the
> theatre of it . . . . The temper of our own natives was then unknown,
> and if the Zulus once began making raids into Natal a far larger
> force than we possessed would be required to protect our own border,
> and at the same time to carry the war into the enemy's country . . . it
> was only by acting on the offensive and taking up positions in
> Zululand that we could hope to preserve our own Colony from
> the horrors of Zulu invasion.[57]

Yet for all the support which the strategy of pre-emptive aggression
apparently enjoyed in Natal immediately prior to the war, the colonists
were by no means unanimous in their enthusiasm for the conflict. For
example, concern was expressed about those 'who are apt to take too
sanguine a view of the situation, and who see in the immunity from native
wars enjoyed by the Colony in the past a sort of assurance against their
occurrence in the future.'[58] On the question of settling simply for a
renewal of Cetshwayo's coronation agreement, Frere himself was disturbed
by the 'great disposition among many persons in Natal, to be satisfied
with such promises of amendment — a fatal error as I think — but what
security can we demand likely to bind so faithless a tyrant?'[59] By December
1878 he was complaining bitterly to Shepstone of the colony's apathetic
attitude towards his policy:

> I do not think that even with all your knowledge of Natal you fully

recognize the difficulties we are in with our own countrymen here . . . how half-hearted is the support we get not only from gun runners and pseudo-philanthropists, but from a mass of half informed and prejudiced people, who to much contempt and ill-will towards the Transvaal Boers, add a curious sort of sympathy for Cetywayo, such as one might feel for a wolf or hyena one had petted. Then there are many who, from habit, mistrust all we do because it is done by government or by what they call 'imperial', and not by Colonial people. The net result is that our own countrymen hereabouts are only half of them heartily with us, in all we do, and our difficulties are as much from our own people as from Cetywayo's.[60]

A week after Frere penned this complaint, Harriet Colenso quoted a visitor to Pietermaritzburg as having observed 'that every one he meets in town speaks of war as probable — if not inevitable, but that he does not think that the *desire* for war is general.'[61] For their part, the Colenso family hotly disputed the necessity for conflict with the Zulu and had long-since decried 'the lying rumours industriously promoted about their doings or rather about their intentions.'[62] The bishop himself remained convinced that Cetshwayo had 'done all in his power to have the dispute with the Transvaal Government' — in other words with Sir T. Shepstone — 'settled in an amicable manner by arbitration' and that he had no intention whatsoever of invading Natal.[63] He and his family were drawn to the conclusion that 'there is a party here who would like to drive the Zulus to some act of hostility in order to have an excuse to take Zululand by force of arms' and that it had become Shepstone's policy 'to bring on such a war.'[64] Not least, Colenso feared Frere's thinly veiled intentions, commenting that 'if any one of the three great men, Sir H.B., Lord C., and Sir B.F., wishes for war, it is the *last named* alone.'[65] By the end of 1878 he found public opinion in Pietermaritzburg strongly inclined to the view that 'it is intended to force Cetshwayo into war' and he hinted at the possibility that Frere (like Wolseley in 1875) had harnessed the services of local newspapers to plead his policy, for 'some of them . . . seem to have been inspired from high authority.'[66] In support of that contention, the *Mercury* and *The Times of Natal* were both subsequently accused by the *Witness* of being 'subsidized serpents', because of their defence of the authorities in contrast to the criticisms of the *Witness* and of the *Natal Colonist.*[67]

Indeed, the notion that Natal's war-psychosis had been actively promoted was not beyond the realms of possibility. Bulwer had already observed the colony's predilection for panic:

> People are prone in these times to circulate and believe in rumours,
> some of them absurd rumours . . . . One great thing that we have
> to do here is not to show panic, to which there is always, I fear,
> too strong a tendency on the part of many; and, I am sorry to say,
> on the part of some at Maritzburg . . . who ought to know better . . . .
> For 30 years the bare possibility of such an event as a Zulu invasion
> has been a fertile source of alarm, and enough to engender in many
> persons, although 30 years have passed without any confirmation
> of their fears, a chronic habit of vague, and it must be said often
> most unreasoning apprehension.[68]

But if the disposition of some colonists to assume the worst of their
Zulu neighbours really was 'inspired from high authority', as Colenso
suggested, Bulwer was certainly not a party to the scheme. He had been
quick to appreciate that Shepstone's annexation of the Transvaal had
effected a radical change in the fragile political equilibrium of southern
Africa and that Cetshwayo's consequent encirclement by British-protected
territories could produce a clash, most likely 'with English authority in
the Transvaal, and, if with English authority in the Transvaal, with English
authority everywhere',[69] including Natal, for 'now that we have stepped
into the Dutchman's shoes, we have succeeded to his claims, we have
taken them up as our own, and look upon them in a very different light
to what we did.'[70] Yet Bulwer steadfastly refused to accept that the
dispute concerning the Blood River Territory could not be 'settled without
a single shot being fired'[71] and he urged Frere and Shepstone not to 'rush
into war so long as it can be avoided.'[72] The realization of their true
intentions had obviously come as a shock to him when he wrote that
'we are looking to different objects — I to the termination of this dispute
by peaceful settlement, you to its termination by the overthrow of the
Zulu Kingdom.'[73]

On this evidence the rumour was doubtless true that Bulwer signed
the Ultimatum, finally delivered to Cetshwayo on 11 December 1878,
with great reluctance and under pressure from Frere, in spite of his own
personal dislike of the Zulu King for his refusal to surrender those who
had killed chief Sirayo's wives.[74] Doubtless too, at least some of the Natal
colonists were as dubious as was their bishop and their governor as to the
necessity for war with the Zulu people — which might explain Frere's
complaint that 'our own countrymen hereabouts are only half of them

heartily with us.'[75] None of the colonists could seriously have disputed the assertion that the Ultimatum requiring 'the "disbandment" of the king's regiments is tantamount to asking the Zulus as a nation to commit self-emasculation.'[76] At the same time, it was confidently believed that, in the campaign which must follow, 'Zululand will fall after the first engagement into the Confederation,'[77] even though Lord Chelmsford had declined local advice concerning the adversary and terrain before him on the grounds that 'the broad principles of tactics hold good in Africa equally as well as in Europe, and the idea of South African colonists that there is a spécialité in African fighting is quite a mistake.'[78] Yet, just a week before his disaster at Isandlwana, Chelmsford was himself advising subordinates that 'the great thing will be for you to make yourself thoroughly secure wherever you may take up your position.'[79]

Natal received the news of the defeat with understandable panic and even Colenso eventually conceded that Cetshwayo 'may be driven to desperation' by the failure of his peace overtures and resort to invasion.[80] Barricades were thrown up and laagers formed throughout the colony, the laager midway between Helpmekaar and Greytown subsequently acquiring the appropriate name *Fort Funk*.[81] In northern Natal many Boer farmers sent their families across the Drakensberg to the relative safety of the Orange Free State, as they had done during the crisis of 1873, while part of Natal's black population disappeared into forest and other natural seclusions. On a tour of inspection between the colonial capital and Ladysmith, Frere was struck by 'the evident haste and temporary character of the defensive measures undertaken by the English part of the population' and (interestingly enough) considered this an indication of their inadequate sense of 'the real insecurity of their position' prior to Isandlwana.[82] In Pietermaritzburg the whirl of social activities which usually surrounded the observance of the Queen's birthday in May was forgotten as the colonists were 'plunged into the deepest mourning.' Business was suspended, a nine-foot high redoubt made its appearance in the centre of town and Frere and Bulwer both took the precaution of having their bedding transferred to the gaol in preparation for the expected siege.[83] In Durban all shipping bound for the Cape was crammed with women and children. A Town Guard was formed to reinforce the Royal Durban Rifles, encamped on the Umgeni flats, as well as the emergency corps which had already been raised by Harry Escombe and was popularly known as 'Escombe's Stinking Half-Hundred' because 'the only uniform procurable for them was that horrid moleskin stuff with its sickly smell.'[84] As one observer of the Natal scene concluded:

> The whole thing is at this moment in a state of most utter chaos,
> and any 'military dictator', from Cromwell down to yourself,
> would be a God's blessing to this wretched country. This state of
> prostrate and abject funk will, it seems to me, continue more or
> less until the reinforcements arrive.[85]

The arrival of more troops and the turn in the tide of battle did indeed
enable the colonists to recover their equanimity but Isandlwana hill had
cast a long shadow over Natal and subsequent events in Zululand did
little to dissipate its impact. Frere's subsequent censure and recall produced
expressions of sympathy reminiscent of Pine's departure from Natal
in 1875, although many were outraged when the publication of the
relevant despatches revealed the extent to which the High Commissioner
had apparently provoked the crisis with Cetshwayo, in order to further the
confederal scheme for southern Africa.[86]

Prior to his recall in September 1880, Frere continued to believe
that the cause of confederation was not yet lost and, with one eye on the
unfavourable mood of the Cape Parliament and the other on the impending
expiry of Natal's Constitution Amendment Act of 1875, he confidentially
suggested that 'the next move should come from either Natal or the
Transvaal.'[87] But such expectations were misplaced. In so far as it is
discernible, Natal's attitude towards the idea of confederation for southern
Africa had wavered indecisively during the course of the 1870s. On the
one hand there was the security which appeared to lie in some form of
closer connection with the Cape Colony and, on the other, there was the
promise of further commercial advantage, in more favourable competition
with her coastal neighbour, which was offered by a confederal alliance
with one or both of the interior republics. The notion of union with the
Cape, if not outright annexation, was particularly attractive during times
of crisis, notably the Langalibalele episode in 1873–1874 and the immediate
pre-war period in late 1878 and early 1879, whilst the alternative of
political alliance with the Boer states of the hinterland was never more
seriously entertained than just after Shepstone's annexation of the Transvaal in 1877.[88]

But by 1880, for Natal no less than for her prospective political partners,
neither of these schemes, nor any other confederal proposal, was still a
feasible or desirable proposition. Immediately prior to the outbreak of
war, the colony's Legislative Council had passed a resolution expressing

its willingness to participate whenever 'the Cape Government shall have signified its intention of holding a conference of delegates from the various South African communities, for the purpose of discussing, in all its bearings, the important subject of Confederation.'[89] During the war-crisis the report of a sub-committee of the Natal Executive Council, appointed in November 1878 to consider the matter of permissive confederation, was shelved so that the Executive Council's deliberations on its findings could be postponed to a more convenient time.[90] At a subsequent meeting in August 1879, the Executive Council resolved that this report was now no longer applicable to prevailing circumstances and decided instead to refer all the relevant papers to a committee of the entire Council, for preparation of a report on the whole subject of Natal's interests with regard to any future confederal association.[91] What emerged from this report, which was duly forwarded to the Colonial Office, was the extent to which the adequate representation of black interests in any future confederation had loomed large in the Executive Council's deliberations on the subject. It is also evident that the related problem of the conflicting 'native' policies and franchise qualifications which were currently operating in the Cape and Natal had become a further source of concern.[92]

Events in the Cape had contributed towards this deflation of the pre-war enthusiasm for confederation in Natal. Under the Molteno ministry, the Cape's government had been consistently cool towards the idea of a confederal association in which it was intended to be the senior partner and the Langalibalele episode had done nothing to encourage the idea of closer union with Natal.[93] In February 1878 the advent in office of Sprigg's 'Eastern or Confederation party' and its avowed support of Frere's confederal policy, was greeted in Natal with an enthusiasm which soon proved to be unfounded.[94] Before long it was apparent that the Cape Colony was still reluctant to shoulder the responsibilities involved in confederation and that it might be persuaded to do so only if offered the security of imperial protection, until such time as a confederated South Africa was better able to undertake its own defence. Such an attitude was understandable, in view of the Cape's own financial difficulties at that time, the unsettled state of affairs on the borders of Natal and the Transvaal and the resounding defeat suffered in the Cape House of Assembly by a private member's motion that the Cape government should be authorized to convene a conference on confederation.[95]

The Anglo-Zulu War and the subsequent settlement of Zululand proved to be decisive in confirming the Cape Colony's disenchantment with the policy of confederation. The Cape press expressed the opinion that it was now 'not a thing of this year, nor the next, and perhaps not for a generation to come . . . with Sir Garnet Wolseley and John Dunn's Zulu settlement, confederation would be the dream of a madman.'[96] A Cape ministerial minute on the subject concluded that 'the settlement of Zululand does not rest upon a satisfactory basis. It is not a settlement to which Ministers would have assented had they been consulted' and disappointment was expressed that the Cape government had not been counselled in this connection.[97] Wisely, Sprigg delayed raising the confederal issue for debate in Parliament but when he eventually did so in mid-1880, out of obligation to Frere for his initial appointment to the premiership and honour-bound to his own successful electoral platform a year later, he was forced to withdraw his motion in the face of strong opposition.[98] Thereafter, Sprigg continued to decry the 'snail-shell policy' which prevailed in the House but it was obvious that the Cape Colony had firmly turned its back on assuming the uncertain responsibilities which the imperial government had acquired in the Transvaal, Zululand and Natal. When Sprigg's ministry eventually fell in May 1881, any remaining possibility of a Cape-inspired confederation conference had already disappeared.[99]

In Natal, the Cape's official attitude towards confederation had always been a matter of public interest but Sprigg's failure to carry a conference proposal through Parliament was not a source of great disappointment, for severe misgivings about the confederal idea had already been expressed there.[100] It had been suggested in the colony that Natal should assure itself of an adequately strong voice in any future central Parliament by insisting that such representation be based on revenue as well as population at the time of confederation. In this connection, the loss of local revenues derived from the hut tax and from customs duties, which would inevitably accompany confederation, was viewed with some disfavour. Moreover, it was feared that the uniformity of customs duties which a confederal association would impose on each of its members, would deprive Natal of the lower customs rates which had been her only advantage in competition with the superior transport facilities of the Cape Colony's ports for the trade with the interior.[101]

The financial sacrifices which lay in confederation may not have weighed very heavily outside governing and commercial circles but, as in the Cape, the traumatic experience of the Anglo-Zulu War and the uncertain settlement of Zululand which followed it proved, in the opinion of the colony's leading newspapers, to be decisive in turning 'the public mind against confederation, the establishment of which, with the consent of the colonists, appears to us to be now further off than it seemed to be four years ago.'[102] The Colenso family expressed much the same opinion when they asserted that 'there will be trouble there yet — and confederation is an absurdity . . . . A more absurd attempt at "Settlement" could never have been made.'[103] In similar vein, Shepstone confided to Frere that 'bad and dangerous as it would be to restore Cetywayo, the present arrangement is worse and more dangerous and will, before long, produce much more fatal consequences.'[104] Any surviving notions of an eastern confederation, comprising Natal and her overberg Boer neighbours, disappeared in December 1880 when the Transvaal resorted to force in order to recover its independence from British rule.[105] Consequently, when Natal held its Legislative Council elections in 1882 it did so not only in the shadow of Isandlwana but of Majuba hill as well. By then the attractions of self-rule, whether in the form of confederation for southern Africa or even of responsible government for Natal, had little appeal for a substantial majority of the colony's electorate, which unequivocally indicated its preference for the retention of the more certain security of imperial protection.[106] Shortly before relinquishing his post as Officer Administering the Government in Natal, Sir Evelyn Wood had already expressed the mood in which the colony entered the 1880s:

> About Natal's future, I feel as uncertain as the Mexican lady who answered . . . as to who was the Father of her baby, 'Quiem Sabe? . . . . What with Zulus, Colenso and Boers my successor will have a lively time.[107]

While acknowledging the aforementioned difficulties involved in establishing the precise nature of public opinion in Natal at the time of the Anglo-Zulu War, the limited evidence available does suggest that the white colonists were by no means unanimous, either in accepting the necessity for such a conflict, or in lending the imperial war effort their wholehearted support.[108] Indeed, Chelmsford complained that they had not 'done as much as they ought for the defence of the Colony.'[109] Arguably, it was only in the immediate aftermath of the disaster at Isandlwana that the colonists demonstrated a complete identity of interest, anticipating as they did a common fate at the hands of invading Zulu impis and reacting to the crisis in a collaborative defensive effort as they had done in 1861.[110]

The influence of events across the Thukela upon Natal's attitude towards confederation was clearly indicated in the elections of 1882, though other factors undeniably had a bearing on their outcome and, by then, other issues which affected the colony's political life had re-emerged.[111]

As far as the responsibility for the war was concerned, both Colenso and Bulwer were adamant that the colonists were in no way liable for its provocation, nor could it in any sense be justified as being essential to their security. Some opportunistic settlers may have seen the war as a means to abundant labour and land, while it is also evident that the 'presence of the troops . . . had the effect of a minor boom on the Colony's economy.'[112] But the latter benefit proved to be shortlived, the colonists actually complained of an exodus of Natal 'natives' to Zululand during the immediate post-war period[113] and Colenso, whose unpopularity hardly gave him cause to defend the settlers, seriously doubted that 'there is any ground for charging them with wishing to occupy Zululand. I doubt if there is a single colonist (except perhaps some low trader) who has any desire to possess a farm in Zululand.'[114] With reference to the accusations levelled at Natal from abroad, he went so far as to add:

> I think the colonists have been harshly and unjustly judged in England in respect of this War. Speaking of them generally I have no hesitation in saying that they never urged it on, or even dreamt of it, until Sir B. Frere came up here, and wheedled them into following his lead . . . the colonists, who left the right and justice of his proceedings to be settled between Sir B.F. and the English Government and English People, gave their voice at public meetings in support of his policy, when it was too late for him to stop, because they believed that it would relieve them from a danger, which some few perhaps actually dreaded, but which all felt to be there, in spite of the fact that Cetshwayo had never once threatened the Colony and personally desired to be on friendly terms with the English Government. To this extent alone, I firmly believe, can the colonists be charged with 'self-interest'.[115]

Colenso's views were subsequently endorsed by Bulwer, who was similarly convinced that 'an invasion of Natal was one of the last things that would have occurred to the Zulu King to undertake, and one of the last things that would have found favour with the Zulu people.'[116] It was Bulwer's contention that the fatal deterioration in Anglo-Zulu relations was a direct consequence of the British annexation of the Transvaal, whereas no point of dispute existed between Natal and Zululand until

the Sirayo incident in July 1878 and that the notion of conflict with the
Zulu kingdom which eventually gained currency among the colonists
'was imported at the time of the arrival of the troops and the Head-
Quarters Staff from the Cape Colony.' Their appearance in Natal was,
in Bulwer's opinion, premature and 'gave rise to the belief that it was
intended to bring matters to an issue with the Zulu king', serving only
to agitate the colonists and arouse Zulu suspicions. Bulwer insisted that,
while Natal's interests had undoubtedly been promoted by the war, it
could not be held 'primarily responsible' for it — 'an idea which appears
to have been greatly due to the circumstance that the Colony was the basis
of operations.'[117]

In their efforts to exonerate the colonists from the burden of blame
for the war, Colenso and Bulwer both overlooked the earlier speculation,
favouring 'strong measures' against the Zulu, which had preceded the
appearance of Frere's entourage in Natal, though not his own arrival in
southern Africa.[118] Moreover, as Colenso conceded, some at least of their
number were guilty of allowing themselves to be 'wheedled' by Frere 'into
following his lead and supporting him in his undertaking to relieve them
from the "standing menace" of the Zulu Power.'[119] In his relationship
with the Natal colonists, Frere did enjoy a decided advantage, for even if
there was a consensus of opinion and purpose among them, which is not
discernible in the available evidence, the absence of responsible government
in the colony made it impossible for them to exert any control or
significant influence on the official policy adopted towards their Zulu
neighbours.[120] Far from acting in response to the pressure of white public
opinion in Natal, Frere found a useful pretext for his policy of provocation
in the colonists' traditional fear of Zulu invasion, as well as an obvious
staging-ground for Chelmsford's three-prong strategy of invasion. Yet no
Zulu incursion eventuated and no evidence has been produced to prove
that such an inroad was ever seriously considered.[121] By the same
token, although some colonists apparently believed that, at Cetshwayo's
command, 'the Natal natives would rise and murder the whites who lived
amongst them', no such holocaust materialized.[122] On this the centenary
of the Anglo-Zulu war, coinciding as it does with yet another period of
crisis in southern Africa, the behaviour of the Natal colonists merits
contemplation.

NOTES

1   Natal Archives, Shepstone Papers: Bulwer to Shepstone, 27 Feb. 1878.

2   See C. F. Goodfellow, *Great Britain and South African Confederation,
     1870–1881* (Cape Town, 1966); also W.J. De Kock, 'Federation and Con-
     federation in South Africa, 1870–1880, with Special Reference to the Cape
     Colony' (unpublished M.A. thesis, U.C.T., 1938); and A. Don, 'Confederation
     in the Seventies' (unpublished M.A. thesis, Rand, 1936).

3   See, for example, E.H. Brookes and C. de B. Webb, *A History of Natal*
     (Pietermaritzburg, 1965), chapters XIII and XIV.

4   See W.R. Guest, 'Natal and the Confederation Issue in the 1870s' (unpublished
     M.A., Natal, 1967) upon which this paper is, in part, based.

5   The part played by Natal's black population in the war-crisis of 1879 is
     only briefly touched upon in this paper and presents itself as a potentially
     fruitful topic in its own right.

6   See Frere's despatches insisting that the Zulu were a threat to their white
     neighbours in *Br. Parl. Papers* LII of 1878–79, C.2220 and C.2222, passim;
     also LIV of 1879, C.2454, pp.129–142: Frere to Hicks Beach, 30 June
     1879; see also notes 114 to 117, below. Br. Parl. Papers hereafter cited as
     BPP.

7   Brookes and Webb, pp.17, 30, 63–71, 158.

8   Natal Archives, Sutton Papers: Lawton to Sutton, 18 Sept. 1876; T.R.H.
     Davenport, 'The Responsible Government Issue in Natal, 1880–1882',
     Butterworth's South African Law Review (1957), pp.122–124. See also
     C.A. Gillitt, 'Natal 1893–1897: the Alignment of Parties and the Fall of the
     Escombe Ministry' (unpublished Honours Long Essay, Natal, 1965), pp.2–5.

9   Killie Campbell Africana Library, Colenso Papers: Colenso to Bunyon, 21 Dec.
     1878; Colenso to Shaen, 14 Dec. 1873; Mrs. Colenso to Mrs. Lyell, 20 June
     1874; Natal Archives, Shepstone Papers: Bulwer to Shepstone, 25 July 1877;
     Guest, *Natal and the Confederation Issue in the 1870s* pp.vii-ix.

10   *Times of Natal*, 17 May 1878; BPP LX of 1877, C.1748, pp.214–215: Bulwer
     to Carnarvon, 31 Oct. 1876; LV of 1878, C.1961, pp.152–3: Bulwer to
     Carnarvon, 4 Oct. 1877; LVI of 1878, C. 2079, pp.3–4: Shepstone to
     Carnarvon, 25 Dec. 1877, enclosing statement of messengers from Swazi Chief.

11   *Natal Witness*, 13 April 1869; *Natal Mercury*, 5 March 1878.

12   BPP LI of 1880, C. 2584, p.196: Bulwer to Hicks Beach, 10 March 1880.

13   Ibid.; and Natal Archives, Govt. House Records, Vol.1220, pp.392–3: Bulwer
     to Carnarvon, 12 June 1876.

14   Goodfellow, p.2; F. Wolfson, 'Some Aspects of Native Administration in
     Natal under Theophilus Shepstone . . . 1857–1875' (unpublished M.A.,
     Rand, 1946), pp.3–4; D. Child (ed.), *The Zulu War Journal of Colonel Henry
     Harford, C.B.* (Pietermaritzburg, 1978), p.9.

15   Ibid., p.10.

16   Natal Archives, Sir Evelyn Wood Papers: Wood to Col. A. Mitchell, 8 March
     1881.

17   Natal Archives, Govt. House Records, vol. 1219, p.213: Bulwer to Carnarvon,
     15 Jan. 1876; Brookes & Webb, p.79; E.D. Campbell, *The Birth and Develop-
     ment of the Natal Railways* (Pietermaritzburg, 1951), p.72.

18 BPP LII of 1876, C. 1401, 1, pp.5–12: Wolseley to Carnarvon, 15 July 1875, enclosing Report by Major Butler on Immigration, 3 July 1875.

19 *Grahams Town Journal*, 21 Aug. 1871.

20 Goodfellow, p.2; D. Hobart-Houghton & J. Dagut, *Source Material on The South African Economy*, vol. I, p.36, quoting *Colony of Natal Blue Book, 1871*.

21 *Natal Govt. Gazette*, vol.XXII, p.52, No. 1219, 1 March 1870, publishing despatch Granville to Keate, 6 Dec. 1869; and vol.XXIV, p.156, No. 1364, 23 July 1872, publishing despatch Kimberley to Musgrave, 20 May 1872.

22 Goodfellow, pp.1–2 (the figure for blacks excluding Basutoland and Transkei).

23 Natal Archives, Shepstone Papers: Frere to Shepstone, 20 Oct. 1877; see also B.A. Le Cordeur, *The Relations Between the Cape and Natal, 1846–1879* (Ph.D. thesis, Natal, 1962, published in Archives Year Book, 1965, vol.I), pp.283–287.

24 Natal Archives, Shepstone Papers: Frere to Shepstone, 26 April 1877; *Times of Natal*, 12 Nov. 1870 and *Natal Mercury*, 20 Aug. 1870, 6 April 1872, 18 Nov. 1875; Le Cordeur, pp.271–277.

25 *Natal Mercury*, 6 May 1878.

26 Le Cordeur, pp.277–287.

27 Natal Archives, Shepstone Papers: Notes Explanatory of Returns (1864), p.61; Wolfson, p.4.

28 See G.B. Nourse, 'The Zulu Invasion Scare of 1861' (M.A. thesis, S.A., 1948) and L.M. Young, 'The Native Policy of Benjamin Pine in Natal, 1850–1855' (M.A. thesis, N.U.C., 1941).

29 *Natal Mercury*, 23 Sept. 1873.

30 See W.R. Guest, 'Langalibalele: the Crisis in Natal, 1873–1875' (Durban, 1976), pp.31–38.

31 *Natal Mercury*, 18 Nov. 1873.

32 *Natal Govt. Gazette*, Jan–Dec. 1873, p.363, 4 Nov. 1873, publishing Bill No. 12 of 1873.

33 Guest, *Langalibalele*, p.38; and see N.A. Etherington 'Why Langalibalele Ran Away', *Journal of Natal and Zulu History*, vol. I (1978), pp.12–15, 24.

34 Guest, *Langalibalele*, pp.29–30.

35 Ibid., pp.45–47, 59–60, 92–94.

36 A.F. Hattersley, *Carbineer* (London 1950), p.183.

37 H.E. Lugg, *Historic Natal and Zululand* (Pietermaritzburg, 1948), pp.41–2.

38 Natal Archives, Govt. House Records, vol. 1325, p.134: Pine to Barkly, 15 Jan. 1874 and p.137: Pine to Brand, 15 Jan. 1874.

39 *Natal Mercury*, 8 Jan. 1874.

40 BPP XLV of 1874, C.1025, pp.43–76: Pine to Kimberley, 16 Feb. 1874, enclosing Minutes of the Trial.

41 *Natal Mercury*, 29 Nov. 1873: and *Times of Natal*, 11 Feb. 1874; see also *Natal Witness*, 27 Jan. 1874.

42 *Natal Mercury*, 5 Nov. 1874; *Cape Argus*, 12 June 1875; BPP LII of 1876, C.1399, pp.29–35: Barkly to Carnarvon, 20 Oct. 1875, enclosing Memorandum accompanying Minute of Ministry on Confederation Conference.

43 Natal Archives, Govt. House Records, vol. 1501, No. 323: Frere to Hicks Beach, 20 Dec. 1878.

44 Natal Archives, Shepstone Papers: Statham to Shepstone, 26 July 1878.

45 KCAL, Colenso Papers: Colenso to Bunyon, 28 April 1878.

46 KCAL, Cetywayo Papers: Bulwer to Shepstone, 21 Nov. 1877 (typescript); Natal Archives, Shepstone Papers: Bulwer to Shepstone, 26 Dec. 1877 and 22 March 1878.

47 Natal Archives, Shepstone Papers: Frere to Shepstone, 10 Sept. 1878.

48 *Times of Natal*, 2 May 1877.

49 *Natal Witness*, 7 and 18 Dec. 1877; *Natal Mercury*, 15 Dec. 1877 and 24 Jan. 1878.

50 Natal Archives, Govt. House Records, vol. 1411: Memorandum on 'Defence of the Colony' by G.H. Mitchell, J.Shepstone and J.E. Dartnell, 7 Oct. 1878; *The Times of Natal*, 30 Dec. 1878.

51 Natal Archives, Robinson Papers: Robinson to R. Jameson, 13 and 28 Sept. 1878.

52 Natal Archives, Govt. House Records, vol. 281, pp.391–395: Bulwer to Hicks Beach, 26 July 1878; *Natal Mercury*, 19 Oct. 1878.

53 See J.L. Smail, *With Shield and Assegai* (Cape Town, 1969), pp.150–7; and J.P.C. Laband and P.S. Thompson *A Field Guide to the War in Zululand, 1879* (Pietermaritzburg, 1979).

54 KCAL, Allison Papers: Cato to Allison, 31 Oct. 1878; also, Hawkins Papers: Fannin to Hawkins, 23 Dec. 1878.

55 Natal Archives, Govt. House Records, vol. 1411: Draft of Confidential Minute, Natal Col. Sec. to Res. Magistrates, 30 Oct. 1878; and vol. 1412: Minute, Bulwer to Natal Co. Sec., 27 Nov. 1878.

56 Natal Archives, Shepstone Papers: Frere to Shepstone, 15 Nov. and 20 Nov.1878.

57 BPP LIII of 1879, C.2316, pp.17–21: Frere to Hicks Beach, 1 March 1879: also LIV of 1879, C.2454, pp.129–142: Frere to Hicks Beach, 30 June 1879.

58 BPP LIII of 1879, C.2367, pp.107-119: Frere to Hicks Beach, 8 Nov. 1878, enclosing Memorandum of observations on Frere to Hicks Beach of 30 Sept. 1878, dated 25 Oct. 1878.

59 Natal Archives, Shepstone Papers: Frere to Shepstone, 15 Nov. 1878.

60 Natal Archives, Shepstone Papers: Frere to Shepstone, 3 Dec. 1878; see also *Natal Colonist*, 22 Aug. 1878 and *Natal Witness*, 18 Jan. 1879.

61 KCAL, Colenso Papers: H.E. Colenso to Frank Colenso, 10 Dec. 1878.

62 KCAL, Colenso Papers: Colenso to Bunyon, 22 Oct. 1877; also F.S. Colenso to Mrs. Lyell, 23 June 1875.

63 KCAL, Colenso Papers: Colenso to Miss J.E. Hughes, 4 March 1878; and Colenso to Bunyon, 21 Dec. 1878.

64 KCAL, Colenso Papers: F.S. Colenso to Mrs. Lyell, 2 Jan. 1879; and Colenso to Miss J.G. Hughes, 23 June 1878.

65 KCAL, Colenso Papers: Colenso to Chesson, 6 Dec. 1878.

66 KCAL, Colenso Papers: Colenso to Chesson, 29 Dec. 1878.

67 *Natal Witness*, 8 March 1879; *Natal Colonist*, 3 April 1879; *Natal Mercury*, 3 April 1879.

68 Natal Archives, Shepstone Papers: Bulwer to Shepstone, 22 March 1878 and 9 Oct. 1877; BPP LIII of 1879, C.2367, pp.107−119: Frere to Hicks Beach, 8 Nov. 1878, enclosing Memorandum by Bulwer, 25 Oct. 1878.

69 Natal Archives, Shepstone Papers: Bulwer to Shepstone, 11 July 1877.

70 Natal Archives, Shepstone Papers: Bulwer to Shepstone, 14 Nov. 1877.

71 KCAL, Cetywayo Papers: Bulwer to Shepstone, 9 Jan. 1878 (typescript copy).

72 Natal Archives, Shepstone Papers: Bulwer to Shepstone, 21 Nov. 1877.

73 Natal Archives, Shepstone Papers: Bulwer to Shepstone, 16 Jan. 1878.

74 KCAL, Colenso Papers: Colenso to Chesson, 23 May and 21 March 1880.

75 See Note 60 above.

76 *Natal Mercantile Advertizer*, 10 Dec. 1878.

77 P. Lewson (ed.), *Selections from the Correspondence of J.X. Merriman, 1870−1890*, pp.58−9: J. Sivewright to Mrs. A. Merriman, 6 Dec. 1878.

78 Natal Archives, Shepstone Papers: Chelmsford to Shepstone, 10 Aug. 1878.

79 Natal Archives, Sir Evelyn Wood Papers: Chelmsford to Wood, 16 Jan. 1879.

80 KCAL, Colenso Papers: Colenso to Chesson, 22 June 1879.

81 Natal Archives, Sutton Papers: Diary of Geo. Sutton 1879, entries for 24 Jan. and 10 Feb. 1879; KCAL, Jameson Papers: 'Directions for putting our house in a state of defence in the event of the Zulus reaching Durban . . .' by R. Jameson, Feb. 1879; BPP LIII of 1879, C.2318, pp.32−37: Frere to Hicks Beach, 28 March 1879 and 4 April 1879; D. Child (ed.) p.61.

82 BPP LIII of 1879, C.2318, pp.32−37: Frere to Hicks Beach, 28 March 1878.

83 *Natal Witness*, 1 Feb. 1879; KCAL, Colenso Papers: H.E. Colenso to Mrs. Lyell, 22 June 1879 and Colenso to Chesson, 7 Feb. 1879; KCAL, Memoirs of Robert James Mason (typescript copy).

84 KCAL, Zulu War Papers: Article by A.A. Shuter in *Natal Mercury*, 22 Jan. 1929, 'Zulu War Commemoration' edition. N.B. Royal Durban Rifles, formed in May 1873, are not to be confused with the Durban Mounted Rifles (see note 37, above).

85 Lewson (ed.), pp.69−70: J. Sivewright to J.X. Merriman, 9 Feb. 1879.

86 *Natal Witness*, 1 Feb. 1879; *Natal Mercury*, 5 May and 7 July 1879, 4 Aug. 1880; *Natal Mercantile Advertiser*, 18 Sept. 1880; *Natal Colonist*, 16 Sept. 1879; Natal Archives, Shepstone Papers: Broome to Shepstone, 11 Sept. 1879.

87 Natal Archives, Govt. House Records, vol. 686: Frere to Colley, 10 July 1880 (Confidential) enclosing Frere to Kimberley, 6 July 1880. Natal's Constitution Amendment Act (1875), increasing the number of Executive members in the Legislative Council had been successfully introduced by Sir Garnet Wolseley and came into effect on 24 Sept. 1875. See Natal Archives, Govt. House Records, vol. 1219, pp.91−94: Wolseley to Carnarvon, 1 June 1875.

88 See Guest, *Natal and the Confederation Issue in the 1870s*, pp.33−40, 102−105, 85−86, 94, 129.

89 BPP LIII of 1879, C.2252, pp.7−11: Bulwer to Hicks Beach, 28 Dec. 1878, enclosing resolution of Natal Legislative Council, 3 Sept. 1878.

90 Natal Archives, Govt. House Records, vol.1501: Broome to Colonial Secretary, 14 Nov. 1878, Minute Paper on Legislative Council Debate re appointment of delegates to confer on confederation; vol.1220, pp.145−149: Bulwer to Hicks Beach, 15 Nov. 1879.

91   Natal Archives, Executive Council Minutes, vol. 10, p.415, No.21 of 1879,
     12 Aug. 1879; Govt. House Records, vol. 1501: Broome to Colonial Secretary,
     13 Aug. Minute Paper.

92   Natal Archives, Govt. House Records, vol. 1220, pp.145–149: Bulwer to
     Hicks Beach, 15 Nov. 1879.

93   See De Kock, passim; Le Cordeur, pp.334–338.

94   *Times of Natal*, 8 Feb. 1878; *Natal Mercury*, 11 June 1878.

95   *Cape Argus*, 18 July 1878 Supplement (Cape House of Assembly Debates
     16 July 1878); Cape Archives, Govt. House Records 23/24: Frere to Hicks
     Beach, 22 July 1878; J.H. Hofmeyr, *The Life of Jan Hendrik Hofmeyr* (Cape
     Town, 1913), pp.147, 150–151.

96   *Cape Argus*, 28 Aug. and 4 Sept. 1879; *Cape Times*, 16 Sept. 1879.

97   BPP LI of 1880, C.2584, pp.49–52: Frere to Hicks Beach, 26 Jan. 1880,
     enclosing Minute of Cape Ministry, 24 Jan. 1880.

98   Natal Archives, Govt. House Records, vol. 686: Frere to Colley, 10 July 1880
     (Confidential), enclosing Frere to Kimberley, 6 July 1880 (Confidential).

99   Ibid.; Cory Library, Sprigg Papers, PR1932: Sprigg's Speech, June 1880.

100 *Natal Mercury*, 29 June 1880.

101 Natal Archives, Govt. House Records, vol. 1501: Report of Sub-Committee
     of Natal Executive Council, 29 Nov. 1878 and Memorandum by T. Polkinghorne
     (Treasurer), 8 May 1879.

102 *Natal Mercantile Advertizer*, 12 and 28 Feb. 1880; see also *Natal Witness*,
     27 Sept. 1879; *Natal Colonist*, 27 Sept. 1879; *Natal Mercury*, 2 Sept. 1879;
     Times of Natal, 15 Sept. 1879.

103 KCAL, Colenso Papers: Mrs. Colenso to Mrs. Lyell, 30 May 1880; Colenso
     to W.H. Domville, 21 June 1882; *Times of Natal*, 28 Jan. 1880; Natal Archives,
     Shepstone Papers: Cato to Shepstone, 29 Sept. 1879.

104 Natal Archives, Shepstone Papers: Shepstone to Frere, 31 May 1880.

105 Natal Archives, Govt. House Records, vol. 1220, pp.489–493: Colley to
     Kimberley, 26 Dec. 1880; *Natal Mercantile Advertizer*, 10 Feb. 1881; *Natal
     Mercury*, 28 March 1881; *Natal Witness*, 8 April 1881.

106 Natal Archives, Govt. House Records, vol. 1221, pp.285–300: Bulwer to
     Kimberley, 31 Oct. 1882; see also T.R.H. Davenport, op.cit., pp.84–133.

107 Natal Archives, Sir Evelyn Wood Papers: Wood to Hercules Robinson, 10 Oct.
     and 17 Oct. 1881.

108 Natal Archives, Shepstone Papers: Frere to Shepstone, 3 Dec. 1878.

109 BPP LIV of 1879, C.2374, pp.87–89: Bulwer to Hicks Beach, 22 May 1879,
     enclosing Chelmsford to Bulwer, 7 May 1879.

110 See Nourse, pp.37–46.

111 See Davenport, op.cit., pp.118–124.

112 *Natal Almanac and Yearly Register, 1879* (Pietermaritzburg), p.iv.

113 *Times of Natal*, 22 Dec. 1879.

114 KCAL, Colenso Papers: Colenso to Chesson, 23 Nov. 1879.

115 Ibid.

116 BPP LI of 1880, C.2584, pp.141–144: Wolseley to Hicks Beach, 13 Feb.
     1880, enclosing Bulwer to Wolseley, 4 Feb. 1880.

117 BPP LI of 1880, C.2584, pp.196–207: Bulwer to Hicks Beach, 10 March 1880.

118 See references in notes 48 and 49 above.

119 KCAL, Colenso Papers: Colenso to Chesson, 23 Nov. 1879.

120 Natal's Constitution Amendment Act (1875) had actually increased the number of non-elected members in the Legislative Council. See note 87, above.

121 See Brookes and Webb, pp.135, 141.

122 BPP LIII of 1879, C.2367, pp.13–14: Frere to Hicks Beach, 24 March, 1879; Natal Archives, Shepstone Papers: Shepstone to Windham, 29 May 1879.

PETER COLENBRANDER

The Zulu Political Economy
on the Eve of the War

It is almost a commonplace to suggest that the key to understanding the
emergence of the centralised Zulu monarchy in the time of Shaka and
its structural continuity is to be found in the tradition of the *ibutho*
system which persisted in modified form throughout the sixty year lifespan
of the kingdom; that is the system of enlisting the large majority of Zulu
males in their late teens into *amabutho* or age sets. The crucial characteristic
of this institution was that its members were forbidden from marrying
until the expiry of their period of service some fifteen to twenty years
later, during which time they were attached, generally on a permanent
basis, to the various royal homesteads (*amakhanda*) that were scattered
throughout Zululand.[2]

Women too were formed into *amabutho* and were prevented from
marrying at will, but they remained at the homes of their fathers and
were not required to perform direct service for the king.[3] Despite these
organisational and functional differences, female age-sets were, as will
later be demonstrated, a vital element in the political economy of Zululand.

Turning first to the male *amabutho*, many scholars of nineteenth
century Zulu history have emphasized their politico-military significance.
Thus it is argued that the very manner in which they were constituted
tended to fuse hitherto disparate groups into one larger national entity.[4]
Moreover, they provided the Zulu political elite with the coercive potential
to deter and suppress rebellion, to administer and protect the kingdom
effectively, to undertake raids and to extract tribute from other communities.[5] In more recent years, our appreciation of the role of the
amabutho has been extended and refined as a result of a shift in emphasis,
particularly evident in the work of Dr. Jeff Guy and John Wright, away
from the study of political and military events towards a materialist

analysis of the processes of social change.[6] Central to this re-interpretation is the realisation that the segmentary patrilineal lineage system, of which the homestead (*umuzi*) was the physical expression, and which constituted the social framework for the organisation of production amongst the northern Nguni peoples prior to the emergence of large states, had endured in easily recognisable form into the nineteenth century.[7]

In addressing himself to the problem of how these many thousands of homesteads were united into a single polity under one king, Guy has stressed what many historians have neglected. The *amabutho* had not only military and police duties to perform, they were in the words of another student of Zulu history, 'multifunctional, organised labour gangs'.[8] They had not only to defeat the king's enemies, but also to construct and refurbish the many *amakhanda*, in each of which a portion of his household resided, as well as to work his fields and tend his cattle.[9] Guy concludes that the *amabutho* were thus the means by which the king was able to divert the labour power of young adult males into the service of the state for up to one third of their productive lives.[10]

Furthermore, if Zulu royal power was rooted in the extraction of labour, it was reinforced by the prudent redistribution among the king's most important subordinates of the various resources the *amabutho* had made available to him.[11]

In sum, the material bases of royal power were realised in the form of control over the producer, rather than over the means of production.[12] This is more clearly perceptible when it is recalled that though the Zulu king had the authority to allot the land and if necessary relocate families, in practice it was seldom exercised, for in Cetshwayo's day, people were usually left in undisturbed possession of the land that their forbears had held before them. Moreover the king, it would appear, had no right of absolute dispossession.[13] However, there is evidence to suggest that individual Zulu did on occasion make presents of their daughters to the king in exchange for agricultural implements,[14] but whatever the extent of the monopoly that Shaka and Dingane may have been able to exercise in this regard, Mpande's reign witnessed the advent in significant numbers of peripatetic traders from Natal, from whom hoes were freely available.[15]

But the control over production which the *ibutho* system allowed the king to exercise was not limited to enlisted men. Homesteads, though materially self-sufficient (with the exception of ironware), did not produce wives, who had to be obtained from other homesteads in exchange for cattle, and who were responsible for the production both of crops and of children.[16] They were not only direct producers, but were also the begetters of the work force of the next generation. Matrimony led to a further segmentation of the patrilineal lineage and the creation of new homesteads. Thus, the restriction on marriage achieved through the agency of the male and female *amabutho* involved much more than the regulation of biological reproduction; it gave the king control over the extension of kinship relations and the formation of new production communities (homesteads), and in so doing gave him a decisive influence over the productive process throughout the kingdom.[17] The labour power of the members of the female *amabutho*, like that of the older womenfolk, was also extracted for the immediate benefit of the state. They produced grain in the fields attached to their respective homesteads and this was siphoned off to feed their relatives in the male age-sets who were provided only with milk and, less frequently, meat by the king.[18]

The dimensions of the social, economic and political changes wrought by the process of state formation in the early nineteenth century now become more apparent. Whatever the degree of continuity in *form* and *structure* of pre-Shakan socio-economic organisation, its *function* had been radically transformed by the 1820s.[19] At the risk of oversimplification, it may be conjectured that in the pre-*Mfecane* period men and women worked for the most part to sustain the immediate community in which they resided. Furthermore, the homestead head (*umnumzana*) had limited powers to delay the distribution of bridewealth among his young adult sons, and so to prevent them from establishing their own households free from his control.[20] After the Shakan revolution, the labour power of both sexes was utilised for considerable lengths of time by a dominant and largely exclusive elite for purposes of its own, namely the maintenance of the state which was the source of its wealth and power. The homestead now formed part of the productive base of the state to which it had become politically subordinated.

Hence, while one may not be able to speak of exploitation of labour on the basis of class in eighteenth century Nguni society, except perhaps on a limited scale,[21] one can plausibly do so in relation to the Zulu kingdom. In this regard the words of the French anthropologist Terray, related though they are to West Africa, seem to be particularly apposite.

> Exploitation would be present if the elder (read king) were in a position to interrupt the process of circulation of wives, or divert it to his advantage, or if he could take the surplus product of the juniors without obtaining wives for them.[22]

This does not take into account the productive role of women. It does, however, mirror the position of the king and of male *amabutho* in the Zulu political economy.

* * * * *

The student of the history of the Zulu polity in its twilight years is confronted with a seeming paradox. Despite the continued enrolment of *amabutho*[23] and despite the comprehensiveness of the control this enabled the king to exercise, there are clear indications that the Zulu kingdom in Cetshwayo's day was politically and economically less monolithic and cohesive than it is thought to have been in the reign of Shaka. Indeed, it was in a condition of fairly acute disequilibrium on the eve of the conflict of 1879. The purpose of this essay is not, however, to uphold the extreme view of Cetshwayo's kingdom as expressed by one colonial official, and shared by many of his contemporaries,[24] that, 'anarchy among the people prevailed everywhere, and the country seemed hastening to ruin.'[25]

Nonetheless, the extent of the domestic difficulties which confronted the king should not be obscured by the heroic and concerted response of the Zulu people to the war. The impulse behind Zulu resistance must also be construed as deriving from the lengthy and bitter territorial dispute and the repugnant ultimatum that prefaced the conflict, as well as the aggressive character of the British campaign.[26]

Some insight can be gleaned from the words of Cetshwayo himself. Late in 1876 he angrily repudiated the interference of the Natal official establishment in the governance of Zululand, and stated further,

> Did I ever tell Mr. Shepstone I would not kill? . . . I do kill, but I do not consider that I have done anything yet in the way of killing. Why do the white people start at nothing? I have not yet begun . . . . My people will not listen unless they are killed . . . . Go back and tell the English that I shall now act on my own account . . . .[27]

This message may have been little more than an impetuous outburst, conditioned by the incipient decline in accord between Natal and Zululand[28] and its tone may have been misrepresented by messengers inimical to Cetshwayo's interest.[29] Nonetheless, the sense of political tension conveyed is also apparent in other of his statements. Perhaps it is most explicitly expressed in a letter written in 1881, when he was in exile at the Cape, to Sir Hercules Robinson.

> The many disorders that have existed in Zululand lately are the outcome of so many men pretending royalty, keeping assemblies, and not allowing my people to come and serve me as in the days of old.[30]

I wish to suggest that at base Cetshwayo's political predicament was the result of something approaching a major resource crisis. More specifically, as European observers did not fail to point out, there existed a serious insufficiency of cattle in his kingdom.[31]

Cattle clearly played a pivotal role in nineteenth century Zulu society. They were a man's most prized possession and a considerable amount of labour time was devoted to animal husbandry. Furthermore, they were treasured not only as suppliers of hides, meat and *amasi* — one of the two staples in the Zulu diet — but also, and quite apart from their ritual significance, for their social value, most obviously as the means by which wives and hence children were obtained. In short, cattle represented both expended labour and potential labour power. Moreover, self-aggrandisement and social mobility depended on the acquisition of additional stock; status and power being measured largely in terms of the number of cattle possessed. In the form of patronage and fines, they were for the king important instruments of political control.[32] It follows therefore that a shortage of cattle would pose a threat to the king's position and to the political integration of the state, and would have serious implications for the production of food and for the reproduction of the society.

Several factors may have contributed to this dearth in the 1870s. The first was cattle disease. Anthrax, quarter evil and *nagana* were in evidence in Zululand but it is probable that stock keepers as experienced as the Zulu were able to minimise fatalities by careful management of herds.[33] However, white traders from Natal brought new sicknesses including tuberculosis and redwater and most importantly bovine pleuropneumonia (lung-sickness).[34] Introduced in the late 1850s, this disease soon reached epidemic proportions, inflicting such casualties on the national herd, that in late 1858, according to one trader, Mpande was obliged to send to the Transvaal Boers to make good the losses.[35] The same commentator reported that of the hundred cattle he had purchased in the Zulu country, all but seven had succumbed to the disease, and another visitor observed that by 1861 Mpande's herds had been so decimated that the king had called upon John Dunn to shoot 800 buffalo in order to guarantee a sufficient supply of meat.[36] Given the high concentration of cattle that the natural environment of Zululand made possible, and the failure to control the ingress and movement of traders, traditional strategies for containing losses probably proved relatively ineffectual and the Zulu were obliged as a last resort to slaughter a large part of their herds.[37] Even so, the disease was still prevalent in many parts of Zululand in the early 1870s.[38] Indeed, though there is some mention of the effectiveness of inoculation,[39] lungsickness may have had its most devastating impact after Cetshwayo had inspected all his herds at the time of his succession in 1872, as a consequence of which this and other illnesses were spread throughout the kingdom. An illustration of the resultant casualties is that in one year alone during this period a single firm of Durban merchants reportedly exported 90,000 hides from Zululand.[40] Improbable as this figure may seem, a recent study of Lozi society bears testimony to the disastrous consequences of this disease.[41]

A second factor is that of long-term pasture degeneration. It is likely that Shaka's raiding activities[42] and the period of forty years of generally good rainfall[43] that ensued led to a considerable increase in cattle. This in turn may have led to overstocking, the ill effects of which would no doubt have been compounded by the Zulu practice of repeated grass-burning,[44] and there is evidence in one traveller's account of the extent of soil erosion in some areas of the kingdom.[45] Normally the depletion of cattle herds by disease would be expected to relieve pressure on pasturage, thereby permitting its rehabilitation for the next generation of cattle.[46] Such, however, was probably not the case in Zululand in the 1870s.

This leads directly to a consideration of weather patterns during the period. Contemporary or near-contemporary accounts make reference to at least two droughts in the decade which, if not of a calamitous order, nonetheless occasioned considerable hardship in certain localities.[47] More suggestive are the results of dendroclimatological research[48] which indicate that the weather in the two decades preceding the war was passing through a protracted period of reduced precipitation and, indeed, that rainfall declined with each consecutive year during the 1870s to an almost unprecedentedly low level in 1878/9. These data must be used with caution since they are based on a single sample, but they are perhaps useful in as much as they denote a general trend. Significant reductions in rainfall over an extended period would tend to lead to continued and intensified pressure on pasturage, both in terms of overgrazing and increased trampling of grass cover in the vicinity of scarce water resources. Of much greater and more immediate moment would have been the protraction, and possibly the exacerbation, of the dearth of cattle occasioned by epidemic. Milk yields would have declined further, cattle would have become increasingly susceptible to the diseases that prevailed, and conception rates would have fallen drastically.[49] Simultaneously, maize yields would have diminished, necessitating in extreme cases the destruction of herds for consumption.[50]

A further dimension to be considered is the long-term increase in the Zulu population. Attention must first be drawn to a number of factors impinging upon population growth. It would seem that polygamy does not necessarily have significant repercussions on the rate of reproduction.[51] There were, in addition, customary proscriptions on the impregnation of lactating mothers and as children were not weaned until between one and three years of age, a minimum of two years elapsed between the births of successive children.[52] It has, moreover, been argued that the *ibutho* system, in addition to its other functions, tended to retard the pace of demographic growth by delaying the marriage of women until they were as much as thirty-five years old.[53] Since the period of fertility in women spans the years between fifteen and forty-nine,[54] the impact of the enrolment of *amabutho* on child-bearing would, it is claimed, have been notable.

Nevertheless, such figures as are available point to a sustained and marked demographic enlargement during the kingdom's existence. These statistics must, however, be used with considerable caution. They are the fruits either of guesswork by observers whose competence and objectivity is not always above suspicion, or of the computations of a scholar (Bryant) whose methodology was by modern standards unsophisticated. Population trends were, moreover, distorted by historical circumstances, including the extensive and ferocious campaigns undertaken by Shaka and Dingane, the bloody intestine strife that characterised the middle period of Mpande's reign, and the smallpox and influenza epidemics of 1864,[55] all of which would in varying degree have inflated mortality rates. The outflow of refugees to Natal after 1824 and particularly in the 1840s and 1850s must also be borne in mind.[56]

Although Fynn was to claim that in the mid-1820s the Zulu army totalled 50,000 men, given Captain Gardiner's reckoning that 900 'soldiers' were present at Dingane's capital in 1835, and that Shaka, according to Bryant, enrolled fifteen *amabutho*, Farewell's estimate of an army of 14,000 in 1824 is not unreasonable. The upper age limit of these men is said to have been 40.[57] Extrapolating from this figure, Bryant has calculated that the total population at this time amounted to between 75,000 and 96,000 people.[58] By the 1890s, when much of the territory of the old Zulu kingdom had been alienated, official estimates of the total population varied between 163,000 and 196,000.[59] On the eve of the Anglo-Zulu war Lord Chelmsford reckoned that there were 34 *amabutho*,[60] of which seven were of limited military value, being constituted of men older than 60. The effective force at Cetshwayo's disposal was put at 41,900 men,[61] a figure not significantly at variance with other contemporary estimates.[62] Of these, 4,500 were aged between fifty and sixty years, 5,900 between forty and fifty, 14,500 between thirty and forty, and 17,000 between twenty and thirty. Even allowing for the higher mortality rate among men over forty,[63] and the more turbulent times their generation had witnessed, this statistical breakdown points to a veritable population explosion.

Exaggerated though this image almost certainly is, there existed circumstances which were consistent with demographic growth. During much of Mpande's reign, weather patterns favourable to food production[64] and generally more peaceful conditions prevailed. Furthermore, it must be emphasized that the formation of female *amabutho* may have inhibited, but did not check, population increase, particularly as women were perhaps seldom as old as thirty-five at the time of marriage. Thus for example, the IsaNgqu *ibutho* married girls from eight to ten years younger than themselves. One may assume that these women were in their late twenties or early thirties and that, for the most part, they were still capable of producing sizeable families. On other occasions, the differences in marriage age ranged from nine to twenty years, suggesting that there may have been periods when the birth-rate was unusually high.[65] Whatever the origins and the dimensions of growth, the size of the population in the later kingdom is said to have been a great talking point among the Zulu, and Cetshwayo, according to one tradition, sent to the Secretary for Native Affairs in Natal a sack of millet with the challenge that, 'if you can count the grains then you will also be able to count the Zulu people.'[66]

Against the backdrop of the growth in population, the consequences of the livestock epidemic and of inclement weather were all the more serious. The gravity of the problem of social reproduction, for instance, can be better appreciated when it is noted that, of the twenty-seven active *amabutho*, sixteen comprised unmarried men.[67] Conditions such as these contained within them the germs of intensified discontent, friction and instability.

The shortage of cattle cannot, however, be explained solely in terms of natural factors. It has been said that trade with Natal had essentially superficial consequences for the Zulu political economy in that, with the exception of firearms, no new products were introduced which came to be seen as essential to the Zulu way of life and which could not, if necessary, be manufactured by the Zulu themselves. Moreover, imported commodities were exchanged in the main for cattle and hides, the main surplus product of the kingdom, so that changes in existing techniques and relationships of production were not effected.[68] The extent to which trade with European settlements was assimilated into existing forms of Zulu economic activity is, it has been suggested, further illustrated by the manner in which goods of European origin were exchanged by the Zulu for African products from Zululand's northern neighbours.[69] In sum, without dislocating the domestic economy to any appreciable degree, trade with whites served to perpetuate older patterns of exchange. Such an assessment is too bland, and in my view the penetration of Zululand by Natal commercial interests had far-reaching repercussions for the traditional political and economic order. This is especially true of the period after the late 1840s which saw the growth of the settler community in Natal and, in all probability, led to increased truck with the Zulu.[70] The influence of traders was the greater since they not only purchased cattle but, as has been noted, were responsible for the introduction and the recurrence of the fatal stock diseases that wrought such havoc upon the national herd.

The deficiency in cattle numbers notwithstanding, trade between the two communities remained fairly active. In 1878, for example, the Standard Bank estimated the annual value of exports from Natal to Zululand at £12,000 and put the profit margin at an extremely handsome 75%, a clear if partial illustration of the unequal terms on which trade between the two communities was conducted (and, incidentally, a marked contrast to the pattern of exchange between Zululand and her northern neighbours which generally took the form of tribute extraction[72]). Indeed, there are some suggestions that the volume of exchange during the 1870s may have increased. The ravages of lungsickness in Natal may have boosted demand there for beef and for the hardy Sanga type Zulu cattle.[73] Above all, and not subsumed under the foregoing estimate, the trade in firearms burgeoned in the decade that preceded the war. At least 8,000 guns, and perhaps as many as 20,000,[74] plus a large volume of powder, ammunition and percussion caps were introduced into Zululand during this period.

How is one to reconcile the continuation and probable intensification of trade with the suggested insufficiency in cattle? In the first instance, hides, as indicated above, were often obtained from stock that had succumbed to disease. Secondly, the acquisition of firearms was no ordinary matter, but an issue of some considerable political significance. Cetshwayo obtained his first large consignment when his succession to the kingship was clearly imminent and the possession of firearms would have given him an obvious advantage over any potential usurpers. Moreover, guns were perceived as a vital necessity to national self-preservation at a time when other black chiefdoms were arming, when settler communities had grown in strength, and when the Boers were pressing more urgently on the northern and north-western boundaries of Zululand.[75] Thirdly, it would appear that, as a result of the importation of considerable amounts of ironware — particularly hoes which had to be replaced at fairly frequent intervals — the indigenous iron-working and iron-smelting industry had declined. The Zulu had therefore become increasingly reliant on regular imports for the agricultural implements basic to survival.[76] In fine, the disruption of the iron industry and the depletion of cattle herds are an index of the degree to which the capitalist economy, through the agency of its mercantile out-riders, had impinged upon the productive processes in Zululand and undermined the essential autarky of the traditional political economy.

The gradual transfiguration of the once independent and self-reliant Zulu people into an impoverished labour-exporting peasantry in the period after 1879 is presaged in a further development during this period. Against the background of severe stock losses, Cetshwayo resorted to payment in cash for the weaponry he so earnestly desired. Though he stated emphatically that no Zulu had worked on the Diamond Fields,[77] in order to raise the requisite moneys, he manipulated the tributary powers he exercised over certain Tsonga chiefdoms in the vicinity of St. Lucia Lake, forcing them to send labourers to Natal. This device, which was not fundamentally dissimilar from the slave-trading practices indulged in by political elites elsewhere in Africa, seems to have been resorted to on at least two occasions. In about 1872 some 300 to 400 men were involved, and Cetshwayo appropriated five of the six monthly payments of eight shillings per head, thereby enriching himself to the tune of £600 to £800. On the second occasion in 1876/7, 800 men were affected, and not only did he extract one third of their wages (a deduction that netted £1701), he was also paid by the Natal agents, with whom he was actively co-operating, a fee of £1 for every labourer enlisted.[78] Whatever the long-term implications of this trend for the Zulu themselves, in transposing the pressure they were experiencing on to the productive bases of societies tributary to them, they contributed to the underdevelopment of the area to north-east of Zululand.[79]

Predominant among the Zulu traders in Cetshwayo's reign were members of the richest and most powerful class.[80] Among other things, this involves the question of social and economic stratification which, I wish to suggest, had become more conspicuous by the 1870s. It is against this background that the tensions to which the shortage of cattle gave rise can be delineated with a little more precision.

Fundamentally, increased social stratification stemmed from the presence in Zululand of ecological conditions eminently suited to pastoralism. The corollary was a lesser dependence on grain. As has been observed elsewhere, African societies in the sub-continent which concentrated on grain production were characterised by a greater measure of social and economic equality.[81] It arose, furthermore, out of certain conventions governing marriage, a phenomenon which must be considered from two angles. In the first instance, differential control over stock was, as we have seen, on the basis of age and was associated with the *ibutho* tradition. To recapitulate, regulation of marriage had as its concomitant a retardation of the age at which a man reached social maturity and could thus control his own patrimony and establish his homestead. Hence, at any one time Zulu society was divided into two disparate groups. The one made up of men over 35 or 40 commanding both cattle and the labour power of their womenfolk and children. The other, comprising the sons and younger brothers of the former group, exercised direct control over neither.[82] In the second instance, unequal access to cattle was on the basis of kinship and arose out of the conjunction of patrilineage with certain other traditions affecting marriage. Professor Monica Wilson has written that, 'Only the combination of patrilineal descent, polygyny and marriage with stock allows wealthy lineages to increase fast at the expense of poor.'[83]

Moreover, it has been calculated that a seven year difference in marriage age between men, the older partners, and women would allow 20% of the former to have more than one wife.[84] Though the precise figures do not apply to the Zulu, the general pattern clearly does.

Male members of wealthy lineages would be at an obvious advantage in this regard, particularly as there is evidence that women sometimes showed a preference for men of substance, even if they were considerably older than other males eligible for marriage.[85] Thus, whilst Mpande it is said, had some twenty spouses,[86] according to Cetshwayo there were 'many men in Zululand who have no wives'.[87] Between these two extremes were commoners constituting perhaps 90% of the population,[88] who had 'a couple of wives',[89] and the aristocratic hierarchy who had from six to twelve depending on their wealth.[90] Nor was the difference in the number of wives all that distinguished rich lineages from poor. Whereas the usual rate of *lobola* was from three to ten cattle, a man of importance might demand between 20 and 100 cattle for a daughter.[91] Thus, wealthy lineages rapidly increased their wealth, in terms of clients and cattle. The gap between rich and poor would therefore tend to widen with each generation.

Discrepancies in wealth were not simply the product of social dynamics and the peculiarities of Zulu marriage practices, but were both distorted and accentuated by the tradition of appointing heads of dominant lineages to positions of the highest political importance.[92] As a supplement to the lineage resources available to them, they were in receipt of gifts of cattle and women from both the king and their own subjects. From the latter they were also able to extract surplus in the form of fines and tribute.[93]

One is struck by the quantity of the evidence attesting to the influence these men exercised in Cetshwayo's day in the administration of the state and on the formulation of policy in respect of foreign affairs and a wide range of domestic issues. They had the right to overrule the king and, as Cetshwayo's statement of 1881 cited above makes plain, often acted in a highly independent manner.[94] It would seem that most of the executions arising from witchcraft practices were instigated by *izikhulu* without the king's knowledge or consent and even against his will.[95] These chiefs who indulged in lucrative long distance trading activities, did so without restraint, and at least one harboured distinct ambitions to secede.[96]

The growth of chiefly power derives from the civil war of 1839/40, from the succession crisis that exploded in 1856, and from the power vacuum which resulted from the subsequent struggle for supremacy between Cetshwayo and his father, a contest that was resolved only in 1867. All of these events served to loosen former ties of allegiance to the monarchy and, while weakening its capacity to control, increased its dependence upon subordinate political authorities.[97]

These developments must also be considered in conjunction with, and give content to Basil Sansom's hypothesis that the physical environment of Zululand, characterised by small, repetitive and largely self-sufficient ecological units, resultant upon the broken topography of the area, made for economic fragmentation and administrative decentralisation.[98]

Furthermore, the presence of overmighty subjects must be comprehended in terms of the limitations of the *ibutho* system as an instrument of centralised control. The most obvious anomaly is that, except in so far as it delayed the age at which a man could set up home, and allowed for the extraction of fines and the 'eating up' of herds belonging to citizens guilty of crimes against the state or, in some instances, of becoming too wealthy in stock,[99] it did not interfere with the accumulation of cattle. This is because cattle are a self-regenerating resource and because, in comparison with agriculture, stock-keeping requires a small labour input[100] and could be, and indeed was, carried out by the residual manpower in each homestead. Moreover, the practice of *ukusisa*, (farming out cattle to poorer families) had the effect of increasing the labour resources available to wealthier men.

Intrinsic structural inadequacies aside, it is clear that neither in space nor time was the enrolment of *amabutho* uniform or universal. Thus it would seem that not all enlisted young men were stationed at royal homesteads,[101] or were called up for more than occasional service.[102] Moreover, according to the account of two prisoners taken during the Anglo-Zulu war, 'in the coast and outlying districts there were large numbers of people who retained their liberty and married as they pleased but that strict loyalty was the *fashion* near the court.'[103]

Hence, in addition to being able to draw upon the labour power of the women and juniors within, as well as without, their large families, together with that of the older men released from duty (who were in Cetshwayo's day summoned only at the time of the *umkosi* ceremony,[104] and were in any event increasingly reluctant to obey such calls or were prevented from doing so[105]), certain *izikhulu* could draw on young men to work their fields, herd their cattle or to act as instruments of coercion.[106] It is noteworthy that the *izikhulu* located in the marches of the kingdom tended to predominate in the political system and in the civil upheavals that rent Zululand apart in the 1850s and 1880s. Here one thinks of Masiphula, Maphitha and his son Zibhebhu, Hamu and Mnyamana.[107] They were also favourably placed to profit from long distance exchange, and it is not surprising that among their number were those who were most actively involved in trade.[108] Some enjoyed the additional advantage of being able to obtain tribute from neighbouring Tsonga groups.[109]

It may thus be concluded that the *izikhulu*, who were at the outset wealthy and strong by virtue of their positions in their own lineages, were vested with power and authority and commanded manpower which they were able to use with increasing impunity for the aggrandisement of themselves, selected members of their lineages and the growing personal following which they would thus have been able to attract. The obverse facet was the pauperisation of weaker groups in the society,[110] a trend which in all likelihood became more marked in the wake of the decline in cattle herds, and which found expression in the considerably greater incidence of witchcraft accusation in the 1860s and 1870s.[111]

In fine, distinctions in wealth were the function of a dynamic interplay of factors including age, location, kinship and political affinity. One may reasonably surmise that they were reflected in microcosm, and in varying degree, in the *fracas* which occurred in late 1877 between the older, married men of the Thulwana *ibutho* and the younger Ngobamakhosi men.[112]

Cetshwayo's response was threefold. In the first place, he sought to reassert his authority by revitalising and redisciplining the *amabutho*. This took the form of a rigorous enforcement of both the marriage provisions and the attendance of the older men at the annual levy. His actions culminated in a number of deaths and yielded cattle by way of fines.[113] Moreover, he adopted a more hostile attitude towards the missionaries, who represented an alien and corrosive influence in the land.[114] Beyond these policies, he was to address repeated pleas to the governments of Natal and the South African Republic for permission to raid the Swazi.[115] Raiding was an obvious solution at a time when his cattle herds, and those of the nation, had been depleted; when by virtue of population growth unprecedentedly large numbers of men were in his service and were dependent on his resources; and when he was unable to expropriate cattle from his powerful subordinates without risking a major confrontation. In undertaking a military expedition, he would add to his prestige, divert and sublimate the potentially dangerous resentment his young men harboured against the more privileged members of the society, and satisfy their frustrated yearnings for distinction.[116] Cattle thus obtained would have compensated for his recent losses and augmented his breeding stock, thereby enhancing his capacity to maintain

and reward the younger *amabutho*, his most important political prop.
Furthermore, he would have been better able to distribute patronage
more widely in the kingdom, and in so doing, to counter the fissiparous
forces manifest in it. It is worth recalling that, according to one account,
the last major challenge to kingly authority, the civil conflict of 1856,
arose in part out of a shortage of war booty.[117] In addition to relieving
the crisis of political integration, raiding would also have alleviated the
problems of food production and social reproduction in the society at
large. The blank refusals with which his requests were met, not surprisingly
led to increased disenchantment on the part of Cetshwayo and his younger
'soldiers' in particular.[118]

* * * * *

This brief survey suggests that during Cetshwayo's reign the Zulu political
economy, while showing a high degree of structural continuity, was
clearly in a state of some stress. This arose in part out of events beyond
the control of man. It was also partly endogenous in so far as it was both
the result and the manifestation of the not inconsiderable changes in
the balance of political and economic forces that had occurred since the
death of Shaka. But to a crucial degree it was the consequence of
European penetration into south east Africa, the effects of which long
antedated the political and economic subordination which followed the
military destruction of the Zulu state in 1879.

NOTES

1   The conclusions arrived at in this chapter, based as they are on uncompleted
    research, are necessarily of a tentative order. For a definition of political
    economy see J.B. Wright, 'Pre-Shakan Age-group Formation among the
    Northern Nguni', *Natalia*, 8 (Dec. 1978), p.24. I have relied heavily on this
    source in the first part of this chapter.

2   Ibid., pp.22–30.

3   A.T. Bryant, *Olden Times in Zululand and Natal Containing Earlier Political
    History of the Eastern Nguni Clans* (London, 1929), p.645.

4   J.D. Omer-Cooper, *The Zulu Aftermath: a Nineteenth-Century Revolution in Bantu Africa* (London, 1966), p.24–48.

5   J.J. Guy, 'Production and Exchange in the Zulu Kingdom', paper presented to workshop on precapitalist social formations and colonial penetration in southern Africa, National University of Lesotho (July 1976), p.9; Wright, op.cit., p.25.

6   J.J. Guy, 'Ecological Factors in the Rise of Shaka and the Zulu Kingdom', paper presented to conference on southern African history, National University of Lesotho (Aug. 1977); Guy, 'Production and Exchange'; Wright, op.cit., p.25.

7   Guy, 'Ecological Factors', p.11–14.

8   H. Slater, 'Transitions in the Political Economy of South-east Africa before 1840' (unpublished D. Phil. Thesis, University of Sussex, 1976), p.307, cited in Wright, op.cit., p.25.

9   Guy, 'Production and Exchange', p.8.

10 Ibid.

11 Ibid., pp.10–11; E.J. Krige, *The Social System of the Zulus*, second edition (Pietermaritzburg, 1950), p.241.

12 C. Meillassoux, 'From Reproduction to Production', *Economy and Society*, 1, (1972), pp.93–105; E. Terray, *Marxism and 'Primitive' Societies* (London and New York, 1972), pp.95–186, especially pp.163–86.

13 C. de B. Webb and J.B. Wright, (eds.), *A Zulu King Speaks: Statements Made by Cetshwayo kaMpande on the History and Customs of His People* (Pietermaritzburg and Durban, 1978), pp.82, 84–5, 91.

14 J.Y. Gibson, *The Story of the Zulus* (London, 1911), pp.31–2.

15 Ibid., pp.100, 110; *Precis of Information concerning Zululand with a map prepared by the Intelligence Division, War Office* (London, 1895), p.109.

16 Guy, 'Production and Exchange', pp.4–5.

17 Guy, 'Ecological Factors', p.16; 'Production and Exchange', pp.10–11.

18 Ibid., p.8; Gibson, p.131; Webb & Wright, *A Zulu King Speaks*, p.90.

19 In this regard there are highly suggestive analogies with Inca society. See M. Godelier, *Perspectives in Marxist Anthropology* (Cambridge, 1977), pp.186–95; see also S. Marks, 'Natal, the Zulu Royal Family and the Ideology of Segregation', *Journal of Southern African Studies*, vol. 4, 2 (April 1978), pp.172–94.

20 Guy, 'Production and Exchange', pp.2–3, 5; Wright, op.cit., pp.26–7; see also Terray, op.cit., pp.169–70.

21 Meillassoux, op.cit., p.101; Terray, op.cit., p.167; Wright, op.cit., passim. A further investigation of the role of women may well modify this characterisation.

22 Terray, op.cit., pp.169–70. My insertion.

23 A comprehensive list of *amabutho*, including dates of birth and enrolment may be found in Bryant, *Olden Times*, pp.645–6.

24 R.L. Cope, Shepstone and Cetshwayo, 1873–79' (unpublished M.A. thesis, University of Natal, 1967), p.220.

25 F.B. Fynney, 'The Rise and Fall of the Zulu Nation', in F.B. Fynney, *Zululand and the Zulus . . .* (Pietermaritzburg, no date, reprinted Pretoria, 1967), p.32.

26   E.H. Brookes and C. de B. Webb, *A History of Natal* (Pietermaritzburg, 1965), pp.124–35.

27   Br. Parl. Papers LX of 1877, C.1748, p.216, no. 165, enclosure 1: Statement by Barjeni and Mantshonga, 2 Nov. 1876. Hereafter cited as BPP.

28   Cope, pp.145–7.

29   F.E. Colenso (assisted by Lt. Col. E. Durnford), *History of the Zulu War and its Origin* (London, 1880), pp.230–1.

30   Webb & Wright, *A Zulu King Speaks*. p.61.

31   Natal Archives, Colenso Collection, Box No. 3, Bishop Colenso, Annexure to Letter Received: R. Robertson to John Sanderson, 20 April 1877, pp.4–5; BPP LV of 1878, C.1961, pp.43–50, no. 12, enclosure 1: Fynney to Osborn, 4 July 1877.

32   See for example, Guy, 'Production and Exchange', pp.10, 13; C. de B. Webb and J.B. Wright (eds.), *The James Stuart Archive of Recorded Oral Evidence Relating to the History of the Zulu and Neighbouring Peoples*, vol. 1 (Pietermaritzburg and Durban, 1976), passim.

33   A.T. Bryant, *The Zulu People As They Were Before the White Man Came*, second edition (Pietermaritzburg, 1967), p.336; Gibson, pp.129–30.

34   Bryant, *The Zulu People*, p.336.

35   D. Leslie (Edited by the Hon. W.H. Drummond), *Among the Zulus and Amatongas: with Sketches of the Natives, their Language and Customs . . .* (Glasgow, 1875), p.185. There may also have been political motives behind this move.

36   Cited in Bryant, *The Zulu People*, p.336.

37   G.H. Mason, *Zululand: a Mission Tour in South Africa* (London, 1861), pp.199–200.

38   Mrs. Wilkinson, *A Lady's Life and Travels in Zululand and the Transvaal during Cetewayo's Reign . . .* (London, 1882), p.71.

39   Ibid., p.67.

40   Natal Archives, Colenso Collection, Box No. 3, Bishop Colenso, Annexure to Letter Received: R. Robertson to John Sanderson, 20 April 1887, p.5.

41   L. van Horn, 'The Agricultural History of Barotseland, 1840–1964', in R. Palmer and Neil Parsons, (eds.), *The Roots of Rural Poverty in Central and Southern Africa* (London, 1977), p.156.

42   Bryant, *The Zulu People*, p.538.

43   M. Hall, 'Dendroclimatology, Rainfall and Human Adaptation in the Later Iron Age of Natal and Zululand', *Annals of the Natal Museum*, vol. 22, 3 (Nov. 1976), pp.698–9.

44   Bryant, *The Zulu People*, p.538.

45   The Hon. W.H. Drummond, *The Large Game and Natural History of South and South East Africa* (Edinburgh, 1875), p.352.

46   There are interesting parallels with the situation in Botswana in the late nineteenth century. See. N. Parsons, 'The Economic History of Khama's Country in Botswana, 1844–1930', in Palmer and Parsons, p.128.

47   Fynney, *Zululand and the Zulus*, p.14; C. Vijn (ed. and trans. by J. W. Colenso), *Cetshwayo's Dutchman, being the Private Journal of a White Trader in Zululand during the British Invasion* (London, 1880), p.13; Wilkinson, pp.124–32.

48 Hall, op.cit., p.698–9.
49 D.I. Bransby, 'The Ecology of Livestock Production in Natal and Zululand', paper presented to workshop on production and reproduction in the Zulu kingdom, University of Natal, Pietermaritzburg (Oct. 1977), p.8.
50 Hall, op.cit., p.700. See also D. Beach, 'The Shona Economy; Branches of Production', in Palmer and Parsons, p.44.
51 M. Wilson, 'Changes in Social Structure in Southern Africa: the Relevance of Kinship Studies to the Historian', in L.S. Thompson, (ed.), *African Societies in Southern Africa* (London, 1969), p.79.
52 Bryant, *The Zulu People,* p.637; Krige, p.73.
53 Guy, 'Ecological Factors', pp.15–16.
54 G.A. Willis, 'Some Basic Concepts in Demographic Analysis', paper presented to workshop on production and reproduction in the Zulu kingdom, University of Natal, Pietermaritzburg (Oct. 1977), p.2.
55 R.C.A. Samuelson, *Long, Long Ago* (Durban, 1929), p.22; Webb and Wright, *The James Stuart Archive,* Vol. 1, pp.31–2.
56 D.R. Edgecombe and J.B. Wright, 'Mpande kaSenzangakhona' (unpublished typescript), pp.8, 13. [I am indebted to these authors for permitting me to make use of this work.]
57 Bryant, *Olden Times,* p.80.
58 Ibid.; Bryant, *The Zulu People,* p.29.
59 Bryant, *Olden Times,* p.81; *Precis of Information,* p.79.
60 This figure is not significantly at variance with the list in Bryant, *Olden Times,* pp.645–6.
61 *Precis of Information,* p.112.
62 Colenso, p.318 (footnote); F.B. Fynney, *The Zulu Army and Zulu Headmen,* second edition, revised (Pietermaritzburg, 1879), p.4.
63 Willis, op.cit., p.4.
64 Hall, op.cit., pp.698–9.
65 Bryant, *Olden Times,* pp.645–5; Gibson, pp.133–5.
66 Cited in Gibson, p.120.
67 *Precis of Information,* p.112.
68 Guy, 'Production and Exchange', p.12.
69 C. Bundy, 'African Peasants and Economic Change in South Africa, 1870–1913, with particular reference to the Cape' (unpublished D. Phil. thesis, University of Oxford, 1976), p.224. Now published as *The Rise and Fall of the South African Peasantry* (London, 1979).
70 Some indication can be obtained from Mason, pp.199–200.
71 BPP LII of 1879, C.2222, pp.213–15, no. 55, enclosure 1: Extract from letter from E. Thomas, Manager, Durban Branch, Standard Bank, 16 Dec. 1878.
72 Webb and Wright, *The James Stuart Archive,* vol. 1, pp.63–8.
73 Colenso, p.35; Wilkinson, p.111.
74 Cope, p.80; J.J. Guy, 'A Note on Firearms in the Zulu Kingdom with Special Reference to the Anglo-Zulu War, 1879', *Journal of African History,* vol. XII, 4 (1971), pp.557–70.

75   Guy, 'A Note on Firearms', p.559.

76   Bryant, *The Zulu People*, p.388; Gibson, pp.4–5. The Shona replaced their
      agricultural implements at intervals of from two to five years. Beach, op.cit.,
      p.48.

77   Webb and Wright, *A Zulu King Speaks*, p.92.

78   BPP LII of 1878, C.2220, pp.172–94, no.66, Enclosure 1: Report by Attorney
      General on 'Employment of Native Labourers in Natal', 22 Aug. 1878;
      Enclosure 1: Extract from *Natal Mercury*, no date; Enclosure 3: Durban
      Circuit Court, 16 April 1878; Leslie, 187–8; see also C. Ballard, 'The Role
      of Tributary Labour in the Zulu Political Economy', paper presented to
      conference on the history of opposition in Southern Africa, University of
      the Witwatersrand (Jan. 1978), p.68–9; C. Ballard, 'Migrant Labour in Natal,
      1860–79, with Special Reference to Zululand and the Delagoa Bay Hinterland',
      Journal of Natal and Zulu History, vol. 1 (1978), p.40.

79   There are interesting parallels with the situation in Ovamboland in the late
      nineteenth and early twentieth centuries. See W.G. Clarence-Smith and
      R. Moorson, 'Underdevelopment and Class Formation in Ovamboland,
      1845–1915', *Journal of African History*, vol. XVI, 3(1975), pp.365–81.

80   Colenbrander Papers (in the possession of Dr. J. Colenbrander, Pietermaritzburg):
      C.W. Wheelwright to Marquis del Moral, no date, pp.4–5; J.J. Guy, 'The
      Destruction of the Zulu Kingdom: the Civil War in Zululand, 1879–1884',
      (unpublished Ph.D. thesis, University of London, 1975), pp.35–9. Now
      published as *The Destruction of the Zulu Kingdom* (London, 1979).

81   B. Sansom, 'Traditional Economic Systems', in W.D. Hammond–Tooke (ed.),
      The Bantu-speaking Peoples of Southern Africa, second edition (London,
      1974), pp.135–76 and especially pp.135–57.

82   BPP LV of 1878, C.1961, pp.43–50, no. 12, enclosure 1; Fynney to Osborn,
      4 July 1877.

83   Wilson, op.cit., p.79.

84   Ibid., p.77.

85   Webb and Wright, *The James Stuart Archive*, vol. 1, pp.316–7.

86   Edgecombe and Wright, op.cit., p.12.

87   Cited in Webb and Wright, *A Zulu King Speaks*, p.72. It is clear from the
      context that Cetshwayo's reference is to men eligible to marry.

88   Bryant, *The Zulu People*, p.438.

89   Ibid., p.412.

90   Ibid., pp.412, 576.

91   Ibid., p.591.

92   Guy, 'Production and Exchange', p.10–11; Webb and Wright, *A Zulu King
      Speaks*, pp.2–3.

93   Bryant, *The Zulu People*, p.481; Guy, 'Production and Exchange', pp.10–11;
      Webb and Wright, *The James Stuart Archive*, pp.316–7.

94   Bryant, *Olden Times*, p.647; Colenso, p.109, pp.223–4, p.407; Cope,
      pp.145, 232–39; Webb and Wright, *A Zulu King Speaks*, pp.67, 70, 75,
      79–84, 93–4; Webb and Wright, *The James Stuart Archive*, vol. 1, pp.314–5.

95   Samuelson, pp.34–5.

96   Colenbrander Papers (in the possession of Dr. J. Colenbrander, Pietermaritzburg):
      C.W. Wheelwright to Marquis del Moral, no date, pp.4–5.

97 Edgecombe and Wright, op.cit., pp. 6, 13, 16, 18.

98 Sansom, op.cit., pp.135–57.

99 Guy, 'Production and Exchange', p.9; Webb and Wright, *The James Stuart Archive*, vol. 1, p.317.

100 Sansom, op.cit., pp.151–2.

101 Bryant, *The Zulu People*, p.467; see also the list of chiefs in Fynney, *The Zulu Army*.

102 Webb and Wright, *The James Stuart Archive*, vol. 1, p.310.

103 Cited in Colenso, p.228 (footnote).

104 Webb and Wright, *The James Stuart Archive*, vol. 1, p.32.

105 Webb and Wright, *A Zulu King Speaks*, pp.19, 60–1.

106 Bryant, *Olden Times*, p.647; Bryant, *The Zulu People*, p.463: Sansom, op.cit., p.148.

107 Edgecombe and Wright, op.cit., p.12; Guy, 'The Destruction of the Zulu Kingdom', passim.

108 Colenbrander Papers: C.W. Wheelwright to Marquis del Moral, no date, p.4.

109 Leslie, pp.134, 288.

110 Webb and Wright, *The James Stuart Archive*, pp.314–17.

111 Webb and Wright, *A Zulu King Speaks*, pp.19 (footnote), 20.

112 Gibson, pp.135–7; Webb and Wright, *The James Stuart Archive*, pp.31–2.

113 Gibson, pp.133–5: Webb and Wright, *A Zulu King Speaks*, pp.19, 60.

114 Colenso, p.213–226; N. A. Etherington, 'The Rise of the *Kholwa* in Southeast Africa; African Christian Communities in Natal, Pondoland and Zululand, 1835–1880' (unpublished Ph.D. thesis, Yale University, 1971), pp.181–98. Now published as *Preachers, Peasants and Politics in Southeast Africa, 1835–1880* (London, The Royal Historical Society, 1978).

115 BPP LX of 1877, C.1748, pp.150–1, no. 121, enclosure 1: Burgers to Bulwer, 29 Aug. 1876; ibid., p.198, no. 156, enclosure: Reply to message from Bulwer, 9 Oct. 1876; ibid., p.216, no. 165, enclosure 1: Statement by Barjeni and Mantshonga, 2 Nov. 1876; BPP LV of 1878, C.1961, pp.43–50, no. 12, enclosure 1: Fynney to Osborn, 4 July 1877.

116 Webb and Wright, *A Zulu King Speaks*, p.25.

117 Revd L. Grout, *Zululand: or, Life among the Zulu Kafirs of Natal and Zululand* (London, 1863), pp.347–8.

118 Natal Archives, Government House, vol. 1326; no. 96: Bulwer to Frere, 12 June 1878, p.105.

ELAINE UNTERHALTER

Confronting Imperialism:
the People of Nquthu and the
Invasion of Zululand

The Nquthu district lies in the west of Zululand on its border with Natal.[1]
It was the western boundary of this area that was the subject of the
investigations of the Boundary Commission of 1878; it was from this
area in 1878 that Mehlokazulu and his brothers crossed the Mzinyathi
River to seize two of their father's wives, so providing the British with
a *casus belli* for the invasion of Cetshwayo's kingdom in early 1879;
the famous battle of Isandlwana took place in the Nquthu district and
it was in this district that the Prince Imperial was killed. However, this
paper is not concerned with revising these well known events but with
looking at the Nquthu district for the detailed information and insight
which its history provides about the people of Zululand during the
invasion of their country.

The Nquthu district had been brought into the Zulu kingdom as a result
of Shaka's campaigns in the early 19th century which destroyed the
independent kingdoms there. Many of the inhabitants fled. Those who
remained had to accept the rule of the Zulu monarchy which was enforced
by administrators and settlers, placed in the district by the king.

In northern Nquthu Shaka established the *ikhanda* of Qulusi. Members
of *amabutho* were stationed at the *ikhanda*, as was usual elsewhere in Zululand. After their period of service was over, the *amabutho* at Qulusi did
not return to their homes elsewhere in Zululand, but settled around the
ikhanda on land granted to them by the king. They formed a settler
population in Nquthu with strong ties of loyalty to the monarchy on
whom they depended for their land. Because of this strong bond with the
monarchy, the Qulusi *amabutho* were not required to gather at the royal
capital to render tribute labour but were allowed to perform this at
Qulusi.[2] This relationship between the monarchy and the Qulusi settlers

continued to 1878. In that year the commanding officer of the *ikhanda* was Seketwayo kaNhlako Mdlalose.

The people of central and southern Nquthu, once incorporated into the Zulu Kingdom, were ruled by an *induna* appointed by the monarchy to apportion land and organise *amabutho* to perform tribute labour for himself and the king. In about 1850 Mpande appointed Mfokazana kaXongo Ngobese as his *induna* in this area. There was a very close connection between Mfokazana's family and the Zulu ruling family, this being celebrated in stories of common origin.[3] Mpande's appointment of Mfokazana to rule the Nquthu district can thus be seen as an attempt by the monarchy to tighten its control over this border region.

In the Zulu Civil War of 1856 Sihayo kaXongo, Mfokazana's brother, supported Cetshwayo and the Usuthu party. Sihayo continued this support during the subsequent struggle between the prince and the king.[4] In 1872 Cetshwayo assumed the crown. He ratified Sihayo's inheritance of his brother's title. He probably did this because Sihayo had been an Usuthu supporter and because, like Mpande, he was aware of the family ties that made the Ngobeses suitably loyal administrators for the Zulu monarchy.

Sihayo built his capital at Sokexe, opposite Rorke's Drift. He appointed three headmen to assist him in the administration of the district. In 1878 his headmen were Dwaba kaMpunzi, Mvemve, and Sombitshana kaYoto. Sihayo's brother Magumdana also acted as a headman. According to Fynney's estimates in 1878, Sihayo had command over the labour power of three hundred men who served in *amabutho* summoned by him.[5]

Sihayo used his position as *induna*, with control over the surplus labour of the people he ruled, to accumulate considerable wealth in cattle. These cattle were exchanged for guns and horses in Natal, where Sihayo had considerable status as a trader.[6] Thus, despite Sihayo's political relation with the king and his history of loyalty to Cetshwayo, the economic base of his power had come to derive less from relations within the Zulu Kingdom and more from his connections with colonial Natal. This contradiction in his position was similar to that of other powerful *izinduna* in Zululand like Zibephu in the northern districts.[7]

It may have been a dispute over trade in which women were involved as part of the exchange agreement that led Mehlokazulu kaSihayo and his brothers to attack the *umuzi* of Mswagele near Shiyani Hill in the Msinga district of Natal. This excursion was a dangerous step to take from the point of view of the Zulu Kingdom as subsequent events were to show. It was probably only the concerns of the Ngobese family as traders in

Zululand with interests more connected to Natal than Zululand that made Mehlokazulu undertake the expedition. Sihayo's trading exploits had always made Cetshwayo regard him with some ambivalence[8] and during the war other members of the Zulu ruling class regarded Sihayo's sons with hostility and wanted to surrender them to the British.[9] The contradictions of Sihayo's position — political allegiance to the monarchy and economic interests at odds with it — are an example of the structural contradictions which occurred within the Zulu Kingdom as a whole.[10] These contradictions should be seen as central to the causes of the Anglo-Zulu war. It was not just an accident that Mehlokazulu's raid on Natal was the *casus belli* for the Anglo-Zulu war. That incident epitomised the reasons for the war — the involvement of the people of Zululand with the people of Natal and hence with British imperialism.

The rulers of the central and northern Nquthu had strong attachments to the Zulu crown. In southern Nquthu, the ruling class had a tradition of independence from the monarchy. The Cunu people who lived in the area of the Mzinyathi valley were ruled by the *izikhulu* (hereditary noblemen) Matshana kaSitshakuza from his capital at Dayingubo. His family had ruled the Cunu people in pre-Shakan times. During Shaka's reign, they had decided it was preferable to join the Zulu Kingdom rather than suffer an attack. As a result, Shaka had allowed the ruling family to continue in power as long as they provided him with the labour tribute and any other services he required. Throughout the history of the Zulu Kingdom, tensions had existed between the need of the crown for centralisation and the demands of the *izikhulu* for autonomous control of the labour power of their subjects. Matshana kaSitshakuza, like former rulers of the Cunu people, wished to establish an autonomy and it was his search for support in this conflict that led him to incline towards the Natal settlers and made Fynney doubt his allegiance to the Zulu king.[11]

In 1878 southern Nquthu around Qudeni was settled by Sithole people, ruled by Matshana kaMondisa. Matshana's grandfather, Jobe, had been appointed *induna* over the major part of the Nquthu district by Shaka. Jobe had used this position to establish claims on the labour power of the people he ruled. In Dingane's reign his position had frequently brought him into conflict with the monarchy. He moved his capital into Natal and in the late 1830s made an alliance with the Boer invaders of Zululand against the Zulu king. The Boers, and later the British, recognised Jobe's claim to land in Northern Natal and his people remained settled there until 1858 when Matshana kaMondisa had to flee from the Natal administration because he had been involved in witchcraft accusations. Mpande gave him and his people land in Nquthu.

Matshana kaMondisa's relation with the Zulu monarchy was an anomalous one. Historically it was a relation of conflict, but Mpande's land grant had created a state of dependence. The power Matshana's father and grandfather had exercised over their followers was more in the nature of an *isikhulu* than an *induna*. These anomalies made the Natal settlers conjecture that, on an invasion of Zululand, Matshana would bring his 700 men into alliance with them as Jobe had done in 1839.[12]

Thus, on the eve of the Anglo-Zulu war, a number of contradictions characterised the relation of the people of Nquthu, and especially that of the ruling class, to the monarchy. The people of the northern Qulusi district were loyalists. Sihayo was a monarchist by inclination but the economic base of his power put him at odds with the monarchy. Matshana kaSitshakuza was drawn towards the colonists in Natal because he wished to consolidate his autonomy. Matshana kaMondisa had similar inclinations but had experienced living under Natal rule and had enjoyed the generosity of the Zulu king. However, despite these contradictions, the rulers of Nquthu and the peasantry all supported Cetshwayo in the war of 1879. Sihayo's brother Magumdana was the only member of the ruling class in Nquthu who deserted and none of his people followed him.[13]

Apart from the obvious strategic need to defeat the invading army before more imperial troops could be brought in, it may have been a suspicion of the loyalty of the border areas under Matshana kaSitshakuza and Matshana kaMondisa that led Cetshwayo and his generals to decide to fight a pitched battle with the invading imperial army so close to the border with Natal. Some of the king's advisers also doubted the loyalty of Sihayo and blamed him for the war because of the action of his sons.[14]

Since October 1878 the Zulu army had been assembled at the king's military headquarters at Nodwengu.[15] Members of *amabutho* from Nquthu had been sent to muster there by the *izinduna* and *izikhulu* of the district. Among the men Sihayo provided was a mounted detachment armed with firearms who were to act as scouts.[16] Sihayo himself with his sons went to join the king at Ulundi as did Seketwayo, who was the commanding officer of the Nodwengu regiment.

Although a large number of men from every area of Nquthu went to the capital to prepare for war, a fair sized force remained in the district to garrison it. Some of Sihayo's sons commanded a force stationed at Sokexe to guard the approach from Rorke's Drift. A section of the Qulusi remained at their *ikhanda* near Hlobane and Matshana kaMondisa remained around Mangeni, commanding a detachment of 700 men.[17]

These details of the preparations for war by the rulers of Nquthu bear out Guy's general observations on the coherence of the Zulu Kingdom when faced with invasion.[18] Even *izikhulu* and *izinduna* with interests directly opposed to the monarchy remained loyal in Nquthu, although British Intelligence had supposed they would abandon the king as had happened during the Boer attack on Dingane in 1839. It is probable that the reason for this was that by 1879 the people of Zululand knew from what had happened in Natal what subjection to imperialism meant. They knew about hut taxes, passes, forced labour, the deposition of *izikhulu* and *izinduna* and their replacement with appointees of the Secretary for Native Affairs, subject to the orders of his magistrates. The ruling class and the peasants both stood to suffer if the imperial invasion succeeded.

Cetshwayo voiced what must have been a general sentiment in July 1879 when he was in hiding at Mnyamana's *umuzi*. He sent Maphelu kaMkhosana to Qudeni to herd together 140 royal cattle to send to the British as a peace offering, but remarked while giving the order: 'The whites are not interested in cattle, they want land.'[19]

The ruling class of the Zulu Kingdom fought against the invasion to protect its control over the land and the people of Zululand. The peasants of Zululand obeyed orders to assemble for war because their land and livelihood depended on obedience to the ruling class. They also knew that an imperialist victory would threaten the basis of their survival. It was in expression of this awareness that the British would rob them of their land that the men of Nquthu guarding Sihayo's capital taunted Chelmsford's column riding to attach them:

> What are you doing riding along down there? Try and come up. Are you looking for a place to build kraals?[20]

The column of the imperial army that invaded Nquthu made its first attack at Sokexe on 12 January 1879. The defenders, commanded by Sihayo's son Mkumbikazulu, were armed with rifles and able to position themselves in rock shelters. But they were outnumbered by the British troops who also had faster firing guns. The imperial army captured all Sihayo's cattle that were at the capital and burnt Sokexe to the ground.[21] The column then moved to the encampment at Isandlwana.

After the attack on Sokexe the British did not molest the women or children and did not burn any *imizi*.[22] However, the presence of troops led to most of the women taking their children into hiding.[23] From late 1878 the *imizi* along the Mzinyathi River had been abandoned.[24] In early January 1879, when Chelmsford sent reconnaisance parties riding through the Nquthu district toward Isipezi, they found the countryside deserted,[25] as Chelmsford himself discovered when he rode from Isandlwana toward Mangeni on 20 January 1879.[26] Thus, in the first weeks of the war, those people of Nquthu who did not arm and join the *amabutho* at the capital or station themselves to guard a strategic point in the district, went to safe places so that children and food supplies could be protected.[27]

For all the people of Nquthu, the first weeks of the war involved a complete overturning of the pattern of daily life. Virtually all the men of military age were mobilised. Virtually all the older people, women and children went into hiding. However, after the battle of Isandlwana and the withdrawal of the survivors of the imperial column from Nquthu, those who had fought returned with their families to their *imizi*. They buried some of the men who had been killed at the Isandlwana battle.[28] Families probably buried their relations. It was probably the bodies of soldiers from other districts which were left unburied and found by imperial troops returning to the site in May 1879.[29]

H.H. Parr, who visited the Isandlwana battlefield just after the battle, estimated that from 2 600 to 3 000 Zulu soldiers had died in the engagement.[30] The people of Nquthu who returned to the district knew that they had won a great victory but at some cost. The invasion was by no means over. They had to regroup for a new phase of the war.

In the second phase of the war, after the three pitched battles at Isandlwana, Khambula and Hlobane, the imperial army, strengthened by the arrival of reinforcements, moved through Zululand to attack Cetshwayo's capital at Ulundi. It was during this phase of operations that imperial troops first returned to the Nquthu district in May 1879. Although one of the first tasks they undertook was the burial of the men who had died at Isandlwana,[31] this concern did not divert them from carrying out an intensive attack on the people of Nquthu. The troops rode through the district burning *imizi* and confiscating cattle.[32]

The Zulu Kingdom's resistance to the invasion had been concentrated in the three major battles. However, the people of Zululand also made considerable use of guerilla tactics to harass the invading troops. In Nquthu, where many imperial troop movements took place, a large number of guerilla groups operated. In the north, the Qulusi people made constant raids on the South African Republic. In the south, strong armed bands of people attacked the Natal farms along the Mzinyathi River.[33] The Msinga district was frequently attacked by the people of Gamdana (Sihayo's brother who had deserted from the Zulu Kingdom) who, unlike their headman, fought to resist the attack on their land.[34] Imperial troops were constantly harassed while making their way to Ulundi through Nquthu. In one such encounter the Prince Imperial was killed.

While the members of the guerilla bands were probably all men detailed from the *amabutho*, the women of Nquthu also played a significant part in the war. They took their children and cattle into hiding and provided the fighting men with food. In May 1879 the correspondent of the London *Times* noticed a large number of waggons leaving Sihayo's district laden with food, presumably for members of the *amabutho* stationed in other districts.[35] This food must have been harvested and loaded by the women, as most of the men were engaged in the fighting. The women of Zululand felt as strong a hatred of the invaders as the men did, and their will to resist was as fierce. This is illustrated by the words an old woman near Telezini hurled at the military party who went to bury the Prince Imperial:

> They killed your great inkosi. They are gone now to the king's kraal to fight you white men. What do you come here for? We don't want you. This is Zululand. Keep to your own side.[36]

In the last months of the war, the majority of the people not engaged in fighting went into hiding again. W.E. Montague, riding through the Nquthu district towards Telezini at the end of May 1879 remarked that there was no sign of life; no smoke, no labourers in the mealie fields; just dead silence.[37]

In October 1879 Montague returned to Nquthu and found much of the district still deserted.[38] The people were still in hiding in forests and caves, protecting their children and cattle. It was necessary for them to continue to evade the imperial army in this manner because, after the battle of Ulundi in July 1879, columns moved through Zululand burning *imizi*. Montague accompanied one such column that rode throught the Nquthu district, passing up the valleys and setting the *imizi* alight.[39] Operations of this nature were particularly intensive in the Nquthu district as the Qulusi guerilla bands continued to attack British troops there even after they had news of the defeat at Ulundi. It was only after Maphelu kaMkhosana brought a message from Cetshwayo, who had been captured, ordering them to demobilise because '. . . the impi of the Whites will kill us'[40] that Seketwayo dismissed the Qulusi troops. In response, Chelmsford sent a force which pacified the Qulusi district with considerable ferocity, killing men and taking cattle and arms in an attempt to enforce submission.[41]

The Nquthu district thus saw the first engagements of the Anglo-Zulu war and the last. The people of the district experienced troops invading their land, looting their food, burning their homes and killing their relations. They fought to defend themselves against this attack which they knew stemmed from Britain's desire to annexe their land, and which they feared would result in their losing their children as servants and their cattle as plunder.[42] They fought heroically to protect their land. They inflicted a great defeat on their attackers at Isandlwana. That they themselves were defeated in 1879 was because of the superior military technology and vast forces their attackers could bring against them at that time.

Although in a Colonial Office memorandum on the Anglo-Zulu war in 1880 it was noted that the war had 'been declared against Cetshwayo and not against the Zulu nation',[43] the war engaged the Zulu people who suffered both its immediate effect of death and deprivation and also its long-term effect which brought Zululand into the British Empire. The ruling class and the peasants of Zululand were both attacked and fought together to defend their land and their livelihood. They were defeated together. However, under imperial rule, their fate diverged.

* * * * *

After a few days in Zululand in January 1879 Chelmsford wrote:

> The more I see of the Buffalo border the more convinced I am that we *must* hold both sides of the river if Natal is to be made secure in the future from raidings . . . with the border belt in our possession and Zululand parcelled out into small divisions under chiefs Natal will be quite secure.[44]

Chelmsford's limited view of the reasons for the conquest contrast with Wolseley's wider ambitions. After the end of the war Wolseley reported to the Colonial Office:

> I have laboured with the great aim of establishing for her Majesty's
> subjects in South Africa, both white and coloured, as well as for
> this spirited people against whom, unhappily, we have been involved
> in war, the enduring foundations of peace, happiness and prosperity.[45]

It is evident that Wolseley not only wished to establish a military buffer
to protect the Natal border. He had a wider perspective which entailed
political and economic domination. The British government's final settlement of Zululand in 1879, however, while embodying much of the spirit
of Wolseley's plan, was closer to Chelmsford's original formulation.

The Zululand peace settlement entailed the division of the kingdom
into thirteen areas, each of which was put in the charge of a chief appointed
by the British. These appointed chiefs were, according to the Colonial
Office, each to be independent rulers in their own territory. The nature
of this independence was in the future years of civil war to be a matter
of dispute. In 1879 the Colonial Office wanted to establish British
dominance in Zululand by enforcing the settlement but wished to leave
to the appointed chiefs the arduous tasks of local administration. As
Wolseley wrote in 1879:

> The settlement is based on expediency because any statesman
> unbiased by the colonial avarice for more land must feel how
> important it is to refrain from adding to the already serious and
> heavy responsibilities of Empire in South Africa.[46]

Yet, despite Colonial Office stress on the independence of the appointed
chiefs, Wolseley was concerned to make clear to them and their subjects
the limits of their power. Shortly after the British victory at Ulundi,
he made a speech to members of the Zulu royal family, *izikhulu* and
izinduna, amongst whom were some of the men who were to be appointed
chiefs. Wolseley indicated that Cetshwayo's fate should be a warning to
them. He stated that the people of Zululand were to live subject to the
British as the people of Natal did and that the Resident appointed by him
would ensure that the dictates of Britain were carried out by the appointed
chiefs. He was explicit that the appointment of the chiefs was an 'act of
grace' by Britain.[47] The local authority which the Colonial Office wanted
to grant the new rulers was interpreted as a very limited one by their
representatives in Zululand.

Generally, the men appointed as chiefs to the thirteen areas into which
Zululand was divided were members of the Zulu royal family, *izikhulu*,

or *izinduna*. For example, Seketwayo, who had commanded the Qulusi *ikhanda* in northern Nquthu, was appointed chief of one of the central districts. The two southern districts that bordered Natal, however, were placed under men of non-Zulu origin. John Dunn, the Natal trader, was given charge of the area from the coast to the Nkandhla forest. Hlubi Molife, a Sotho headman, who had fought with the Natal Native Corps for the British during the war, was appointed to rule the Nquthu district.[48] Both these men were considered by the British to be suitable rulers of the sensitive border areas because it was thought that their interests coincided with those of the imperialists. In appointing these two men as chiefs, the influence of Chelmsford's idea of creating a buffer zone can be seen.

In October 1879 Hlubi Molife arrived with twelve mounted men at the magistracy in Msinga. H.F. Fynn, the Resident Magistrate, took them into the Nquthu district and, with Fynn's policemen as guides, Hlubi's party was shown round the area.[49] It was quite clear that he was coming to rule the district under direction from imperial masters.

The terms of Hlubi's appointment as chief were similar to those governing the other appointed rulers of Zululand. His territory was to be defined by the Imperial Boundary Commission. He was forbidden to sell or alienate any land within that area. Any successor to his title as chief was to be approved by the British government. A number of other conditions was imposed, mostly vague and full of unspoken assumptions. Hlubi was enjoined to 'govern, order and decide in accordance with ancient laws and usage' of his people, to forbid the continuation of the Zulu military system, and the practice of witchcraft. He was to allow men to marry when they chose and to permit them to work in Natal or the Transvaal or wherever they chose. The agreement also stipulated that all the inhabitants of the area were to be allowed to remain there, provided they recognised the appointed chief. There were to be no wars between chiefs without the sanction of the British government, and any dispute in the territory involving a British subject was to be referred to the Resident.[50]

Imperial strategy in Nquthu and the other areas of Zululand after the invasion was thus based on indirect rule. Britain gave Hlubi almost complete control over the land and labour power of the people of Nquthu. He was directed to dismantle the Zulu military system and to encourage men to go to work for wages but no explicit pressures were placed on him to ensure that this was done. The appointment of chiefs, while saving the imperial administration the cost of employing magistrates, did not necessarily provide them with compliant rulers. Indirect rule was to have many pitfalls as colonial administrators were to find in the subsequent years of civil war in Zululand.

Despite the wide-ranging powers given to him on paper, Hlubi seems to have modified these considerably in practice. He reached agreements with most of the members of the ruling class in Nquthu that more or less accommodated their interests. Matshana kaMondisa and Matshana kaSitshakuza in the southern region both remained in authority over the people they had commanded before the invasion. Hlubi apparently did not interfere with the manner in which they distributed land to their followers or extracted surplus labour from them.[51] They probably provided Hlubi with a small tribute payment and he did not interfere further.

The Qulusi *ikhanda* in northern Nquthu was destroyed by Wolseley's troops in the final operations of the war. Seketwayo, the *induna* there, was appointed one of the thirteen chiefs. The Qulusi general Manyonyoba was taken prisoner by the imperial army and brought with a small following to Hlubi's capital near the Mzinyathi at Masotsheni, where they were settled on land apportioned to them by British Government officials in the hope that, cut off from the main Qulusi forces, Manyonyoba would not instigate further fighting.[52]

When Hlubi first arrived in Nquthu he was anxious to take possession of the Qulusi lands which Seketwayo had governed. He ordered Seketwayo's nephew Mpiyake Mdlalose and other members of his family to leave the district and to go to join Seketwayo. Mpiyake refused. Through negotiation, he and Hlubi came to an agreement whereby, under Hlubi's direction, Mpiyake would apportion the Qulusi lands and administer them. Mpiyake would also provide Hlubi with any revenue or labour tribute he required. In return, Hlubi undertook to recognise Mpiyake alone as the successor to Seketwayo, and not to consider the rival claims of other members of the Mdlalose family.[53]

The only members of the ruling class of the Zulu Kingdom in Nquthu with whom Hlubi reached no agreement were Sihayo's family. Mehlokazulu had been taken prisoner after the battle of Ulundi and was held in gaol in Pietermaritzburg until October 1879. He was then released and returned to Nquthu, where he began to rebuild Sokexe. By that date Sihayo, who had been held captive at Fort Cambridge, had also returned to Nquthu and had settled at one of his *imizi*, Nusu.[54] A clash of interest and authority immediately developed between Sihayo and Hlubi. Sihayo began to allocate land to his people who had spent the war in hiding. Hlubi considered the apportionment of land to be his right. Sihayo ignored

Hlubi's claims and forbade Hlubi access to the best land in the district.[55] Hlubi appealed to Wolseley for help in expelling Sihayo from Nquthu. Wolseley's response epitomised the indirect rule view. He wrote in October 1879:

> Hlubi is a sovereign chief in his own territory and he must show his capacity to exercise sovereign rights by expelling Sihayo.[56]

Hlubi's problem in asserting his authority over Sihayo was finally solved for him not by the British government, but by Cetshwayo's chief minister Mnyamana. After Cetshwayo's capture, Mnyamana ordered that, as Sihayo and his people were responsible for the outbreak of the war, all their cattle were to be seized. Six hundred head of cattle were taken from Sihayo and five hundred head were taken from his people.[57] This impoverishment of the Ngobese family and their punishment by a representative of the Zulu monarchy made it difficult for them to assert authority in Nquthu. Hlubi capitalised on this. He moved Sihayo and his sons to the outskirts of the Nquthu district and settled them at Qudeni.[58] According to Osborn, the British Resident, they lived there subject to Hlubi until 1883.[59]

Thus, by the end of 1879 the old ruling class in Nquthu had either been deposed or had accepted Hlubi's rule. However, Hlubi had learnt some of the meanings of indirect rule through his experience with the British over the expulsion of Sihayo. It was clear that imperial authority could not be relied upon and it was necessary to find an alternative support. To secure this, Hlubi granted land in Nquthu to settlers from the Orange Free State and Natal. He hoped to gain from these people, whose allegiance was not intertwined with the relations of production of the Zulu Kingdom, a following who would help him to consolidate his power.

Natal people from the Dundee and Msinga districts had been grazing their cattle in Nquthu and paying Sihayo a small fee for this before 1879.[60] Hlubi allowed them and former tenants from white-owned farms in Natal to settle in Nquthu.[61] The headman he placed over them was Gadeleni Mazibuko. Natal *Kholwa* (Christian converts) and prosperous peasant farmers (some of them, like the Mtembu family, had connections with the Nquthu district from pre-Shakan times[62]) were given land at cost considerably below that which they would have paid in Natal.[63] In his first year in Nquthu, Hlubi also gave land to 100 Sotho settler families from Natal and the Free State.[64] Hlubi hoped that these settlers, dependent on him for land, would support him in any conflict with the ruling class of the Zulu Kingdom and their followers.

The entrance of considerable numbers of immigrants into Nquthu under Hlubi's patronage probably limited the access to land of the people who had lived in the district before the invasion.[65] It is likely that the peasants who had been ruled by Sihayo felt this most intensely because the expulsion of Sihayo meant that Hlubi could alter the distribution of land in central and southern Nquthu without reference to pre-1879 land-holdings. In the other areas of Nquthu, the retention of some control by members of the old ruling class probably meant that no large scale confiscations of land were undertaken. The immigrants were settled mostly in the areas formerly under Sihayo's control. These were Masotsheni, Nquthu Hill, Raladu, Isandlwana and Hlazakazi. These comprised some of the most fertile land in the district. As a result, Sihayo's people probably felt the pressures of conquest most intensely of all the people in Nquthu.

The people of Nquthu accepted the settlement in the months after the war for two reasons. First, the war had been fought with particular ferocity in the district. As late as October 1879 people were still living in caves around Isandlwana, expecting further attacks.[66] The district had borne a great burden during the war and, in the months after its end, the mood of the people was to retreat in a spirit of *reculer pour mieux sauter*.[67]

The second reason why the people of Nquthu did not immediately reject the settlement was that Hlubi had reached an accommodation with some sections of the former ruling class. These men were able to demonstrate to their followers that the basis of their livelihood had not been much disturbed as a result of the war. It was this aspect of the policy of indirect rule that appealed to British imperialist strategists, and Hlubi earned praise for his successful implementation of it.[68]

The people of Nquthu's initial acceptance of the settlement at the end of the war appeared to Osborn, the British Resident, an indication of 'good order and quietness'.[69] In the subsequent years of civil war, Osborn's lack of perception was to be revealed. However, over a longer period of time, Britain's armed victory of 1879 did enable imperial administrators to alter politically and economically the lives of the people of Nquthu and all Zululand. They created an impression of order, which belied the fact that it was constantly challenged, both overtly and covertly. Thus the short term and long term effects of the war must be distinguished.

One of the immediate short-term effects of the war was a famine throughout Nquthu because of the devastation of crops carried out by the imperial troops, and because supplies had been requisitioned from the district by the commanders of the Zulu army. The suffering caused by this famine was noted by the chairman of the Boundary Commission, in September 1879[70] and by Charles Johnson and members of the Jenkinson family, who arrived to do mission work in Nquthu early in 1880.[71]

A second short-term effect of the war was that Hlubi assumed considerable powers. He was authorised to settle disputes between people that previously had been referred to the king.[72] Osborn sanctioned the imposition of a 14/- annual hut tax,[73] later reduced to 10/- in keeping with taxes imposed by the other appointed chiefs.[74] He had access to the surplus labour of the people he ruled and, in common with other chiefs in Zululand, sent some of them to Natal so that wages in cash could be remitted to him.[75]

However, the powers vested in Hlubi must be distinguished from the power he was actually able to wield. He arrived in Nquthu with only a small force of men, largely ignorant of the people they were to rule. Fynn ordered Hlubi and his party to make a tour of inspection of Nquthu in October 1879.[76] The tour probably revealed more to the people of Nquthu of the smallness of Hlubi's entourage than it gave him insight as to how he should govern. Hlubi's authority could not be challenged too openly because it was backed up by imperial arms, and because after 1881 his enlarged force of Sotho troops was armed.[77] However, he did not have a large enough police force to exert the kind of legal control Osborn had hoped for, nor could he collect the hut tax.[78] It was only from his immediate followers and from those immigrants to whom he had given land that he was able to extract revenue. Because of his policy of indirect rule, he did not antagonise the *izikhulu* and *izinduna* of the former Zulu Kingdom by demanding further labour tribute from their followers. It was only from those settlers to whom Hlubi had given land that the chief was able to demand tribute labour.[79]

In February 1883 Charles Johnson wrote, reviewing Hlubi's rule of the Nquthu district, that the chief had striven to conciliate the people placed under him.[80] This had been as much a consequence of Hlubi's limited administrative power as it had been a diplomatic manoeuvre to keep the people contented. This conciliation was in marked contrast to the more stringent application of imperialist administration which the people of Nquthu were to experience after the district was annexed by Britain as part of the Reserve in 1883.

The third short-term effect of the war was a loss of cattle by some of the people of Nquthu. As has already been indicated, the cattle of Sihayo and his people were seized by Mnyamana in late 1879.[81] Wolseley had ordered that all Cetshwayo's cattle, including those *sisa'd* throughout the kingdom, should be taken by the imperial army.[82] But in effect these attempts at cattle confiscation in Nquthu were not as devastating as they were intended to be. While some royal cattle in Nquthu were taken, many were successfully hidden at the Ntabankulu and Qudeni.[83] In late 1879 Wheelwright, the British Resident, gave permission for the cattle and other livestock which Mnyamana had taken from Sihayo's subjects to be returned to them. Sihayo's property, however, was to be taken by the government.[84]

These short-term effects of the war — temporary famine, some loss of cattle, and the conciliatory, rudimentary government of Hlubi — were very different from the long-term effects which altered the whole structure of the people's lives. But it was in the long-term effects, which emerged only obliquely in the year after the invasion, that the essence of imperial control lay.

As a result of the invasion of 1879, British authority was established in Zululand. Although at the end of 1879 this amounted in Nquthu and the rest of Zululand only to the military boundary commission determining the territory of each of the thirteen chiefs, to the attenuated presence of the British Resident, and to occasional visits from Natal magistrates, the precedents for later intervention had been established. British control was *de jure*; it was not yet *de facto*. The agreement with the thirteen chiefs which opened with the words: 'I recognise the victory of British arms over the Zulu nation . . .'[85] and then went on to give each chief 'sovereignty' indicates this.

Whenever the strict terms of the settlement did not meet the needs of imperialism in Zululand, British forces intervened. Although the terms of the settlement insisted that no land should be alienated, the British sanctioned the arrival of settlers in Nquthu because they knew that, without the support of these settlers, Hlubi would be a powerless and inefficient ally.[86] Although the thirteen appointed chiefs were, according to the settlement, independent, the British Resident, Osborn, gave them unsolicited advice and instructions which they were compelled to obey.[87] In 1881 the British Resident called a meeting of all the independent chiefs at which they had to consent to levy a uniform 10/- hut tax throughout Zululand, to pay the salary of the British Resident, to make and maintain the roads in their areas, to prevent the importation of liquor, and to suppress rebellion.[88] British control of Zululand, established by the defeat of the Zulu army at Ulundi and the capture of the king, was expressed in these small ways in the early 1880s. The footholds gained in this manner led to the annexation of the country in 1888 and to subsequent attempts to extend wideranging controls.

The war disrupted the relations of production of the Zulu Kingdom. In the early years after the conquest this was not marked. *Izikhulu* and *izinduna* still had access to the surplus labour of their people, and they could still mobilise armies to fight, as illustrated by Mehlokazulu's attack on Mnyamana for the return of the cattle of Sihayo's people[89] and the mobilisation of the Qulusi people in Nquthu against Hamu in 1882.[90] It was this control of surplus labour that British incursions into Zululand during the periods of the civil war sought to wrest from the old ruling class.[91] The imperial authorities not only wanted to reduce the military threat, although this was a real enough problem for them when appointed chiefs like Hamu and Zibephu were attacked. They were also concerned about the control which *izikhulu* and *izinduna* had over the surplus labour of the peasants because this prevented the free movement of labourers, essential to the development of capitalism elsewhere in South Africa. In 1879 the agreement with the thirteen chiefs had included a clause which compelled the chiefs to:

> ... allow and encourage all men within my territory to go and come freely for peaceful purposes, and to work in Natal or the Transvaal or elsewhere for themselves or for hire.[92]

In November 1880 Osborn observed that the only men going to work outside Zululand for wages were going under direction from the chiefs, and that the chiefs would not permit people to go to sell their labour as they pleased.[93] The discovery and development of the Witwatersrand gold mines in the late 1880s, the growth of the coal mines on Natal's border with Zululand and the emergence of large-scale capitalist farming in Natal, made pressing the need for labour from Zululand and the destruction of the relations of production of the Zulu Kingdom.

The invasion of 1879 also led to a reduction in land available to the people of Zululand. In Nquthu, this was felt initially only by those people whose land was taken by the settlers Hlubi brought in. But the trend started by Hlubi was to continue through subsequent decades. In 1883 people from Natal were given land. In the 1890s, gold prospectors at Nondweni were given a township there, and in the early twentieth century white settlers were given farms. Although the British policy in Zululand had never been designed to deprive the people of access to the land, other necessities of imperialist rule required that the people's right to the land be continually circumscribed.

The war of 1879 meant that a missionary presence was established permanently in Nquthu. The Norwegian Mission Society had had a mission station there since 1865. Missionaries had been periodically active in Zululand from Dingane's time but, as a result of the 1879 invasion, missionaries for the first time enjoyed the backing of the Colonial Office.

Although the Society for the Propagation of the Gospel viewed the settlement with the thirteen chiefs with some indignation because it seemed to deny the protection of the imperial power to missionary endeavour,[94] and although Wolseley's instructions to the British Resident directed him to hold himself '. . . entirely aloof from all missionary or proselytisation enterprise',[95] these actions were only an expression of the indirect rule policy. Wolseley made this point clear when he replied to the Archbishop of Cape Town, Bishop Jones's complaint against imperial policy toward the missionaries. He wrote:

> Although Your Lordship is a Protestant Bishop, I cannot in any way whatever admit for a moment that you are in any degree, no matter how slight, in the least more interested in the spread of Christ's religion than I am. You may possibly think that when an army has beaten a native people in battle the opportunity should be seized for altering the land laws of that subdued people so as to allow missionaries to become landed proprietors at the expense of the conquered. I don't take this view of Christ's teaching or the practice of his disciples . . . I must remind Your Lordship that missionaries have now a better opening in Zululand than they ever had and I look forward to the good they may do with great hope.[96]

The missionaries in Nquthu, Charles and Margaret Johnson, came to the district at the request of Hlubi and, like other settlers, were given land there because he believed that they could help him consolidate his power. Through decades of mission activity in Nquthu, large numbers of people were converted to Christianity. Although there is no precise correlation of conversion to Christianity with imperial rule, the penetration of Christianity into Nquthu (as well as Zululand) was intimately linked with its conquest.

The invasion of Zululand in 1879 fundamentally changed the lives of the people of Nquthu and all Zululand. Some people experienced only changes associated with the conflicts of the war; others were affected by the settlement and the immediate after-effects of the war; many experienced over decades the real nature of imperialism and the meaning of their confrontation with it.

NOTES

ABBREVIATIONS AND GUIDE TO UNPUBLISHED SOURCES

A *Official records of the Colony of Natal in the Pietermaritzburg Depot of the South African Archives.*
   BPP   British Parliamentary Papers.
   GH   Government House (Zululand) Papers of the Governor of Zululand.
   NMC   Nquthu Magisterial Correspondence.
   NML   Nquthu Magisterial Letterbook.
   ZA   Zululand Archives. Papers of the Resident Commissioner of Zululand.

B *Papers in the Archives of the University of the Witwatersrand, Johannesburg.*
   CPSA Papers of the Church of the Province of South Africa.

C *Papers in the Archives of the United Society for the Propagation of the Gospel, London.*
   SPG   Papers of the missionaries of the Society for the Propagation of the Gospel.

D *Papers in the Public Record Office, London.*
   CO   Colonial Office Confidential Print Series.

E *Papers in private hands.*
   The Pollack Papers. Journals of the Rev. Charles Johnson in the possession of Mr D. Pollack, Babanango.

F *Oral interviews.*
   Conducted by me during field work in South Africa in 1977.

1 In this paper the Nquthu district is taken to be broadly the same area as covered by the present Nqutu district of Kwazulu. The present borders of the district have been adjusted at various times by British, Natal and Union of South Africa governments. Thus the area referred to in the paper is slightly more extensive than the present district's boundaries. (See map, p.

2 J.J. Guy, 'The Destruction of the Zulu Kingdom: the Civil War in Zululand, 1879–1884' (University of London, Ph.D. thesis, 1975), p.36. Now published as *The Destruction of the Zulu Kingdom* (London, 1979).

3   A.T. Bryant, *Olden Times in Zululand and Natal* (London, 1929), p.130.

4   P.A. Kennedy, 'The Fatal Diplomacy: Sir Theophilus Shepstone and the Zulu Kings, 1839–1879' (University of California Los Angeles, Ph.D. thesis, 1976), p.175.

5   F. Fynney, *The Zulu Army and the Zulu Headmen* (Pietermaritzburg, 1879), pp.9–10.

6   Ibid.

7   Guy, p.38.

8   CO 879/17, Confidential Print Africa, No. 215. A: Zulu Boundary Commission Report; G. Villiers report 1879: 'Zululand from a military point of view'.

9   CO 879/16: Bulwer to Frere, 7 June 1879.

10   Dabulamanzi, Hamu and John Dunn also used their position in the Zulu Kingdom to build up trading interests, frequently at odds with the monarchy. Guy, p.36.

11   Fynney, pp.7–8.

12   Ibid.

13   ZA, vol. 21: Fynn to British Resident, 26 Dec. 1879.

14   KCAL, Zulu Society Papers: typescript 'uMaphelu kaMkhosana', pp.11–12.

15   C. Vijn, *Cetshwayo's Dutchman* (London, 1880), p.6; BPP, C.2260: Report of J. Dunn, 10 Oct. 1878; Report of F. Fynney, 24 Oct. 1878.

16   CO 179/132: Chelmsford to Secretary of State for War, 14 Feb. 1879, Encl.(b): 'Statement of a Zulu deserter regarding the Sandhlwana battle'.

17   D.R. Morris, *The Washing of the Spears* (London, 1966), p.340.

18   Guy, p.6.

19   KCAL, 'uMaphelu kaMkhosana', p.2.

20   H.H. Parr, *A Sketch of the Kafir and Zulu Wars* (London, 1880), p.183. Parr was present at the engagement and reported the exact words he heard.

21   Morris, p.328.

22   G. French, *Lord Chelmsford and the Zulu War* (London, 1939), p.72.

23   Nelia Kanyile, in an interview at Nquthu 22 Aug. 1977, described how she was a small child at the time of the British invasion of Zululand and was taken by her mother to hide in caves around Nquthu.

24   Morris, p.321.

25   Ibid., p.330.

26   Ibid., p.335.

27   W.E. Montague, *Campaigning in South Africa: Reminiscences of an Officer in 1879* (Edinburgh, 1880), p.256 and Parr, p.193 both describe how after the battle of Isandlwana the Zulus abandoned most of the food supplies of the imperial troops. This seems to indicate that at that time the Zulu army was reasonably confident that the food supplies in the country were being adequately protected.

28   A. Wilmot, *History of the Zulu War* (London, 1880), p.133.

29   Montague, p.225.

30   Parr, p.247.

31   Wilmot, p.128

32 USPG, Wigram Papers: Johnson to Jenkinson, April 1880; Wilmot, p.133; Montague, p.177; P. Deleage, *Trois Mois chez les Zoulous* (Paris, 1879), p.211.

33 CO 879/16: Robson to Dartness, 27 May 1879, Encl. in no. 188.

34 ZA, vol.21: Fynn to British Resident, 26 Dec. 1879.

35 Wilmot, p.130.

36 Montague, p.177. Montague was present when the speech was made and it was translated to him by members of the Natal Native Corps who accompanied the party.

37 Montague, p.168.

38 Montague, p.250.

39 Montague, p.251.

40 KCAL, 'uMaphelu kaMkhosana', p.3.

41 CO 879/16, Encl. in 115: Wolseley to Frere, 19 Aug. 1879; Encl. in 173: Wolseley to War Office, 11 Sept. 1879; CO 179/132: Wolseley to War Office, 3 Sept. 1879.

42 CO 879/16, No. 315: Campbell to Secretary of Native Affairs, 24 Oct. 1879.

43 CO 879/17, No. 218: Memorandum by A. Pearson, 'The settlement of Zululand'.

44 French, p.82.

45 CO 879/16, Wolseley to Hicks-Beach, 3 Sept. 1879.

46 CO 879/17, No. 218: Memorandum by A. Pearson, 'The settlement of Zululand'.

47 Wilmot, p.218–221.

48 Hlubi kaMbunda was the headman of Tlokwa people who had left southern Zululand during the Mfecane. They moved through Natal and parts of the Free State. Finally a large group of them settled in a location near Estcourt in Natal. Hlubi and some of his followers had fought with the British troops under Col. Durnford against Langalibalele in 1874. Mounted Sotho soldiers commanded by Hlubi had been present at nearly all the engagements of the Anglo-Zulu War.

49 ZA, vol. 1, Encl. in 165/1879: Fynn to SNA, 27 Oct. 1879.

50 CO 879/16, Encl. 1 in No. 136: Form of treaty with each of thirteen chiefs.

51 ZA, vol. 111, Encl. in Desp. 16 of 24 Feb. 1883: Fynn to Bulwer, 6 Feb. 1883. When Cetshwayo returned to Zululand in 1883 both Matshana kaMondisa and Matshana kaSitshakuza were given the opportunity to move into the area under Cetshwayo's control. They both refused although they stated that they recognised Cetshwayo's authority over them. From this I infer that Hlubi had not curtailed their access to land or interfered with their relations with their followers as they had existed under the Zulu king.

52 ZA, vol.21: Shepstone to Wheelwright, 13 Oct. 1879; Shepstone to Wheelwright, 15 Oct. 1879; Memo of D.R. Middleton, 'Instructions as to the disposal of Manyonyoba and his people', 30 Sept. 1879; Madden to Middleton, 15 Oct. 1879.

53 NML, vol. 5/1/8: Hignett to Chief Commissioner, 4 Feb. 1904; CO, 427/19: Proceedings at a meeting of a commission composed of the Resident Commissioner of Zululand and the Resident Magistrate of Nquthu with chiefs and headmen of Nquthu, held at Rorke's Drift 19 and 20 March 1894.

54 ZA, vol. 1: Encl. in Desp. 165/1879: Fynn to SNA, 27 Oct. 1879.

55 GH, vol. 677, Mp. 2063/1879: Fynn to SNA, 31 Oct. 1879.

56 GH, vol. 677: Wolseley to Bulwer, 17 Nov. 1879.

57 ZA, vol. 36, Desp. 33/1880: Osborn to Colley, 23 Sept. 1880.

58 ZA, vol. 21: Statement of Mehlokazulu recorded by Addison, Encl. in minute, 12 Jan 1890.

59 ZA, vol. 22: Osborn to Governor, 27 Nov. 1891.

60 ZA, vol. 41, Desp. 18/1885; Osborn to Mitchell, 15 Dec. 1885.

61 NMC, vol. IV. Robson to Sub-commissioner of Nquthu, 4 June 1888. Interview with Archdeacon P.J. Mbata (b. 1908), Nongoma, 11 Aug. 1977.

62 Interview with Mr G. Mdlalose (b. 1922), Ulundi, 10 Aug. 1977.

63 G.W. Cox, The Life of John William Colenso, vol. II (London, 1888), p.613; J. Mtembu, The Life of Titus Mtembu (London, 1929), p.9. Interview with Archdeacon P.J. Mbata.

64 CO 879/17/264, Encl. (b) in No. 49: Description of each location, Hlubi. NML, vol. II, Desp. 106: Addison to Resident Commissioner, 28 Feb. 1894.

65 Ibid. No figures of the numbers of immigrants to Nquthu in this period have been traced. In this memorandum Addison talks of 'large numbers' of settlers.

66 CO 879/16, Desp. 315: Campbell to SNA, 24 Oct. 1879.

67 This was the spirit of the message Cetshwayo gave to Maphelu to convey to the Qulusi fighters. They accepted his view. KCAL, 'uMaphelu kaMkhosana', p.7.

68 CO 879/16/402, Desp. 136: Wolseley to Hicks-Beach, 3 Sept. 1879; CO 879/17, No. 218: Memorandum by A. Pearson, 'The settlement of Zululand'. GH vol. 677: Mp. 2038: Shepstone to Governor, 29 Oct. 1879.

69 ZA, vol. 36, Desp. 29/1880: Osborn to Colley, 4 Aug. 1880.

70 CO 879/16, No. 253: Villiers to Bulwer, 21 Sept. 1879.

71 T.B. Jenkinson, AmaZulu (London, 1882), 156.

72 ZA, vol. 36, Desp. 29/1880: Osborn to Colley, 4 Aug. 1880.

73 ZA, vol. 36: Report by Osborn, 4 Sept. 1880.

74 ZA, vol. 1, Encl. in 1/1882; Kimberley to Bulwer (?), 2 Feb. 1882.

75 ZA, vol. 36: Osborn to Colley, 10 Nov. 1880.

76 ZA, vol. 1, Encl. in 165/1879: Fynn to SNA, 27 Oct, 1879.

77 ZA, vol. 36: Osborn to Gov. 20 Jan. 1881.

78 ZA, vol. 36: Report by Osborn, 4 Sept. 1880.

79 ZA, vol. 36: Osborn to Colley, 5 Nov. 1880.

80 Pollack Papers, 1883, Letterbook of Charles Johnson: Johnson to Secty SPG, Feb. 1883.

81 ZA, vol. 36: Osborn to Colley, 23 Sept. 1880.

82 CO 179/132: Wolseley to Secty of State for War, 20 Aug. 1879.

83 NMC, vol. 5, Folder 1891, Encl. in Cardew to RC, 4 Nov. 1886: Statements of Matshobolo and Untshalolo. Interview with Mrs Nelia Kanyile (b. c. 1877), Nquthu, 22 Aug. 1977.

84 NMC, vol. 1, Folder 'Boer Affairs in Central Zululand 1885', No. 225, Annexure: Statement of Hlubi, 24 July 1885.

85 CO 879/16/404, Encl. 1 in No. 136: Form of agreement with the thirteen appointed chiefs.

86 CO 879/17, Encl. (b) in No. 49: Description of each location apportioned to thirteen appointed chiefs, Hlubi.

87 ZA, vol. 36: Osborn to Colley, 5 Nov. 1880.

88 ZA, vol. 1: Bulwer to Osborn, 15 March 1882 and encls.

89 NMC, vol.1, Folder 'Boer Affairs in Central Zululand, 1885', No.225, Annexure: Statement of Hlubi, 24 July 1885.

90 ZA, vol. 37: Osborn to Bulwer, 29 June 1882.

91 ZA, vol. 2, No. 9/1883: Bulwer to Shepstone, 12 Jan. 1883.

92 CO 879/17: Agreement to be signed by Chiefs receiving territories in Zululand.

93 ZA, vol. 36: Osborn to Colley, 10 Nov. 1880.

94 CO 179/132: Standing Ctee. SPG to Hicks-Beach, 4 Nov. 1879.

95 CO 879/16, Encl. 2 in No. 136: Instructions to British Resident in Zululand.

96 CPSA, Records of the Archbishops of Cape Town, vol.105, Folder, Zululand: Wolseley to Jones, 19 Dec. 1879.

CHARLES BALLARD

Sir Garnet Wolseley and John Dunn: The Architects and Agents of the Ulundi Settlement

> I recognize the victory of British arms over the Zulu nation and the full right and title of Her Majesty Queen Victoria, Queen of England and Empress of India, to deal as she may think fit with the Zulu chiefs and people and with the Zulu country, and I agree, and I hereby signify my agreement to accept from General Sir Garnet Joseph Wolseley, G.C.M.G., K.C.B., as the Representative of Her Majesty Queen Victoria, the Chieftainship of a territory of Zululand to be known hereafter as

> JOHN DUNN'S TERRITORY,

> subject to the following terms, conditions and limitations:-[1]

Thus read the oath taken by John Dunn and twelve other chiefs appointed by Sir Garnet Wolseley, Her Majesty's High Commissioner for South-East Africa, to rule post-war Zululand under the 'guidance' of a British Resident.[2] The past and present historical literature has generally condemned the post-war settlement of Zululand as destructive, ill-conceived and unworkable in the light of the political circumstances that existed in a Zulu kingdom that had just suffered military defeat at the hands of the British army. The life span of Wolseley's post-war settlement was brief — lasting barely four years, 1879–1883;[3] yet, in this short period the conditions of the settlement were subjected to a withering fire of criticism from practically all quarters of official and public opinion both in Britain and in South Africa. The Bishop of Natal, John W. Colenso, and his daughters Harriette and Frances, were outraged by the exile of Cetshwayo and Dunn's appointment. They looked upon the Ulundi settlement as a cruel mockery of 'British justice' and devoted their formidable political and literary talents to Cetshwayo's restoration and the dismantlement of Wolseley's settlement.[4] Zululand's white missionaries were bitterly disappointed at the lack of consideration and support that Wolseley had given missionary interests in the post-war treaty.[5] A large section of the Natal settler community found the settlement 'perverse and ignorant' for it effectively shut out colonial political and economic activity in Zululand, while doing little to alleviate white fears of possible violence and unrest in a politically unstable African territory.[6] Imperial and Colonial officials of high rank, like Sir Theophilus Shepstone and Sir Bartle Frere were extreme in their criticism of Wolseley's settlement — so irreconcilable were the differences between Shepstone and Wolseley over the post-war treaty that mutual enmity between the two men characterized their relationship after 1879.[7]

Comtemporary historians and journalists have generally reiterated the earlier theme of condemnation concerning the post-war settlement.[8] No historian has ever praised the Ulundi settlement, and those writers who do not castigate it have sought to attach a Machiavellian virtue to Wolseley's tactics in destroying Zulu unity without annexation.[9] C.W. de Kiewiet was particularly vehement in his assessment of Wolseley: 'With a light hearted ignorance of native mentality he divided the country into thirteen parts and over each unlucky part he placed a chief drawn from houses that ruled before the coming of Chaka.' He referred to the appointed chiefs as 'thirteen unpopular *rois fainéants*' whose political impotence was an 'encouragement to unprincipled whites who, acting as the agents of the chiefs, were an immediate source of discord and mal-practice.'[10] Donald Morris says much the same as de Kiewiet in *The Washing of the Spears*: 'The British were hardly out of Zululand before the inevitable consequences of Wolseley's folly began: the thirteen kingdoms he had established were at one another's throats like so many kilkenny cats. No one seemed to care a quarter of a million people were sliding toward anarchy.'[11] Wolseley's settlement was 'patently disastrous'[12] concluded Morris. In the most recently published general history of South Africa, T.R.H. Davenport's *South Africa: a Modern History*, the author has accepted the earlier verdicts of de Kiewiet and Morris. He says that the 'result was disastrous'[13] when Wolseley divided Zululand into thirteen districts and exiled Cetshwayo to the Cape.

Leonard Thompson, in the *Oxford History of South Africa*, vol.II, takes a cold, analytical look at the settlement and, at the same time, upbraids his colleagues for interpretational neglect. He contends that Wolseley's solution was a 'clever one' — a settlement that 'would prevent a revival of the Zulu kingdom' without heavy military occupation expenditures to burden the British Treasury. Thompson takes exception to historians who have criticized Wolseley's settlement because 'they have failed to emphasize its Machiavellian quality.' He makes his point by saying that 'no more astute device could have been found for setting Zulu against Zulu and thus consummating the military victory without further cost or responsibility. Wolseley had improved upon the classic imperial formula. 'Divide and Refrain from Ruling' was a shrewd technique in an area where imperial intersts were merely negative.'[14]

The Ulundi settlement has, in most instances, been mentioned in passing in most general histories of South Africa and Zululand. However, two notable exceptions to the general rule of brevity or neglect exist in the various works of C. de B. Webb and J.J. Guy. The latter has viewed the settlement from a Zulu perspective.[15] Through a detailed study of the Zulu social system Guy has shown how the 'military system' was integrally linked to the economic, social and political framework of Zulu society and how, under the direction of the Zulu king, the coercive manpower of the age-regiments was employed to control economic activity, extend Zulu political hegemony and to determine when the men of a particular regiment could marry — thus regulating the rate of population growth. The defeat of the Zulu army by British forces in 1879 and the disbanding of the regimental system as a national institution, Guy concludes, destroyed the foundations of national unity and brought about the disintegration of the once viable economic and political structure that operated before white conquest. From his Afro-centric stance, Guy interprets the post-war settlement as essentially negative in character — he has appropriately entitled his thesis 'The Destruction of the Zulu Kingdom' to make this position unequivocally clear.

A History of Natal written by Edgar Brookes and Colin Webb, contains the most thorough analysis of the post-war settlement of all the general histories written to date. Brookes and Webb hold to the majority view that the Ulundi settlement was a complete failure: 'The settlement was so short-lived and so completely unsuccessful that it is natural to ask who devised it and why direct annexation was not resorted to.'[16] Through a close and judicious examination of Colonial Office records and the correspondence of important individuals, Webb believes that 'collective responsibility'[17] for the conceptualization of the 1879 settlement rests primarily with three men — Wolseley, Charles Brownlee, Secretary for Native Affairs in the Cape colony, and Theophilus Shepstone, the architect of African administration in Natal.[18]

In a later work appearing in Leonard Thompson's edited series of articles, *African Societies in Southern Africa*,[19] Webb discusses the Ulundi settlement within the wider context of Anglo-Zulu relations during the turbulent eight year interim between the beginning of the 1879 war up to British annexation in 1887. Webb's treatment of the immediate post-war period in Zululand is both concise and comprehensive. He totally rejects mono-causal theories on the Zulu war and its aftermath by focusing on a number of causal factors that contributed to the overall post-war political situation.[20] Webb contends that British party politics, Frere's maverick manoeuvres in precipitating a war with the Zulus, the sting of military disaster at Isandlwana and the resultant tide of British public opinion opposed to further expenditure on territorial aggrandizement in Zululand all played their part in Britain's eight year long policy of indecision and denial of 'responsibility' for Zululand's state of affairs — thus, the Ulundi settlement was formulated in a highly charged atmosphere of heated political struggles in Britain and the abandonment of a confederation scheme in South Africa that was a moral, political and financial liability to Disraeli's Tory government.

This essay does not seek to reinforce either those historians who have condemned the Ulundi settlement or those who have appraised its clauses for its conceptual merits. The intention is, rather, to focus on a long-neglected facet — the role of Wolseley and his principal adviser, John Dunn, in the actual formulation and implementation of the terms of the treaty. Few historians[21] have investigated Wolseley's relations with that handful of traders, missionaries and Natal Colonial officials whose advice on conditions in Zululand he sought. No one has yet fastened on to the significance of Dunn, John Shepstone or Bishop Schreuder as political advisers to the Crown's Special High Commissioner, let alone weighed and analysed the influence these men may have had on the terms of the Ulundi treaty. The terms of the post-war settlement can be better understood once the ambitions, motives and prejudices of the two principals, Wolseley and Dunn, are examined in conjunction with the more controversial clauses of the post-war settlement package. It will be shown that Wolseley and Dunn were responsible, in large measure, for the scrapping of Frere's plans for a defeated and submissive Zulu people and for the exclusion of settler and missionary interests and political influences in Zululand.

In December, 1878, John W. Shepstone, Acting Secretary for Native Affairs in Natal, read the British ultimatum to representatives of the Zulu king near the Lower Drift of the Tugela.[22] The first four demands, to be complied with in 20 days, were related to border incidents for which the British government held the Zulu king ultimately responsible.[23] The last six demands were harsh and substantive conditions that directed the inhabitants of a sovereign African state to repudiate their national traditions and submit to foreign rule; they were:-

1 The stationing of a British Resident in Zululand.
2 The disbanding of the Zulu army.
3 The granting to the young warriors of permission to marry.
4 The observance of the king's coronation promises regarding the unjust shedding of blood.
5 The re-admittance of the missionaries into Zululand.
6 The undertaking only to make war with the consent of the British Resident and the National Council.[24]

The ultimatum of 1879 was the climax of Sir Bartle Frere's two-year campaign to destroy Zulu military power and Zulu independence in the name of South African confederation. He deemed it essential to subjugate the remaining sovereign black states in order to stabilize the frontiers of white settlement in the Cape colony, Natal and the newly annexed Transvaal.[25] That Frere had not received the prior blessing of Disraeli's government to deliver an ultimatum that led inexorably to war is well known;[26] Frere's collaborater in pressing for a British confrontation with the Zulu kingdom was the Administrator of the Transvaal. Recent studies of Theophilus Shepstone have drawn attention to his 'long-term' diplomatic and political efforts to emasculate Zulu sovereignty and annex the kingdom to Natal; new evidence suggests that what is discernable in Shepstone's actions is not an abrupt shift from Zulu to Boer, but a series of initiatives designed to exploit his position as Secretary for Native Affairs and later the office of Transvaal Administrator to reduce Zululand to the status of a British protectorate. Not until 1874 did Shepstone's expansionist goals in Zululand coincide with the policy of the Colonial Office.[27] Frere and Shepstone have emerged as the two figures most responsible for 'manufacturing' the conditions for a war with the Zulu kingdom.

The humiliating British military defeat at Isandlwana has been widely recognised by historians as a watershed event in effecting important changes in Imperial policy and personnel in South Africa.[28] Zulu battlefield victory, combined with Boer opposition to the British annexation of the Transvaal, threatened Britain's South African confederation scheme with disaster. Frere had over-reached the limits of his authority as High Commissioner and was censured for mounting an invasion of Zululand without the full sanction of the Home government.[29] By May of 1879 Disraeli's much-harried Cabinet had adopted a course of action that can best be described as face-saving disengagement from further risk, responsibility and expenditure in Zululand and the Transvaal. Major-General Sir Garnet Wolseley was appointed to supersede Frere as supreme civil and military administrator for all of southern Africa with the latter's power confined strictly to the Cape colony.[30]

Beyond the immediate goal of restoring public confidence in the Tory ministry's ability to retrieve and, at the same time, disentangle itself from the confederation crisis, Wolseley's express task was to bring the Zulu war to a swift conclusion and execute a settlement, and then move to the Transvaal and manoeuvre the Boers into accepting annexation and federation.[31] Disraeli gave Wolseley almost *carte blanche* powers in dealing with the multiplicity of political and military problems attached to the South African situation.[32] The notable absence of instructions from the Cabinet to Wolseley on the conditions to be imposed on a defeated Zululand reveals that late-Victorian penchant for entrusting the specifics of imperial policy initiatives in South Africa to the office of the Cape Governor and High Commissioner.[33] The limitations imposed by time and distance between the metropolitan nerve centre in London and the colonial periphery in South Africa necessitated the concentration of authority in the hands of an imperial proconsul.[34] It is worth noting that when a High Commissioner became a liability to the Home government, as in Frere's case, then that particular official was removed, or his jurisdiction curtailed, not the powers invested in the commission itself. Wolseley's sweeping powers of decree in both civil and military matters in South Africa provide an excellent example of how a special commission is created to meet an imperial emergency. Within the confines of his vague instructions from the Colonial Office not to annex Zululand Wolseley was armed with dictatorial powers and he was not loath to use them.

Until the shock of Isandlwana descended on the Colonial Office, Lord Carnarvon and his successor, Sir Michael Hicks Beach, had transferred the initiative for political change in South Africa to Frere.[35] Hicks Beach, hard pressed by the looming confrontation with Russia in Turkey and Afghanistan, found it necessary, even convenient, to repose the same confidence in Wolseley's judgement and ability to retrieve the deteriorating situation in Zululand and the Transvaal.[36] The Colonial Secretary's response to affairs in South Africa was negative and unimaginative. Beyond his specific instructions not to annex Zululand, Hicks Beach offered few constructive suggestions to Wolseley in drawing up the post-war treaty. Hicks Beach confined his energies to lengthy and detailed critiques of Frere's ultimatum of 11 December. He found practically all of Frere's demands indefensible; 'the appointment of a British Resident' wrote Hicks Beach 'is the solitary measure regarding the necessity and advantage of which I have hitherto heard no difference of opinion.'[37] In short, Wolseley knew what he was not to do — the terms of Frere's ultimatum were to be scrapped almost in entirety — hence, Wolseley was left much to his own devices in designing a new metropolitan policy toward Zululand.[38]

Yet, in retrospect, Wolseley's mission to South Africa was clouded with grave uncertainties and he walked a tightrope between success and failure. He had powerful enemies in their Royal Highnesses Queen Victoria and the Commander-in-Chief of the British army, the Duke of Cambridge, both of whom opposed his appointment as High Commissioner.[39] Wolseley's identification with Lord Cardwell's sweeping army reforms and his ruthless posturing for choice commands in the middle and far eastern theatres of British military operations, at the expense of officers his senior in rank and experience, incurred the wrath of the royal establishment, particularly the Horse Guards and Indian army officers.[40] Furthermore, Wolseley's appointment was tenuous for it was given by a shaky Tory government buffeted by the damaging criticism of the Liberal party, humanitarian lobbyists and a disgruntled electorate over its policy towards Zululand and confederation in general. Most frustrating of all, Wolseley was yoked to a military strategy in Zululand that was not of his making and which was too far advanced by the date of his appointment for him to alter. Preston points to the fact that Wolseley was not a completely 'free agent' in directing Britain's imperial affairs in South Africa for he was

> still technically subordinate to Frere's over-riding seniority and
> civil authority at the Cape, and was bound by all the rules of common
> protocol to keep him informed of his plans and intentions, as these
> might affect the broader issues of South African unity and security.[41]

Wolseley's task was formidable by any diplomatic standard. The assignment given by Beaconsfield was virtually impossible when one considers that he was sent to salvage the wreck of confederation, to implement a plan for the post-war settlement of Zululand and, ultimately, to restore British paramountcy in South Africa. All of these thorny issues were to be resolved by Wolseley who did not have the authority to annex a troublesome Zulu-land — nor did he have the sanction of the Colonial Office to engage in further large scale acquisitive or punitive operations in a bid to bolster Britain's power and prestige throughout the sub-continent.[42]

Amid these handicaps and complications Wolseley arrived in Durban on 28 June 1879. It was his second mission to South Africa in five years. In 1875 he was Lord Carnarvon's instrument for emasculating 'responsible' government in Natal, partly as punishment for the brutal excesses committed by Lieutenant-Governor Pine and Natal settlers against the Ngwe and Hlubi tribes in the wake of the Langalibalele affair,[43] but mainly as one of a series of manoeuvres by Carnarvon to effect the federation of South Africa.[44] Wolseley's well-known 'champagne and sherry' campaign in Natal succeeded in arresting the 'responsible' movement for five years.[45] What is less well known is that Wolseley's first mission to South Africa was crucial in shaping his opinions and impressions of Natal colonists, missionaries and Africans, and the first impressions he gathered in 1875 became the firmly rooted prejudices he carried back to South Africa in 1879, and which coloured, to a large extent, the post-war conditions set out for a conquered Zululand.

Of all the soldiers and imperial administrators of the mid and late-Victorian era, Wolseley must rank as one of the most prolific writers of his generation.[46] His daily diaries and journals written during his two assignments in South Africa were neglected until Adrian Preston recently brought them to light in two volumes, accompanied by a penetrating analysis of Wolseley's controversial career.[47] Wolseley's own private thoughts are especially valuable when compared with his official corres-pondence to the Colonial Office. The diaries are laced with Wolseley's intemperate brand of invective towards policies and people that obstructed his own plans and visions with regard to Natal in 1875 and Zululand in 1879; of course Wolseley's 'official' correspondence could not, in candid language, reveal his 'monstrous contempt for Frere, Hicks Beach, Colenso and Shepstone'[48] as the journals did. Likewise, Wolseley's 1879 journal reveals the prejudice behind his policy of reconstruction for Zululand — his contempt for white colonists, political missionaries and the militant humanitarianism of Bishop Colenso is clearly illustrated in his private correspondence for 1875 and 1879—80. With a soldier's mentality Wolseley

identified the above-mentioned interest groups as 'the enemy' and he
sought to compromise or foil altogether their aspirations in Zululand.

During his brief tenure as Officer Administrator of Natal in 1875,
Wolseley encountered serious opposition to his proposed changes in the
constitution from most of the elected members of the Legislative Council.[49]
Wolseley's contempt for Natal colonists in general was aggravated still
further by the truculence of the settler community's political spokesmen
toward the erosion of their powers of self-government. He was quick to
assume that the colonists were unfit to manage their political affairs
because they were socially and intellectually inferior. 'I don't like colonial
govts' he wrote 'where there is a parliament, a Prime Minister &c., &c.
Indeed a colonial government under any circumstances is hateful from the
inferior style of people you must associate with . . . .'[50] Because the
majority of white settlers desired 'responsible' government, Wolseley
contended that their parochial vision and selfish ends were harmful to the
best interests of Great Britain: 'From the little I have seen I think the men
are about as ill-conditioned a lot as I have ever met with − pettifogging
politicians, self-seeking and regardless of the true interests of the Colony
and the Empire.'[51]

Many imperial officials, such as Frere and Shepstone, regarded Natal
and Zululand missionaries as valuable informants and natural allies in the
subjection of the Zulu kingdom.[52] Wolseley, on the other hand, was
suspicious of missionary motives; he was particularly critical of clerics
who became involved in political activity whether they represented those
Zululand missionaries of the 'war party' who longed for the destruction
of Cetshwayo's power and the traditions of Zulu society,[53] which he
defended and symbolized, or the humanitarian school of the Colenso
family − in fact, Wolseley's animus toward all missionaries was a spinoff
from his initial collision with Colenso.

In the wake of the Langalibalele crisis Wolseley had unpleasant interviews
with Bishop J.W. Colenso. Natal's controversial cleric had led the protest
against the colonial government's harsh treatment of the Hlubi and Ngwe
tribes; and he had protested against the exile and imprisonment of
Langalibalele in the Cape.[54]

Referring to Colenso as that 'pestilent bishop' Wolseley found his
interference in African affairs dangerous and intolerable. An example of
Wolseley's contempt for the Colenso family was recorded in his diary:

Rode with Butler to Bishopstowe to see Colenso. Never will go there again for I was attacked by the whole family about the native policy in very bad taste, the bishop losing his temper and in fact becoming so excited that his voice quavered so that he could scarcely utter. He has lost all position among the white people so he is now endeavouring to constitute himself the great protector of the black people, and to come between the Governor and them, a position that I will never sanction as long as I am here.[55]

Wolseley's antipathy for politically active missionaries surfaced again on his second mission. In 1879 the Colenso family was engaged in a moral crusade against the injustice of British aggression in Zululand, and they later campaigned for Cetshwayo's release and return from exile.[56] Wolseley found Colenso a convenient scapegoat for African unrest; remarking that the bishop

is at the bottom of every native trouble here. How curious it is that wherever ministers of religion can do so, they invariably endeavour to meddle in politics and foreign diplomacy . . . . He is a busybody and a meddler in affairs with which he has no concern.[57]

Wolseley was equally suspicious of missionaries who requested land and economic privileges for their stations. He suspected that commerce rather than Christianity was the top priority among many of them as exemplified by his private rebuke of an Anglican missionary:

. . . this Mr. Dalziel makes money out of the kaffirs when he can. A missionary in the neighbourhood keeps a shop where he sells all the stuff the kaffirs require. I am afraid there is a good deal of the tradesman about many of the Natal missionaries.[58]

On 4th July, 1879, British forces inflicted a serious defeat on the Zulu army at the king's kraal, Ulundi.[59] Cheated of battlefield glory by Chelmsford, Wolseley hastened to finalize his work in Zululand and move as quickly as possible to better military prospects in the Transvaal and eventual employment in the Far and Middle East.[60] He had two tasks to perform in Zululand; first, the fugitive Cetshwayo was to be captured and exiled to the Cape colony;[61] second, Zululand was to be pacified and all royal cattle and firearms confiscated, then a settlement concluded. Wolseley's knowledge of Zululand was more thorough than he has

previously been given credit for.[62] Upon the completion of his 1875
mission Wolseley had returned to England with 'detailed notebooks of
technical information concerning the topographical and strategical
conditions and resources of Zululand'.[63] And he had been briefed in detail
by Sir Theophilus Shepstone on the customs and history of the Zulu and
the Natal Nguni while on tour with Shepstone through Natal in 1875,[64]
and again in 1876 when the latter attended Lord Carnarvon's London
Conference.[65] Yet, there exists a great deal of speculation as to who first
originated the formula on which the Ulundi treaty was grounded. Brookes
and Webb suggest that Charles Brownlee and especially Theophilus
Shepstone were implicated in it.[66] While there is a great deal of agreement
between Wolseley, Shepstone and Brownlee, that the Zulu kingdom should
be politically and militarily decentralized by dividing the country into
petty chiefdoms there was, as Brookes and Webb point out, a great
difference in that Shepstone 'envisaged a British Resident exercising real
power over the "kinglets"'.[67] Several weeks before Wolseley consulted
Shepstone on the settlement, he had already decided to repose greater
authority in several important chiefs and there was no mention of a British
Resident or what functions Wolseley expected him to perform. As early as
8 July 1878, while encamped with General Crealock's coast column at
Port Durnford, Wolseley committed this telling entry to his journal:

> Saw Mr. John Dunn, who in face is very like dear Evelyn Wood. I
> am afraid his honesty of purpose is not like Wood's. However, he
> is a power in Zululand and I intend making as much use of him as
> possible. My idea is to increase his powers by making him paramount
> chief over the district of Zululand lying along the Tugela and Buffalo
> rivers frontiers of Natal. I shall thus secure the civilizing influence
> of a white man over the district of Zululand nearest to us, and he
> and his people will be a buffer between us and the barbarous districts
> of Zululand beyond.[68]

It is clear that Wolseley's view of a settlement with the Zulu was
motivated by strategic and military considerations. Preston has speculated
that Wolseley's Chief of Staff, Colonel Sir George Pomeroy Colley, might
well have provided the initial inspiration for the settlement. If this was
the case, then Wolseley's decision to rule Zululand through compliant
chiefs instead of a British Resident was based on concepts of security
embodied in Indian defence policy — a policy on which Colley's reputation
as a brilliant strategist and military planner was largely founded.[69] Thus

the origins of the Ulundi settlement might well be traced to the British school of Indian defence rather than the schemes of South African administrators of African affairs as Preston suggests:

> The settlement in its final form uncannily resembled that which Lytton originally intended to impose upon Afghanistan; one designed to break Afghan military power permanently into several impotent principalities separately ruled by British residents and agents. Thus it was that Wolseley visualized John Dunn controlling the buffer chiefdom strategically separating the Natal frontier from Zululand proper in much the same way that Lytton envisaged Kandahar providing a bulwark against the more rebellious northern and eastern sections of Afghanistan. To this extent, therefore, the settlement would appear to be Colley's rather than Wolseley's in inspiration.[70]

Wolseley's emphasis on the rule of 'strongmen' instead of Residents in the political reconstruction of Zululand is more compatible with the Indian model of indirect rule than the South African. The concentration of authority in forceful and influential puppet-chiefs placed along the sensitive frontiers with Natal and the Transvaal was Wolseley's strategy for ensuring British paramountcy in Zululand without annexation or costly occupation. Wolseley cast Dunn in the mould of a compliant potentate whose own self-interest would compel him to support British policy for Zululand. He wrote on 8 July

> Dunn is at heart more a Zulu than an Englishman, but he has none of the blood-thirsty and conquering instincts of the Zulu people. It will be in his interest to keep 'peace in his time' and abate as far as possible the warlike spirit of the people he will have to rule over.[71]

Referring to Wolseley's choice of advisers, Donald Morris comments: 'What advice Wolseley did seek, on the basis of which he intended dictating a peace settlement which would affect the future of several British colonies and territories and the kingdom of Zululand, came, of all people, from John Dunn.'[72] A closer analysis of the situation will show that Morris's amazement is unfounded.

John Dunn's career in Zululand was eventful, varied and controversial; it spanned nearly 40 crucial years in Zulu history. At the battle of Ndondakusuka, fought in 1856 between the two royal rivals for Mpande's

throne, Cetshwayo and Mbuyazi, Dunn distinguished himself while fighting
unsuccessfully for the latter, who was defeated and killed.[73] Cetshwayo,
desirous of obtaining the services of a white adviser in his dealings with
the Natal government, invited Dunn to settle in Zululand. He accepted
and moved permanently to the kingdom in 1858 and was given a large
tract of land in the Ngoye forest located in southern Zululand.[74] Between
1858 and 1878 Cetshwayo leaned heavily on Dunn's advice with regard
to Natal and the Transvaal, and his white hunter-trader's wealth and
political power grew rapidly as a result.[75] Dunn was also responsible for
the large-scale arming of the Zulu with guns, especially after Cetshwayo's
1873 coronation.[76] On the eve of the war Dunn had acquired over 3000
head of cattle and ruled as chief over nearly 5000 loyal adherents.[77] He
had numerous wives and children and his chiefly authority was enforced
by his private army of 250 African hunters armed with modern weapons
and trained personally by the chief himself.[78]

However, by 1878 Dunn's political power in Zululand and his influence
with colonial officials in Natal had been seriously eroded by Britain's
confederation scheme. Dunn's deep involvement in the re-export arms
trade from Durban via Delagoa Bay into Zululand had made him unpopular
with Natal colonists and, more importantly, he had fallen into extreme
disfavour with Theophilus Shepstone and Bartle Frere.[79] From the time of
Dunn's entry into Zululand in 1857 until 1876 Shepstone had found Dunn
to be his most accurate and reliable source of information on conditions
in Zululand, and he channelled the bulk of his messages and correspondence
with Cetshwayo through Dunn, who, at the same time, performed the
duties of scribe to the king.[80] In 1873 Shepstone bowed to pressure from
Cetshwayo and appointed Dunn Protector of Immigrants in Zululand at
a salary of £300 per annum.[81] Dunn was instrumental in channelling large
numbers of Tsonga labourers to the sugar plantations and government
railways in Natal during the mid and late 1870s.[82] In 1876 a rift developed
between Dunn and Shepstone when the latter pressed Boer claims for
land in the boundary dispute between the Transvaal and Zululand. As a
consequence Dunn refused to supply information to Shepstone which
might prove injurious to his own interests as well as those of Cetshwayo.[83]
Frere was alarmed and outraged at the proliferation of firearms in Zululand
and Dunn's arms transactions: the High Commissioner referred to him
as a 'soiled rag'[84] and would surely have relieved Dunn of his protectorship
if Dunn had not been the only white resident in Zululand capable of
influencing Cetshwayo's position on the eve of the war.[85]

Initially, the Anglo-Zulu war was a disaster for Dunn. His political and economic base rested on a policy of peace and co-existence between Great Britain and the Zulu kingdom. Frere's brinkmanship and the unreasonable ultimatum caused Cetshwayo to lose faith in Dunn, for his white adviser had always cautioned the king to refrain from risky military demonstrations against the Transvaal and had insisted that the British government would eventually adjust the boundary dispute in favour of Zululand.[86] However, this was not the case and Dunn, in late 1878 wisely returned to his main residence (Mangete) in southern Zululand when a few of Cetshwayo's more militant councillors demanded that Dunn be killed.[87] Dunn crossed over to the safety of Natal on 31 December with 2000 followers and 3000 cattle;[88] his intention was to remain neutral and return to Zululand once the war was over.[89]

The British defeat at Isandlwana was a victory for John Dunn and marks the turning point in his hitherto lagging fortunes. The retreat of the centre column of the British invasion force immediately after Isandlwana had left Colonel Pearson's coast column stranded 50 kilometres in Zululand without flanking support. Pearson fortified Eshowe and awaited the coming of a relief column.[90] At that point Chelmsford was in urgent need of reliable reconnaisance in mounting the relief expedition.[91] Dunn's chiefdom lay astride the line of march to Eshowe and Chelmsford forced a reluctant Dunn to commit himself and his retainers to active service with the British army on pain of forfeiture of his property and position in a post-war Zululand.[92] Dunn served Chelmsford well and was responsible for selecting the easily defensible laager site at Gingindhlovu, where Chelmsford gained his first personal victory of the war over the Zulu army on 2 April.[93] Pearson's column was subsequently relieved on 4 April and Dunn and his scouts received the thanks and praise of Chelmsford. Dunn was then attached to General Crealock's coastal column where he served as Military and Political Intelligence Officer.[94] Crealock found Dunn very useful in pacifying the coastal region where Dunn's influence was greatest. Dunn was most successful in getting many of the coastal chiefs to surrender to British authorities and hand over their firearms and large numbers of royal cattle.[95] Upon Wolseley's arrival at Port Durnford on 7 July General Crealock praised Dunn's role in the work of pacification and recommended his services to the special commissioner.[96] The recommendations of Chelmsford and Crealock were a major factor in influencing Wolseley to employ Dunn. Furthermore, Wolseley had not failed to notice the numerous occurrences of Dunn's name contained in the official dispatches to the

Colonial Office from Natal government officials.[97] Finally, one cannot
ignore the personal factor for Wolseley had met Dunn briefly at the lower
drift of the Tugela in 1875, and his first impression was not unfavourable:

> Mr. John Dunn, Cetewayo's 'white man' came across to see me. He
> lives mostly near the drift although he has kraals elsewhere also.
> He is a very fine looking fellow; very good looking although some-
> what stout. He has a very determined face, the expression of which
> reminded me somewhat of Sir J. Glover's.[98]

When Wolseley met Dunn on 8 July 1879, he had already decided to
rely on his own resources and instincts in drawing up a post-war treaty.
He, therefore, cut himself adrift from the more obvious and acknowledged
sources of information on conditions in the kingdom, namely Frere and
Shepstone. At first glance, this deliberate circumvention appeared illogical
as historians have previously noted.[99] But, one must remember that
Wolseley was the most ambitious and insecure general in the British
army.[100] He had an almost pathological fear of failure where duty was
concerned and he went out of his way to dissociate himself from officials
who were tainted with failure in their political and military assignments.
Frere's policy for Zululand was bankrupt and his advice ignored by the
Cabinet and the Colonial Office.[101] The arrogant Wolseley not only ignored
Frere's suggestions, he refused to supply even the bare minimum of
information to Frere.

Sir Theophilus Shepstone's career was also in decline as his poor
performance as Transvaal Administrator became more apparent to the
Colonial Office.[102] Wolseley corresponded with Shepstone only once
before the Ulundi settlement became effective in September and that
was to get his opinion on how many chiefdoms should be carved out of
the former kingdom. Shepstone recommended that the number be
increased from Wolseley's suggested number of six to roughly a dozen
so as to make them more administratively manageable. According to
Wolseley, he accepted Shepstone's recommendation and constituted
thirteen principalities.[103] Other than this one instance, Wolseley avoided
any further consultation with Shepstone. Natal's Lieutenant Governor,
Sir Henry Bulwer, did not have much more influence on Wolseley's thinking.
Bulwer strenuously petitioned Wolseley to avail himself of John Shepstone's
knowledge and advice on Zulu affairs, but the offer was flatly refused
initially, and John Shepstone would not have joined Wolseley's advisory

staff if another advisor, interpreter, F. Bernard Fynney, had not badly injured his wrist in a carriage wreck on 30 July. On 31 July Wolseley wrote:

> Finney's wrist was too painful to allow of his coming on with us today, so I wrote to Sir Henry Bulwer asking him to send me Mr. John Shepstone . . . . Bulwer has always been in favour of his coming with me, but I have never smiled on the proposal because I believe him to be a stupid man because he is associated in the mind of the Zulus with what they believe to have been treachery and bad faith in the Nutckgana (Matyana) affair, and also since Sir Theophilus Shepstone has fallen into bad odour with the Zulus, his brother might not be regarded with favour by the chiefs of Ulundi.[104]

When charged with specific legal and administrative tasks Wolseley relied on the expertise of his staff. Colley, Broome, Brackenbury and Lanyon – all members of the 'Wolseley Ring' – served in various capacities as colonial secretaries, constitutional advisers, official historians and public relations officers. Wolseley distrusted and usually ignored local advice, especially that of colonials and their elected officials whom he usually held in the utmost contempt.[105] Only when his staff was unable to render an accurate assessment would Wolseley venture outside the 'ring' to seek advice. Wolseley's 'notoriously bookish and doctrinaire' staff might well provide him with an acceptable conceptual framework for the maintenance of paramountcy but they were, as Wolseley realised, almost totally ignorant of local conditions,[106] so he drafted a conglomeration of traders, colonial officials and missionaries to advise him. Prominent among these were Dunn, F. Bernard Fynney, a Natal border agent and author of a remarkably accurate pre-war assessment of Zulu military strength,[107] and Bishop Hans Schreuder, a veteran Zululand missionary of the Norwegian Missionary Society.

An intense rivalry emerged between the three advisers as they jockeyed for position and influence with Wolseley. The special commissioner was fed a host of conflicting reports on the whereabouts of Cetshwayo, who was still at large. He was aware of the rivalry and played his advisers against one another, as his notes indicate:

> There is the greatest rivalry and hatred between Dunn on the one side and dear Maurice and Finney on the other.[108] I work them all separately as far as possible in obtaining news for me then compare

their statements . . . . He (Maurice) is prejudiced very strongly against John Dunn, thinks him a blackguard of the deepest dye, and is carried away so much by this dislike that he cannot see how thoroughly Dunn's interests are wrapt up in ours. I myself see no reason why I should put any trust in Dunn, but I feel that he must, for his own sake, serve us well.[109]

In piecemeal fashion, Wolseley eliminated his advisers when they had served their purpose, or when their information conflicted with Dunn's. The first to fall from Sir Garnet's grace was Fynney. On 20 July he reported that Cetshwayo was amassing a large force to renew the fighting. Dunn's information was just the reverse of Fynney's, 'that the king is virtually alone' and had no hope of continuing the war. Cetshwayo had few followers after the battle of Ulundi, and Dunn's report proved correct. This incident turned Wolseley against Fynney and he remarked acidly: 'Finney is a coward at heart and a dreadful alarmist. He takes a gloomy view of affairs and declares the king has no intention of submitting.'[110]

Bishop Schreuder, the Norwegian missionary, had lived in Zululand even longer than John Dunn. Like most of his colleagues of the Anglican and Hanoverian societies, he had warmly supported Frere's aggression in Zululand[111] and wanted to see Cetshwayo — who had frustrated missionary efforts by removing the rights and privileges of citizenship from Zulus who converted to Christianity[112] — removed from power and the kingdom annexed. Schreuder had, all along, despised John Dunn for his polygamy and he was envious of the wealth and political influence Dunn had enjoyed in the pre-war period. The bishop, however, had a real cause for grievance against Dunn; in 1877 Schreuder had abandoned his prosperous mission station at Entumeni on Shepstone's warning that Zululand was unsafe. Cetshwayo then gave Schreuder's abandoned station to Dunn because it was located in his district, and Dunn initially refused to give the station and its lands back to Schreuder.[113] The bishop received no assurance from Wolseley that he could re-claim his station. Once Wolseley had pumped Schreuder of all useful information his anti-missionary bias surfaced:

Bishop Schreuder left this morning for Durban . . . I was glad to get rid of him: he was of no use and I distrusted his judgement. He was very anxious I should give him some guarantee about his land — 15,000 acres — at Entumeni, which he says Panda (Mpande) gave him and which Cetewayo afterwards acknowledged as his. I told him I could do nothing in the matter as land could not be alienated from the Zulus. I am afraid that when the terms upon which the newly appointed chiefs are to hold their possessions become known there will be a grand howl at me from the missionary world: however, I cannot help that.[114]

Dunn, and to a lesser extent, John Shepstone, emerged as Wolseley's 'native' specialists on Zululand affairs. They were the only two present at the signing of the Ulundi treaty on 1 September. Moreover, it must be noted that John Shepstone did not harbour the same ill-feeling that Fynney, Schreuder and his brother, Sir Theophilus Shepstone, felt toward Dunn and the two men worked together in harmony. Dunn, of course, held distinct advantages over his rivals; his information was generally much more accurate because he had the logistical support of his numerous retainers who formed a useful cadre of scouts and spies. Dunn's men accompanied Wolseley's pursuit units as guides in the ruthless hunt for Cetshwayo. The confidence and growing trust reposed in Dunn was generously expressed in Wolseley's diary entry for 21 July:

> I cannot see what J. Dunn has to gain by deceiving me, for I believe our interests are identical, and I am sure he is more likely to know what is going on north of the Umvolusi river than any other white man in South Africa.[115]

While the man-hunt for Cetshwayo remained Wolseley's most urgent priority, he also devoted a great deal of attention to the pacification exercise, particularly the confiscation of rifles and ammunition. With perverse logic, Wolseley ordered Dunn, the very same man who was responsible for arming the Zulu, to assist in the search and seizure of firearms. On 11 August Dunn's scouts found Cetshwayo's ammunition stores in a cave 16 kilometres from Ulundi. The next day a much pleased Wolseley, accompanied by Dunn, rode to the site and recovered 500 kilograms of powder.[116] Dunn scored another *coup* with Wolseley on 18 August when he led him to a kraal that had served as a powder magazine where BaSotho gunsmiths repaired rifles and cast bullets. The kraal was burned and a large quantity of lead pigs seized.[117] Royal cattle were also seized and Dunn pointed them out as they were surrendered to, or confiscated by, Wolseley.[118]

Finally, Dunn's most important contribution to the character of the post-war settlement was his influence over Wolseley in the selection of the other twelve chiefs. Dunn's future hinged on his being able to acquire

enough political power to counter any opposition to his continued residence
in Zululand that might emerge from those still loyal to Cetshwayo,
particularly the Usutu faction. To do this Dunn needed strong allies who
would also benefit from the ex-king's exile. Chief among these was
Zibhebhu, head of the powerful Mandlakazi faction of northern Zululand.
Zibhebhu was Zululand's most distinguished warrior. He had quarreled
violently with Cetshwayo against going to war with Britain, but he had
remained loyal throughout the war and fought at Isandlwana and Ulundi.[119]
Dunn assured Wolseley that Zibhebhu would oppose any loyalist attempts
to resurrect the power of the kingdom. Largely on Dunn's recommendation
Zibhebhu was offered one of the thirteen chieftainships by Wolseley.[120]
Hamu, a half-brother to Cetshwayo, had deserted to British forces early
in the war and he was offered a chieftainship as a reward.[121] John
Shepstone advised Wolseley in the selection of the remaining chiefs, most
of whom were insignificant individuals who owed their elevation to chieftainship entirely to the whim of Wolseley and his advisers. The selection
of the thirteen chiefs was one of the most crucial factors that coloured
the post-war settlement.[122] It was clearly Wolseley's intention to divide
the Zulu royal house against itself with the appointment of Zibhebhu and
Hamu. In the process, Dunn acquired two erstwhile, yet powerful, allies.

On 28 August 1879 Cetshwayo was captured by a British patrol and
exiled to the Cape colony three days later.[123] The terms under which
the thirteen chiefs would rule Zululand were officially proclaimed before
a large gathering of Zulu chiefs and *izinduna* at Ulundi on 1 September 1879.
Dunn accepted his deed of chieftainship to the largest of the thirteen
districts only after he had extracted Wolseley's written promise that
'under no circumstances should Cetewayo be ever allowed to return to
Zululand'.[124] In the brief time between Wolseley's first meeting with
Dunn on 8 July until his departure from Ulundi on 3 September, the
latter had won the trust, and even admiration, of the special commissioner.
I wish I dared make [him?] King of Zululand [wrote Wolseley] for he
[would] make an admirable ruler; however I am giving him the largest district
in the country, an arrangement that I believe will be the small end of the
wedge of civilization inserted into it.[125]

Dunn owed his post-war political success to a combination of circumstances and factors — the crisis of confederation, Wolseley's reliance on
his 'own limited devices and twisted impulses',[126] and the clear-headed
instincts of the hunter-trader. Theophilus Shepstone grudgingly conceded
to Wolseley that Dunn was a man of 'considerable ability',[127] but

unprincipled. Dunn had the uncanny ability of ingratiating himself with the Zulu king, colonial officials, soldiers and imperial administrators of the highest rank and influence at crucial moments in his career. Theophilus Shepstone wanted information on Zululand's internal affairs and the sugar planters and railway contractors in Natal needed Tsonga labour – Dunn supplied both. Chelmsford desperately needed Dunn and his scouts on the relief march to Eshowe – Dunn's services proved invaluable to the General who, in turn, recommended him for further employment – and Wolseley desired an adviser-cum puppet-chief whose interests were compatible with his own in regard to Zululand. Dunn despised Bishop Colenso and Bishop Schreuder's remark to Wolseley that Dunn hated missionaries was quite correct.[128]   He agreed unreservedly with Wolseley that their mutual interests in Zululand demanded Cetshwayo's permanent exile. Wolseley bade Dunn farewell at Ulundi on 2 September; later that night he wrote what was for him a generous assessment of Dunn's capabilities: 'He is highly pleased with the position assigned to him in the country, and I expect great things from the arrangement . . . .'[129]

The Ulundi treaty contained eleven clauses which the thirteen chiefs pledged to respect. The first clause stipulated that the chiefs 'observe and respect whatever boundaries' the British government assigned to their territory. This condition was a *de facto* recognition of British paramountcy. The terms of the next six conditions called upon the chiefs to disband the so-called Zulu military system, to prohibit the importation of firearms and ammunition into their districts, to pass sentence on those accused of crimes only after a fair and impartial trial, to promptly surrender fugitives from a British colony when demanded by that colony's government, to refrain from making war on other chiefs unless approved by the British government.[130] The seventh clause appears farcical when applied to Dunn, an *abelungu* (European); for the succession to a chieftainship was to be conducted 'according to the ancient laws and customs of my people'.[131] Clauses eight and nine were, however, to be the most controversial for they reinforced chiefly authority and gave them the legal right to bar white colonists and missionaries from acquiring or occupying land in Zululand:

8 I will not sell or in any way alienate, or permit, or countenance any sale or alienation of any part of the land in my territory.

9 I will permit all people now residing within my territory to there remain upon the condition that they recognize my authority as chief, and any person not wishing to recognize my authority

as chief, and desirous to quit my territory, I will permit to quit it, and to pass unmolested elsewhere.[132]

Condition ten compelled the chiefs to abide by the decision of the British Resident in all cases where British citizens were involved. The final clause gave the appointed chiefs the power of discretion in matters that were obscure or not specifically detailed in the ten previous clauses.[133]

Wolseley obviously anticipated a great deal of opposition to the terms of the 'settlement' and especially Dunn's appointment; 'I know I shall catch it pretty heavily from the missionaries and the Colenso family on his account',[134] wrote Wolseley. When the terms of the Ulundi settlement became public, a storm of protest erupted from officials, settlers and churchmen alike. Wolseley's almost total abandonment of Frere's plans for Zululand stirred that humiliated administrator to complain that the settlement only served to 'delight equally Exeter Hall and Manchester; whilst John Dunn's retention in full vigour secures the adhesion of all polygamous bohemians and imperfect Christians'.[135] Sir Theophilus Shepstone penned a lengthy memorandum to Hicks Beach condemning Dunn's appointment. Shepstone said that 'I look upon the necessity for appointing Mr. John Dunn in any capacity over any portion of Zululand as a misfortune, and as likely to produce embarrassment hereafter'.[136] Hoping to absolve himself from further blame for helping to bring on the Zulu war, Shepstone focussed on Dunn's trade in firearms, concluding that 'this traffic tended more than any other circumstance to bring about the Zulu War'.[137] The majority of white settlers in Natal and the Cape shared Shepstone's and Frere's opinions on Dunn. They looked upon him as a renegade from European society, and as a villain for having armed the Zulu. The *Natal Witness* said that 'not a single colonist in Natal has the smallest faith in John Dunn'.[138] The Anglican Archbishop of Capetown, the Right Reverend Jones, echoed the sentiments of churchmen and missionaries of all denominations:

> every single person with whom I have conversed upon this subject has unhesitatingly and loudly condemned the appointment of Mr. Dunn. It is looked upon as a scandal and a reproach, and as a grievous and most uncalled for attack upon the cause of civilization and Christianity.[139]

Wolseley vigorously defended Dunn against his critics' scathing abuse.

Emphasizing Dunn's pre-war eminence in Zululand, Wolseley wrote to
Hicks Beach in October 1879;

> I refer to the fact of J. Dunn being already a chief of such great
> importance, of such wealth and power in Zululand that it would
> have been impossible to leave him out of the list of those to be
> made independent chiefs.[140]

On Dunn's fitness to assume the responsibilities of an administrator,
Wolseley explained:

> I adopted the only practical solution of this difficulty by creating
> him one of the thirteen independent chiefs, a position for which I
> believe him to be better qualified than any man, whether black or
> white, in South Africa.[141]

In the same memo Wolsely demonstrated his contempt for Shepstone and
the Natal settlers:

> I have therefore no hesitation in maintaining that Sir T. Shepstone's
> opinion of that chief's character is based upon erroneous views
> derived from a very slight personal acquaintance with him, and
> that it is I believe strongly tinged with the prejudice felt against
> him by all Natal colonists, who are imminently jealous of his success
> in life.[142]

Hicks Beach held reservations on the propriety of Dunn's appointment
in view of his past activities in the arms trade, but the Colonial Secretary
suffered in silence for he had long ago transferred most of the initiative
for making and implementing metropolitan policy in southern Africa to
Frere, thence to Wolseley.[143]

Adrian Preston perceived at once the 'unique importance' of Wolseley's
South African Journals:

> This lacuna of the crucial year between Chelmsford's destruction of
> Zulu military power at Ulundi and the rise — however momentary —
> of Boer nationalism with Colley's defeat at Majuba, whether
> the result of cultivated neglect or otherwise, was acknowledged
> by contemporaries but has yet to be filled in by some modern
> historian.[144]

The notable absence of published material on Wolseley's 1879 foray into South African politics — indeed, the 'conspiracy of silence' by 'ring' members and associates — Maurice, Brackenbury, Colley's widow,[146] and even Wolseley himself — points to their natural disinclination to discuss a mission that failed so disastrously in its objectives. The contents of Wolseley's 1879 journal sheds an entirely new light on the post-war settlement. The minimal influence of Theophilus Shepstone, Frere, Lieutenant-Governor Bulwer and his adviser John Shepstone, coupled with Colley's pervasive sway over Wolseley's thinking suggests that the Ulundi treaty may well have been wedded to Indian, rather than South African, concepts of defence and strategic security.

In the final analysis, the Ulundi settlement was the product of metropolitan initiatives to maintain British paramountcy in Zululand. The settlement, in its final form, was coloured by Wolseley's own distempered image of the situation. He interpreted his vague instructions from the Colonial Office not to annex Zululand in such a way as to exclude those missionaries and Natal colonists whom he despised from the territory. The goals of missionary imperialists, white settlers hungry for land and labour, and metropolitan administrators were not always one and the same. The controversy emanating from the Ulundi settlement is an appropriate example of this incompatibility of interests between these three distinct strains of European intrusion in Zululand. Wolseley's settlement prevented white settlers from carving up Zululand into farms and plantations and Zululand missionaries were hampered in their efforts or denied altogether the right to occupy their old stations. John Dunn was responsible for the ousting of most missionaries from his large district and he shut down nine stations. His ally, Zibhebhu, made life so untenable for missionaries in northern Zululand that they abandoned his district and did not return until 1887. Moreover, the Ulundi settlement was a double-edged sword that invited, as well as prohibited, white intrusion and exploitation, albeit by indirect means. Wolseley had channelled economic as well as political power into the hands of the appointed chiefs. Dunn and Zibhebhu emerged as willing and effective accomplices in recruiting Zulu as well as Tsonga labour for the expanding capitalist economy in Natal. And, Dunn, Zibhebhu and a few of the other more powerful chiefs used their political power to develop trading and labour recruitment monopolies in their respective districts. Essentially, the Ulundi settlement was the creation of Sir Garnet Wolseley with John Dunn acting as his principal adviser and agent.

NOTES

1 D. C. F. Moodie (ed.), *John Dunn, Cetywayo, and the Three Generals* (Pietermaritzburg, 1886), p.120. Extract of preamble to the Deed of Chieftainship contained in the Ulundi Settlement of 1 September, 1879.

2 *British Parliamentary Papers,* C.2482, 1880, no. 87: Wolseley to Hicks Beach, 3 Nov. 1879. Hereafter cited as BPP.

3 E.H. Brookes and C. de B. Webb, *A History of Natal* (Pietermaritzburg, 1965), p.147.

4 See Frances E. Colenso, *The Ruin of Zululand: British Doings in Zululand since the Invasion of 1879* (London, 1885), and Cornelius Vijn, *Cetshwayo's Dutchman* (London, 1880). This narrative was edited and prefaced by Bishop Colenso.

5 BPP, C. 2482, 1880, Enclosure 2 in no.175: Wolseley to Bishop Schreuder, 4 Oct. 1879.

6 C.W. De Kiewiet, *The Imperial Factor in South Africa* (New York, 1966), p.247.

7 CO 879/14/201, p.452: Wolseley to Hicks Beach, 9 Oct. 1879.

8 *The Daily News,* Durban, 19 July, 1978. Ian Player, Senior Ranger of Zululand, remarked that 'The aftermath of that war was catastrophic, mainly due to the stupidity and arrogance of Sir Garnet Wolseley. We are still living with his mistakes and will have to do so for another hundred years before the political errors of that era will have begun to sort themselves out.'

9 Monica Wilson and Leonard Thompson (eds.), *The Oxford History of South Africa,* vol. II (Cape Town, 1971), chapter V, 'The Subjection of African Chiefdoms'.

10 De Kiewiet, pp. 246 – 247.

11 D. R. Morris, *The Washing of the Spears* (London, 1966), p.592.

12 Ibid.

13 T. R. H. Davenport, *South Africa: a Modern History* (Cape Town, 1977), p.111.

14 Wilson and Thompson (eds.), op.cit., p.264.

15 See J.J. Guy, 'The Destruction of the Zulu Kingdom: the Civil War in Zululand, 1879–1884' (Ph. D. thesis, University of London, 1975). Published as *The Destruction of the Zulu Kingdom* (London, 1979).

16 Brookes and Webb, p.147.

17 The inverted commas are mine.

18 Ibid., pp.147–148.

19 Colin Webb, 'Great Britain and the Zulu People, 1879–87' in Leonard Thompson (ed.), *African Societies in Southern Africa* (London, 1969), pp.302–325.

20 Ibid., pp.302–303.

21 The exceptions are Donald Morris and Jeff Guy, whose works are mentioned in this paper.

22 H.C. Lugg, *Historic Natal and Zululand* (Pietermaritzburg, 1948), pp.85–86.

23 Brookes and Webb, p.134. The demands were: (1) The surrender of Mbilini, a Swazi chief living in Zululand under Cetshwayo's protection, who had made a raid into the Transvaal and killed a number of its African inhabitants. (2) The surrender of the sons and brother of Sirayo. (3) A fine of 500 cattle for Cetshwayo's failure to comply with the Lieutenant-Governor's demand for this surrender. (4) A fine of 100 cattle in connection with the Smith-Deighton case.

24 Ibid. The fourth demand refers to Cetshwayo's 1873 coronation in which Shepstone claimed that the new king agreed to certain 'vows' in regard to the internal affairs of the kingdom, particularly trial and punishment.

25 C.F. Goodfellow, *Great Britain and South African Confederation, 1870–1881* (London, 1966), p.155.

26 Ibid., pp.169-70.

27 See P.A. Kennedy, 'The Fatal Diplomacy: Sir Theophilus Shepstone and the Zulu Kings, 1839–1879' (Ph.D. thesis, U.C.L.A., 1976), p.318.

28 De Kiewiet, pp.231–235.

29 Goodfellow, p.170.

30 Adrian Preston (ed.), *The South African Journal of Sir Garnet Wolseley, 1879–1880* (Cape Town, 1973), p.20.

31 De Kiewiet, pp.234–235.

32 Webb, p.305.

33 For a concise analysis of the powers invested in the Cape High Commission see John Benyon, 'The Cape High Commission: Another Neglected Factor in British Imperial Expansion in Southern Africa' in *South African Historical Journal*, no:5 (1973), p.30.

34 R. Robinson and J. Gallagher, *Africa and the Victorians* (New York, 1968), p.72–75.

35 Goodfellow, p.152.

36 Preston (ed.), *Journal*, p.2.

37 CO 879/14/164: Memorandum on the Zulu Question, p.33: Hicks Beach to Frere, (confidential).

38 Goodfellow, p.152.

39 Preston (ed.), *Journal*, p.11.

40 Adrian Preston (ed.), *The South African Diaries of Sir Garnet Wolseley (Natal) 1875* (Cape Town, 1971), p.89. Preston remarks that 'Since Wolseley invariably moved with some shade of political connivance, his methods upset the delicate mechanism of patronage and provoked the hostility of those rival cliques whose preserves it was his intention to invade.'

41 Preston (ed.), *Journal*, p.20.

42 Webb, p.306.

43 For an analysis based on hitherto unused evidence see Norman Etherington, 'Why Langalibalele Ran Away' in *The Journal of Natal and Zulu History*, vol.1 (1978), pp.1–24.

44 W.R. Guest, *Langalibalele, the Crisis in Natal, 1873–1875* (University of Natal, Department of History, Research Monograph No.2, 1975).

45 Brookes and Webb, p.120.

46 Preston (ed.), *Diaries*, p.3.

47 Ibid., pp.1–139.

48 Preston (ed.), *Journal*, p.2.

49 Goodfellow, p.62.

50 Preston (ed.), *Diaries*, p.10.

51 Ibid., p.30.

52 Norman Etherington, 'The Rise of the *Kholwa* in Southeast Africa: African Christian Communities in Natal, Pondoland, Zululand' (unpublished Ph.D. thesis, Yale University, 1971), p.36. Published as *Preachers, Peasants and Politics in Southeast Africa, 1835–1880* (London, 1978).

53 BPP, C.2220, 1879, Enclosure 1 in no. 129, p.344: Oftebro to Frere, 12 Oct. 1878.

54 Guest, pp.52–54.

55 Preston (ed.), *Diaries*, p.176.

56 Morris, p.592.

57 Preston (ed.), *Journal*, pp.78–79.

58 Ibid., p.69.

59 Frank Emery, *The Red Soldier* (London, 1977), p.233.

60 Preston (ed.), *Journal*, p.2.

61 Brookes and Webb, p.145.

62 Preston (ed.), *Journal*, p.1.

63 Ibid.

64 Preston (ed.), *Diaries*, p.209.

65 Goodfellow, p.104.

66 Brookes and Webb, pp.147–148.

67 Ibid., p.148.

68 Preston (ed.), *Journal*, p.53.

69 Ibid., p.2 and Preston (ed.), *Diaries*, p.106. Preston states '. . . it was upon the Indian model of government and war, derived from Macaulay's essays on Clive and Warren Hastings, that Wolseley's conception of the role of military power in imperial order had always rested.'

70 Preston (ed.), *Journal*, p.318.

71 Preston (ed.), *Journal*, p.53.

72 Morris, p.579.

73 Moodie (ed.), p.14.

74 Ibid., pp.10–13.

75 Ibid., p.26.

76 J.J. Guy, 'A Note on Firearms in the Zulu Kingdom: with Special Reference to the Anglo-Zulu War, 1879' in *Journal of African History*, XII, 4 (1971), pp.559–560.

77 Morris, p.199.

78 Moodie (ed.), p.41.

79   Charles Ballard, 'The Political Transformation of a Transfrontiersman: the
      Career of John Dunn in Zululand, 1857–1879' in *The Journal of Imperial
      and Commonwealth History*, vol. VII, 3 (May 1979).

80   Moodie (ed.), p. 26.

81   S. N. A. 1/1/23: Dunn to Shepstone, 4 Oct. 1873.

82   Charles Ballard, 'The Role of Tributary Labour in the Zulu Political Economy,
      1865–1879', in *Conference on the History of Opposition in Southern
      Africa* (Johannesburg, 1978), pp. 59–64.

83   C. J. Uys, *In the Era of Shepstone*, (London, 1933), p. 224.

84   J. Martineau, *The Life and Correspondence of Sir Bartle Frere* (London,
      1875), vol. I, p. 357.

85   BPP, C. 2222, 1879, no. XXIII, p. 103: Hicks Beach to Frere, 26 Dec. 1877.

86   Ibid., sub-enclosure 10 in enclosure 2 in no. 6, p. 53: Dunn to J. W. Shepstone,
      20 Oct. 1878.

87   Moodie (ed.), p. 72–75.

88   BPP, C. 2242, 1879, no. 5, 12: Dunn to J. W. Shepstone, 30 Dec. 1878.

89   Moodie (ed.), pp. 93–94.

90   Morris, pp. 427, 434, 437 and 452.

91   Op. cit., pp. 98–99.

92   KCAL, John Dunn papers, MS 1459.

93   Morris, p. 452.

94   Moodie (ed.), p. 105.

95   Ibid., p. 113.

96   Ibid.

97   Ibid., p. 74.

98   Preston (ed.), *Diaries*, p. 225.

99   Brookes and Webb, p. 147.

100   Preston (ed.), *Journal*, p. 19.

101   Goodfellow, p. 181.

102   Brookes and Webb, p. 135.

103   Ibid., p. 148.

104   Preston (ed.), *Journal*, p. 68.

105   Preston (ed.), *Diaries*, p. 90.

106   Op. cit., p. 318.

107   Morris, p. 295.

108   Preston (ed.), *Journal*, p. 36. Captain J. F. Maurice was an A. D. C. on Wolseley's
      staff.

109   Ibid., p. 56.

110   Ibid., p. 60.

111   BPP, C. 2220, 1879, Enclosure 1 in no. 129, p. 344.

112   Etherington, 'The Rise of the *Kholwa*', pp. 190–191.

113   Preston (ed.), *Journal*, p.98.

114   Ibid.

115   Ibid., p.61.

116   Ibid., p.84.

117   Ibid., p.90.

118   Ibid.

119   Morris, p.363.

120   Preston (ed.), *Journal*, p.59.

121   Brookes and Webb, p.146.

122   Ibid., p.147.

123   Preston (ed.), *Journal*, p.100.

124   Moodie (ed.), p.125. Extract of letter from Wolseley to the Earl of Derby, 31 Jan. 1883.

125   Preston (ed.), *Journal*, pp.93−94. Wolseley was evidently impressed with Dunn and the two men appear to have taken to each other immediately. He found Dunn 'quiet, self-possessed and respectful without any servility . . .'

126   Preston (ed.), *Journal*, p.19.

127   CO 879/14/168, p.369: Memorandum by Sir Theophilus Shepstone on Wolseley's settlement of Zululand, 23 Aug. 1879.

128   Preston (ed.), *Diaries*, p.195.

129   Preston (ed.), *Journal*, p.105.

130   See BPP, Despatch no. 49, 1880: 'Report of the Zululand Boundary Commission.'

131   Moodie (ed.), p.122.

132   Ibid.

133   Ibid.

134   Preston (ed.), *Journal*, p.105.

135   Martineau, p.357.

136   CO 879/14/168, p.369: Memorandum by Sir Theophilus Shepstone on Wolseley's settlement of Zululand, 23 Aug. 1879.

137   Ibid.

138   *Natal Witness*, 7 Sept. 1879.

139   BPP, C,2505, 1880, Enclosure in No.XII, p.33.

140   CO 879/16/201, p.452: Wolseley to Hicks Beach, 9 Oct. 1879; Reply to T. Shepstone's Memo.

141   Ibid.

142   Ibid.

143   Goodfellow, p.152.

144   Preston (ed.), *Journal*, p.21.

145   Ibid. Wolseley quashed the attempts of Lady Colley to write a 'biographical account of the last controversial years of her late husband's South African administration.'

JEFF GUY

The Role of Colonial Officials in the Destruction of the Zulu Kingdom

The importance of the battle of Ulundi in the events which ended Zulu independence has been greatly exaggerated. Its reputation as a decisive military victory was largely the creation of the British officers who needed an acceptable ending to the story of the invasion of Zululand.[1] A far more significant factor in the cessation of hostilities in Zululand was the message that Wolseley brought to the country after the battle of Ulundi — that if the Zulu people laid down their arms and returned to their homesteads then they would be left in possession of their cattle, their property and their land. With the planting season approaching, and the urgent need to repair the damage caused by the occupation of their country by the invading army, Zulu resistance gradually ceased: the price the Zulu paid for being able to resume the essential processes of production was their king, the centralised state and its army.

Peace however did not return to Zululand. The invasion was followed by a decade of violence of an intensity unequalled since the time of the *Mfecane*. Thousands of Zulu died, the material foundations of the society were devastated, and the independence retained after the invasion, was lost.

In 1879 Wolseley divided Zululand amongst thirteen independent chiefs.[2] Although most of them were drawn from the Zulu political hierarchy as it existed before the invasion, there was a far greater number of men of status and influence who were excluded from positions of authority by the new arrangement. As a result, most of the appointed chiefs found it difficult to exercise their new-found authority and when two of them, Zibhebhu kaMaphitha and Hamu kaNzibe, attempted to do so they met with resistance from groups within their territories who had been closely associated with the deposed royal house. The British

Resident in Zululand received authority to intervene in these disputes, but did so on the side of the appointed chiefs, giving them the confidence to attempt to coerce their royalist rivals. As a result, at the end of 1881, some of the leading members of the royal house were expelled from their homesteads, and over 1000 of their people killed. This onslaught on the supporters of the deposed royal house led to the gradual revival of the royalist party in Zululand — the Usuthu — headed by the closest relatives of the exiled king, Ndabuko kaMpande and the king's son Dinuzulu, and they were joined by an increasing number of Zulu who were disaffected by the new arrangements and who looked to the restoration of the Zulu king as the solution to their difficulties.

It was an effective policy to adopt. The collapse of order and the violence on the eastern border of the Transvaal was causing some concern in London. The British government had just granted the Boer republic its independence, on the assumption that British dominance in the sub-continent could be sufficiently safeguarded by confining the Boers to the interior. The disruption in Zululand appeared to threaten this and an attempt was made to bring order to Zululand by restoring a self-supporting, stable African state between the Transvaal and the Indian Ocean.

However, this policy emanating from London was successfully obstructed by local officials who turned restoration into partition, and who divided the country between the king, his foremost rival Zibhebhu, and, in effect, the Colony of Natal. The Usuthu protested against the partition and, after the king's return, they attempted to drive Zibhebhu from the territory awarded him. They were unsuccessful: in March 1883 Zibhebhu defeated the Usuthu in a battle in which it was said more lives were lost than any other in Zulu history. Then in July Zibhebhu attacked the royal homestead, drove the king into hiding, and killed most of the men who in the old kingdom occupied the highest positions of state and through whom the king ruled.

Cetshwayo died early in 1884 and Zibhebhu and Hamu devastated the northern areas of the country, forcing the Usuthu to take refuge in the caves and forests of the region. Knowing that they faced extinction unless they were able to return to their homesteads by the spring, the Usuthu accepted an offer of Boer fire-power against Zibhebhu. In June 1884 the Boers and the Usuthu defeated Zibhebhu and his people and drove them out of their territory. The Boers then claimed their reward: the land of the Zulu north of the Mhlatuze, from the Transvaal in the west to the Indian ocean in the east.

With the Scramble for Africa then at its height and Germany making feints at the Zululand coast, Britain intervened. Negotiations were started with the Boers and they partitioned Zululand between them. The New Republic was established in the north and west and was soon incorporated into the South African Republic. In 1887 the remainder of the territory was annexed as British Zululand, ruled by proclamation by the Governor of Natal, with a Chief Magistrate and six Resident Magistrates to enforce the law in Zululand. The Usuthu protested strenuously against the division of their country and the loss of political authority. In an attempt to coerce the Usuthu into accepting colonial rule the authorities returned Zibhebhu to his territory in the north. The Usuthu attacked him and drove him from northern Zululand once again. The Zululand authorities, supported by British troops were moved in and the Usuthu surrendered. In 1888—9 their leaders were imprisoned or exiled.

The contrast between Zululand of the 1870s and of the 1890s was stark. The previously self-sufficient, independent kingdom had been laid waste and its population decimated. It was now ruled by outsiders and thousands of Zulu men were travelling beyond the country's borders to labour for wages to pay taxes.

What were the reasons for these changes and why did they take place with such violence? Observers, and participants in the events, were confident in the explanations they gave, but their answers were contradictory. For the local officials, much of the responsibility lay with the British government which, being more concerned with party politics at home than slaughter abroad, refused to give the Zulu people what they desired — the security and prosperity implicit in effective British rule. It thereby allowed the formation in Zululand of an atavistic group of Zulu who would stop at nothing to revive the tyranny of the Zulu royal house. They were assisted and encouraged in this by a group of misguided humanitarians led by the Bishop of Natal, J.W. Colenso, and his family. Those who opposed this interpretation of events, the Colensos and the Usuthu, asserted that the bulk of the people of Zululand wished for the rule of the king, but that a small group of Natal officials hid this fact from the British government by refusing to report truthfully on Zulu attitudes and events. Moreover, by supporting anti-royalist factions within Zululand and spurring them on to violence against the Usuthu, the officials eventually brought disaster to all the peoples of Zululand.

Close empirical analysis can resolve some of the contradictions in these points of view, but for more satisfactory answers one has to move beyond the perceptions of the participants in the events. This essay is an initial attempt to do this.

* * * * *

Any understanding of events in the 1880s must involve a discussion of Zulu society as it existed before the invasion,[3] for although the war disrupted Zulu life, and led to the exile of the king and the termination of the military system, virtually all the men who belonged to the upper reaches of the political heirarchy survived the war. And because the Zulu were allowed to retain possession of their means of production there was considerable social continuity.

At the head of the Zulu state was the king but although he exercised considerable individual authority he could not act without consulting the *izikhulu* – the great men of the nation, who I shall refer to here as chiefs. These chiefs represented the important lineages which had been incorporated into the Zulu kingdom by Shaka fifty years previously and which had retained their positions of importance under his successors. The king could make no decisions on important matters of state without reference to these men. The chiefs were not only lineage heads but also regional governors, responsible for large numbers of people occupying extensive tracts of territory and who were members of different lineages – although these chiefdoms were dominated by members of the chief's lineage.

Authority was delegated from the king, to the *izikhulu*, to chiefs of lesser degree, to local administrators until it reached the individual homestead-heads – the *abanumzana*. It was in the tens of thousands of homesteads and the lands attached to them that production in the Zulu kingdom took place, and upon which the continued existence of the kingdom depended. A certain amount of surplus in the form of grain and cattle, handicrafts, and labour moved up the political hierarchy to the chief in charge of the district. However, the major form in which surplus was extracted was as labour, not for local chiefs but for the king through the Zulu military system. For about twenty years, from the age of puberty until he was given permission to marry – that is, to set up a production community of his own – the Zulu man served the Zulu state as herder, agricultural producer, policeman and soldier. During this time he was supported in part by the king, but primarily by his father's homestead.

It is sufficient for the purposes of this paper to conceptualise the Zulu kingdom as a hierarchical society divided into three levels: the homestead level where production took place; the king at the apex, his power based on surplus extracted from the homestead; and between these the chiefly level, depending on a certain amount of surplus from below, and also from surplus resdistributed by the king in recognition of the chief's role in maintaining the state structure.[4]

The essence of this system — homestead production with surplus being extracted by a dominant stratum — was common to indigenous farming societies throughout southern Africa. But in Zululand the demographic scale and the degree of centralisation was far greater than elsewhere. It was more common to find the chiefdom as the largest discrete social unit. It was the achievement of the Zulu kings that they devised and maintained a social formation which brought under centralised control a large number of chiefdoms which gave them sufficient social power to retain the kingdom's independence and self-sufficiency into the last quarter of the nineteenth century.

The settlement of Zululand devised by Wolseley in 1879 left the homesteads in possession of the *umnumzana*, removed the king and restored to the pre-Shakan chiefdoms 'their independence'. At first sight, the settlement might appear to be a sensible solution to Britain's difficulties in Zululand, dividing Zulu society along existing lines of cleavage, in the spirit of his instructions to bring the war to a speedy end, 'with honour' and without annexation. It was in fact a shallow arrangement. Far from representing the pre-Shakan chiefdoms, two of the chiefs appointed by Wolseley were foreigners to the country, and two were members of the royal house. In other cases, the men chosen were not representatives of the chiefdom's dominant lineage, and frequently many of the appointed chief's followers did not live in the territory awarded to their chief. Moreover, most of the leading men in the country were left without authority. It was a hurried, ignorant scheme, which cannot be analysed in the terms by which it was defended by its creators.

The 1879 settlement was attacked from all sides and particularly by neighbouring colonists, who had been hoping that the land of the Zulu would be opened up for settlement and its inhabitants forced on to the labour market. But the most significant criticism as far as Wolseley and London were concerned came from the retired Secretary for Native Affairs in Natal, Sir Theophilus Shepstone, a man whose reputation as an expert on African affairs was unchallenged in southern Africa.

As Secretary for Native Affairs in neighbouring Natal, Shepstone had a long and intimate experience of the affairs of the Zulu kingdom, culminating in 1873 in his formal recognition of Cetshwayo as Zulu king, his betrayal of the king before the war, and the important part he had played in the events which eventually led to the invasion. Shepstone had always been an expansionist and Zululand for him was a territory which contained large tracts of land which could be profitably occupied by Natal Africans, a pool of labour on the very borders of Natal which it was impossible to tap, and a barbarous system of government from which the common man and the subjugated tribes yearned to be free. Moreover, Zululand lay across the road to the fabled riches of the African interior.

By the mid-1870s Shepstone's interest in Zululand was even more specific. Natal, he believed, had entered a period of crisis as a result of inadequate land for African settlement. About half of the colony's African population was living outside the locations allocated to them as labour or rent-paying tenants, on land to which they had no established legal rights. A dangerous situation would arise when they were evicted and it was absolutely necessary, Shepstone wrote, to find 'A safety valve in the shape of adjoining Territory. . . .'[5]

Wolseley's settlement of 1879 snatched that safety valve from Natal's grasp. In the memoranda which Shepstone wrote when asked to comment on the Settlement by the Colonial Office, he stressed that the future of Zululand and Natal could not be treated separately. He then strongly criticised the terms of the settlement both in terms of justice and practicality. By appointing a number of chiefs over the Zulu, without any check on their actions, the authorities were merely substituting a number of tyrants for a single despot. It was absolutely necessary for the sake of the Zulu people and for future peace, to control the 'fierce avarice' of the chiefs. They should be brought under the overall control of a Resident, with white magistrates appointed to assist each chief, all subordinate to the government of Natal. The cost of the administration could have been covered by the imposition of a hut tax, a move which would be willingly accepted by the Zulu, who fully recognised the implications of conquest, and who wished for the security that such a system would give them.[6]

Shepstone's comments were taken seriously at the Colonial Office and they were forwarded to Wolseley for comment.[7] The High Commissioner's violent rejection was based on the argument that his instructions were not to annex Zulu territory or extend British responsibility and Shepstone's views implied both of these actions.[8] The Colonial Office accepted Wolseley's point of view.

In spite of the rejection of Shepstone's memoranda, they remain significant documents, not only for their criticisms of the settlement but also for those aspects of the 1879 settlement which he accepted by implication. He did not complain about the fact that the Zulu were left in possession of their land, the exile of the king, nor the appointment of the chiefs as the immediate authorities over the people of Zululand. What these memoranda indicate, and this is borne out by his subsequent actions, is that Shepstone believed that conquered Zululand should be administered according to the principles of what has been characterised as the 'Shepstone system'.[9]

The basic tenets of this system were that, at that particular stage in their history and with the imposition of colonial rule, Africans should not be forced off the land, that they should be administered through their chiefs applying customary law but that the chief's authority should be checked by white magistrates who would curb the most barbarous practices and control the abuse of power by acting as a court of appeal. The imposition of a hut tax would not only cover the costs of administration but also force gradual change on the African community. The Governor of Natal assumed the rule of Supreme Chief over the Africans and he could use this position to appoint chiefs and thereby check the power of hereditary ones.

Looking at these ideas in another perspective, we can say that the Shepstone system attempted to ensure that, with the imposition of colonial rule, production at the homestead level was maintained, together with the ideology associated with it, in the form of customary law, the kinship system and chiefly rule, although the chief's authority was circumscribed by the colonial authorities. A proportion of the surplus created by the homesteads was now diverted from the chiefs to the colonial authority either as tax, rent or labour. It was a system developed out of recognition of the distribution of power in colonial Natal, for it avoided the violent freeing of African labour and the threat of African resistance which such a move implied. The Shepstone system was a strategy whereby the colonial authority latched on to the African society and, by preserving a certain continuity, blunted resistance to change, while at the same time altering the existing authority structure to extract surplus. Its success depended on political manipulation, with the white authorities playing commoner against chief, chief against commoner, and chiefdom against chiefdom.

It also depended upon the application of customary law, as interpreted by those whites who alleged that they had acquired the secrets of native custom and tradition and who adapted it when they asserted that it conflicted with civilised practices. But behind these political manoeuvres, and at the heart of the system, lay the continued existence of the homestead system of production, with the homestead-head, his wives and children, producing the surplus which was extracted as tax, rent or labour.

It was such a system that Shepstone sought to introduce in Zululand after the invasion of 1879. For, although Shepstone's advice was not accepted in 1879, this was only a temporary setback and, slowly as the decade progressed he was able to gain increasing influence on the development of policy in Zululand.

The Colensos believed in the existence of what they called the 'Shepstone clique' — that is a small group of officials associated with the retired Secretary for Native Affairs, who successfully controlled the information coming out of Natal about Zulu affairs and who were eventually able to dictate the policy adopted towards the Zulu. While the Colensos undoubtedly credited the group with too much influence in London, there is no doubt that there was such a group of men and that they played a crucial part in the history of Zululand in the 1880s.

From 1880—1893 the senior official in Zululand was Melmoth Osborn. He had served in the Natal civil service from 1853 and was on Shepstone's staff in the Transvaal. From 1880 to 1883 he was British Resident, from 1883—1887 Resident Commissioner in the Zulu Native Reserve before becoming Resident Commissioner and Chief Magistrate in British Zululand. Osborn had to report to the Special Commissioner for Zululand who, before 1882, was also High Commissioner for South East Africa, and afterwards the Governor of Natal. The Governor's residence was in Pietermaritzburg and Sir Theophilus Shepstone also lived there, so that all these officials could call on him for assistance. Shepstone was also described as Melmoth Osborn's 'great friend'[10] and he used his influence to ensure that Osborn kept his job in Zululand.[11]

Although their private correspondence is incomplete, there is sufficient evidence to show that Colley, Bulwer, and Havelock (Special Commissioners from 1880—1881, 1882—1885 and 1886—1889 respectively) relied heavily on Shepstone for informal advice.[12] Evidence of official assistance can be found in the memoranda published in the British Parliamentary Papers. Moreover, Osborn's recommendations for changes in Zululand had frequently been previously discussed with Shepstone who was therefore able to give support to plans which he had already played a part in developing. The Special Commissioners, unable to speak Zulu, with little experience in African administration, could not resist this double thrust, from the one man drawing on a lifetime's experience, and another with the practical knowledge of the man on the spot. And when he looked for another opinion than that of the Secretary for Native affairs, the Special Commissioner found either John Shepstone, Sir Theophilus' brother, or his successor, Henrique Shepstone, Sir Theophilus' son.

* * * * *

We can now examine briefly three major interventions which the Natal officials made in the affairs of Zululand in the 1880s: Osborn's enquiry into the disputes in northern Zululand in August 1881; the partition of Zululand and the establishment of the Zulu Native Reserve in 1883; and the establishment of British Zululand in 1887 and the attempts which followed to bring the Usuthu under control.

From the moment he arrived in Zululand as British Resident in 1880 Osborn was dissatisfied with the terms of the settlement. As he wrote to Shepstone:

> I entirely concur with your view of the Zulu Settlement and do not see how it can possibly stand as it is. More power of control & machinery therefore are necessary. . . .[13]

Working together, Osborn and Shepstone persuaded the Special Commissioner that changes were necessary. Osborn reported that continual appeals were being made to him to settle disputes and that, in spite of his denials, the Zulu insisted on regarding him as the representative of the conquering power with whom lay supreme authority. It was essential, if order were to be maintained, that the British government give the Resident more than just diplomatic powers.

By the end of 1880 serious clashes had occured in the northern part of the country in the territories of Zibhebhu and Hamu. The settlement had placed under these chiefs some of the most important members of the old Zulu kingdom. Mnyamana kaNgqengelele, chief minister to the king and hereditary chief of the powerful Buthelezi people, came under

Hamu, and Ndabuko, the king's full brother and guardian of the king's son, Dinuzulu, was in Zibhebhu's territory. They both alleged that the appointed chiefs had fined them without just cause and seized the property of the members of the royal house.

It is significant that both these appointed chiefs were exceptional in the degree to which they were involved in trade with neighbouring territories. Hamu was addicted to spirits, had a family of white traders living with him, had opposed the king before the war and was the only Zulu of note to go over to the British during the invasion. Zibhebhu's trading activities were intense and extended from Natal to areas far to the north of Zululand. In these activities, he worked with John Dunn, who had been appointed by Wolseley over a large area of southern Zululand. These men led the anti-Usuthu forces in Zululand after the war. Their links with neighbouring territories and their drive to accumulate property suggests why they seized cattle and goods with such vigour from the defeated and unrecognised members of the royal house. And it was these actions which created the antagonisms which were to develop into civil war.

Melmoth Osborn pressed the authorities to be allowed to intervene in the disputes and eventually received authority to 'enquire judicially'. The Usuthu presented their evidence with care and in great detail. They were therefore deeply shocked when, at a public meeting at Nhlazatshe in August 1881, Osborn announced that he had decided in favour of Hamu and Zibhebhu.[14] The two appointed chiefs, now confident that they had the support of the authorities, turned on the men who had complained against them. The royal brothers were driven from their homesteads and the Qulusi, a group which had come directly under the authority of the king, were massacred by Hamu's forces.

Now under severe threat from the appointed chiefs and the authorities, the Usuthu drew together for protection, attracting to their cause other groups, some of which had suffered at the hands of their appointed chiefs, or resented the fact that they had been excluded from positions of authority and felt that their best interests lay in the restoration of the old order under the king. They were encouraged by the news that Cetshwayo might yet return and demonstrations of loyalty were organised. By 1882 the British government was in fact making plans to return Cetshwayo to his country. As Kimberley, the Colonial Secretary had put it:

Cetwayo promises to be most amenable to advice, if returned, and I do not doubt that through him we could exercise the strongest influence without incurring the responsibilities of annexation, and we should thus have a chance of re-establishing a self-supporting Zulu nation.[15]

By adopting this policy the British government was moving in the opposite direction to the wishes of the Natal officials. Shepstone had stated firmly his opposition to the return of Cetshwayo on the grounds that he was 'the representative of the sentiment, and of all those that cherish it in South Africa, that is opposed to civilization, Christianity, and progress. . . .'[16] Moreover by 1881 Shepstone was more convinced than ever that a crisis would develop unless Africans in Natal were given access to more land and 'The Zulu country is the only direction in which relief can be looked for.'[17] He proposed that a strip of territory in southern Zululand be placed under the authority of a British official and that the Zulu in this territory be ruled and taxed as Africans were in Natal. But when Shepstone realised that Britain was determined to return the king, he and Bulwer changed their tactics. Instead of directly opposing the return of the king, they attempted to adapt the restoration so that Natal's interests could be secured.

Thus they argued that, if Cetshwayo were to return, it had to be on condition that a portion of Zululand was set aside for those Africans opposed to the king. It was of course suggested that this area should be in southern Zululand and form a 'native independent territory under British protection and authority', administered by a Resident Commissioner assisted by sub-commissioners, ruling through Zulu chiefs and headmen. The cost would be covered by imposing a hut tax.[18]

Osborn's part in these plans was to convince Bulwer that Zibhebhu had to be left independent of Cetshwayo's rule. His loyalty to the Queen was undoubted; he was sufficiently powerful to be able to defend himself and his people; and the animosity of the Usuthu towards him was so great that, if he were returned to Cetshwayo's rule, civil war would break out immediately.

The Colonial Office found it impossible to resist this pressure and, as a result, plans for restoration were altered to a policy of partition. At the same time, sanction was refused for the imposition of British authority in the southern district. Instead, it was to be called the Zulu Native Reserve and the details of its administration would only be settled once it was known how many chiefs decided to take refuge there, and how many chose to move to Cetshwayo's territory.

In January 1883 Sir Theophilus Shepstone travelled to Zululand to install Cetshwayo. At the meeting, the Usuthu protested against the partition and accused Shepstone of plotting to bring about the king's downfall by encouraging his enemies and of refusing to accept and formulate policy on the premise that there was widespread support for the king in Zululand. However, when violence broke out later in 1883 between the Usuthu and their enemies, Shepstone interpreted it as the consequence of Cetshwayo's refusal to accept the terms of the restoration and to confine his activities to the territory which had been awarded him. Shepstone's views were accepted by the Colonial Office and the responsibility for the failure of Cetshwayo's restoration was held to lie with the Usuthu and their leader.

Before Osborn took over the administration of the Zulu Native Reserve, it was placed in the charge of Shepstone's brother John. It was his task to obtain formal acceptance from the chiefs of the new authority. With an escort of Natal African 'police', he blustered his way around the Reserve, demanding expressions of allegiance, seizing cattle from chiefs who were slow to obey his commands, and from those whose followers had gone north to attend the king. On one occasion, he turned his police on the Zulu assembled to meet him. His lists of chiefs 'loyal to us' were soon contradicted by lists supplied by the king of chiefs from the Reserve loyal to him. To Bulwer it seemed for a moment that 'we must have been all wrong & they must really desire his rule....'[19]

But Shepstone argued that if real authority were established in the Reserve and if Cetshwayo kept to the terms of his restoration, there would be no difficulty. Those Zulu who wished to remain free of the Zulu tyrant would move to the Reserve, while those who wished to remain under the king would move to his territory. As Shepstone expressed it, in language which reveals so clearly the way in which he thought,

> the scheme ... contains so many self-adjusting balances, all the springs of which ... are put into operation by the instincts of self-preservation and self-interest ... will act in the direction of ultimately securing peace to the country....[20]

But most Zulu, as Frances Colenso pointed out, refused to choose between their lands and their king for they wanted both. The officials interpreted the refusal of Zulu to follow their 'instincts of self-preservation and self-interest' as the result of intimidation on the part of the king and 'ultra-Usuthu'.

1883 and 1884 were years of violence and civil war in Zululand. In July 1883 Cetshwayo took refuge in the Nkandla forest in the Reserve. Osborn was convinced that the Usuthu were preparing a rebellion in the territory, and he succeeded in persuading the British to grant him substantial powers and to back them with the presence of British troops in the Reserve. He was unable to collect the hut tax in 1883 but under pressure from the British government he started on this project early in 1884. He met with some resistance from the Usuthu and then attempted to coerce them. The forces at his disposal included the Zululand police, Africans like Hlubi, the Sotho who had been appointed as a chief in 1879, men brought into the country from Natal by John Shepstone and who had been promised land, and some of the Reserve's Zulu chiefs. He also had with him British troops but could not use them for military purposes. Once he assembled these men, the Usuthu fell back on to their strongholds in the Nkandla, from where they raided cattle of loyals. By the winter of 1884 the situation in the Reserve was characterised by cattle raids, skirmishes and confusion as the Zulu inhabitants of the Reserve were driven from one party to the other as they attempted to safeguard their cattle from raiding bands belonging either to the 'government' or to the Usuthu. When the spring rains came, the Usuthu needed to return to their homesteads to plant, and as Osborn realised that it was impossible to continue to use his forces in the rugged terrain of the Nkandla, an uneasy peace was agreed to by both sides.[21]

But these attempts by Osborn to force the Zulu either to support him, or submit to him, were overshadowed by the bloody anarchy taking place in the northern districts. The defeat of the Usuthu in 1883, followed by their revenge on Zibhebhu and the occupation of their territory by armed whites demanding land, drew attention away from the Reserve. Britain intervened in 1886 and at the beginning of 1887 Osborn headed a boundary commission to demarcate the border of British Zululand and the New Republic. The Usuthu protested continuously against this and refused all attempts by the officials to get them to witness the new boundary.

The British government, more wary than in 1883, refused to commit itself on the nature of administration to be established in British Zululand until there had been a clear indication of Zulu opinion on the subject. However, Osborn was unable to get an expression of opinion from the Zulu who knew that it would also imply recognition of their loss of independence. On 5 February however Osborn, on his own initiative, announced that British Zululand would come under the authority of Her

Majesty the Queen. In defending his action and asking for ratification, he argued that it had been necessary to avoid a breakdown of order. He had been unable to obtain an expression of Zulu opinion because

> by Zulu tradition and law, no Zulu whether a Chief or not, may, under any circumstances, voluntarily consent to the transfer of the country or any portion, of the rights and position of the paramount Chief, to any power or person . . . they would only submit on the initiative of that power, as they would thereby be at once relieved of the responsibilities imposed upon them by their own tradition and law.[22]

He was nonetheless sure the Zulu were 'glad of the step taken.'[23]

Shepstone defended Osborn's action, arguing that as a result of Her Majesty's Government's 'feeble and hesitating' policy towards Zululand 'the old trust is badly shaken'. The Zulu were reluctant to commit themselves to British rule 'however much they might secretly wish it.' For the Zulu people as a whole the announcement must have conveyed 'a sense of quiet and rest.' He ended by reminding the authorities of the position of Zibhebhu who, as a result of his loyalty, was exiled from his territory — it should be remembered that 'his influence on the side of the Government would be worth a considerable armed force.'[24]

The Laws and Regulations for British Zululand were adopted from those of British Bechuanaland and they received the stamp of approval from Shepstone. The land left to the Zulu was to be reserved for African occupation. The Governor of Natal was also Governor of Zululand and Supreme Chief of the new territory with 'the powers and prerogatives hitherto attaching to the position of Supreme Chief over Zululand and its Native population.' Osborn was Resident Commissioner and Chief Magistrate and six magisterial districts were to be demarcated with Resident Magistrates handling criminal cases and hearing appeals from the chiefs' court. In his comments on the new administration Shepstone wrote that 'it may be accepted as an axiom . . . that it is impossible to govern effectively a Zulu population . . . without the aid of their own institutions, at the head of which are their Chiefs or Headmen.' To remove jurisdiction completely from the chiefs would not only alienate them but also create 'martyrs' in the eyes of the people, thereby creating 'at the very outset, estrangement and distrust, where confidence was so essentially necessary.' At the same time, the interests of the commoner would be safeguarded by the right of appeal he had to the magistrates. To counteract the influence of the royal family, both the ambitions of and the divisions amongst hereditary rulers, men of influence, and the men recently brought into the country from Natal, should be encouraged. 'These sub-divisions and these ambitions will, I think, furnish the chief executive authority with ample means of reducing to a safe minimum the power for mischief of the members of the Zulu Royal Family.' Their loss of authority should also be compensated with an 'annual money allowance'.[25]

The magistrates in Zululand were young, most of them from Natal, and from the start acted aggressively, and often illegally, towards any chief in their districts who did not obey their instructions. The records show that initially the magistrates courts were used by men (often white traders) to extract alleged debts from the chiefs. When they refused to appear, criminal charges were laid against them by the magistrate. These chiefs were usually old men, highly respected, who resented interference in their areas and were wary of making the sort of public commitment to the new authority that the magistrates demanded. But the authorities were most concerned about the attitude of Dinuzulu and Ndabuko in the Ndwandwe district, where the magistrate reported that they were defying his authority. In Novermber 1887 the Governor travelled to Zululand to inform Dinuzulu and Ndabuko personally that the House of Shaka was 'a thing of the past' and to fine them for activities since annexation. And then he ended the meeting with a chilling announcement: Zibhebhu was to be returned to his territory.

This move had long been suggested by Osborn and now it had the backing of Henrique Shepstone and his father. In a long memorandum Sir Theophilus expressed the view that the return of Zibhebhu was not only an act of justice but also an eminently practical one. The Zululand police was small, the British military force 'must be felt more as the balast of the ship than as intended to actually interfere with the management of it: the real and effective force in the country must be furnished by its own population under the direction of the Government.' He stated that the situation could be compared to the one he faced in Natal in the 1840s, when he had to appoint trusted commoners as chiefs to be used on the side of the authorities.

> The return of Sibebu to his people will at once throw the balance of Zulu power into the hands of the Government; it took some time to do this in Natal, because the process was one of growth, but from the moment it was seen that the Government was furnished with such power, the necessity for using it seldom arose, and so it

be in Zululand in proportion to the weakening of the savage instincts of the people, which their previous Government only served to keep alive.[26]

At the end of 1887 Zibhebhu returned to his district at the head of an armed force, without supplies, women or children. The Usuthu, convinced that he was to be used against them, gathered round their leaders. When he began to evict men from their homesteads and feed his followers on Usuthu crops, they retreated to their strongholds. Civil war broke out again, with some chiefs committing themselves to the authorities in the hope that this course held the best chance of survival, while others joined the Usuthu in the places of refuge. When Zibhebhu killed one of the staunchest Usuthu chiefs, the royalists attacked him under the guns of the British fort at the Ndwandwe magistracy. Having finally defeated Zibhebhu, the Usuthu leaders surrendered and in 1888 and 1889 in Eshowe they were imprisoned or sent into exile for rebelling against the authority of Her Majesty's Government.

But by this time Osborn and Shepstone no longer had any credibility in London. As an official minuted when the news of Zibhebhu's return and the prospect of violence was received in the Colonial Office:

> If civil war break out, Sir A.E. Havelock will have incurred a very heavy responsibility in having pressed for the return of Usebebu to his country; and, in as much as Sir T. Shepstone gave his opinion in favour of the step, Lord Palmerston's wisdom will be illustrated afresh in his saying that 'if you wish to be deceived about a country consult a man who has lived there thirty years and speaks the language.'[27]

* * * * *

What general conclusions can we draw from the nature of the intervention of the Natal officials in Zulu affairs in the 1880s?

Firstly, a major theme is the officials' opposition to the royal house and those who supported it. They based this opposition on the premise that the Usuthu wished to restore the Zulu tyranny, while the bulk of the people of Zululand were opposed to it and desired colonial rule. Events of the 1880s contradicted these assumptions time and again but the officials explained this by asserting that it was the result of the insubstantial authority vested in them by the British government. Outsiders — white agitators, the emissaries of the Colenso family, the Boers — had also been allowed to intimidate and mislead the Zulu people. Without sufficient authority and the symbols of that authority, in which they included coercive force, it was impossible to counter the rumours put about that the Zulu might at some time be handed back to the royal house.

It can be shown empirically that these assumptions were invalid and that there was considerable support for the Zulu royal house which was never (and has never been) successfully crushed. The officials' prejudice against the royal house was rooted in the fact that it represented a way of life that was independent of colonial influence. It possessed both the ideological attraction, and the material strength to resist change as long as the Zulu were left in possession of their means of production. The objectives of the Zulu royal house and the Natal officials were in direct opposition: both parties sought to divert the productive capacity of the Zulu people — one to support a pre-capitalist social formation the other to serve the interests of intrusive colonialism and developing capitalist production.

Secondly, fundamental to the proposals and the policies which the officials sought to impose on the Zulu was the demand that the Zulu should not be alienated from their land. This implied that agricultural production should continue to take place within the homestead, by means of the labour of the homestead-head, his wives, and their children. This provided the subsistence needed for the continued reproduction of the homestead and a surplus, to be extracted largely by means of the hut tax.

The hut tax was a particularly effective form of surplus extraction because the 'hut' was in fact the productive unit within the homestead, headed by a wife in the polygamous household and containing her children. There was therefore a direct correlation between the amount of surplus extracted and the productive capacity of the homestead.

The retention of the pre-capitalist productive system also meant the retention of the ideology which ordered it — the kinship system and customary law being notable features, and also the political order at the chiefly level.

Thus, thirdly, the officials held that the authority of the chiefs should be retained, but under certain conditions: conditions which allowed for overall control by the colonial authorities and the effective diversion of a large portion of the surplus from the homesteads to the authorities in the form of tax.

It was the attempt to gain control of the chiefs which absorbed the energies of the officials in the 1880s and which also led the country into civil war. But, we can only appreciate *why* this was so by understanding the role of the chiefly authority in the pre-capitalist mode, the basis of its power, and how the colonial authorities hoped to adapt and use these features of the Zulu social formation.

A notable feature of the Shepstone system was the use of 'loyal' chiefs against 'recalcitrant' ones and its was the effort of the officials to create and maintain a tractable chiefly class that was such an important factor in the development of the violence of the 1880s. Although Shepstone asserted to the end that Zulu society consisted of a number of tribes yearning 'for their ancient separate existence, relieved of the terrible incubus of the Zulu Royal Family',[28] such an interpretation simply did not apply in Zululand. This, of course, is not to deny that there were many divisions and rivalries in Zululand, including those between chiefdoms and the central authority. But statements of this sort have to be examined within a particular historical context and it must be remembered that the British had not effectively crushed the Zulu state in 1879. The individuals who made up the political hierarchy before the war were still alive in 1880 and were men of prestige, status, social strength and jealous of their rights and privileges, inextricably linked with the Zulu royal house. It was impossible for the colonial authorities to recognise men such as these in post-war Zululand because it would have meant recognising a group of men who would have resisted the demands made on their independence and who would also have had the strength to do this effectively.

It was therefore necessary to exclude from positions of authority the leading chiefs in the kingdom, or at least to reduce their independent power before recognising them. However, the Natal officials did not have the necessary coercive force at their disposal. They therefore drew on African elements which had proved their loyalty to colonial Natal. Most important, they encouraged certain chiefs within Zululand to curb the power of the supporters of the old order. They used men like Dunn and Zibhebhu, whose power and influence was not entirely dependent on the older methods of surplus extraction and distribution, and who had links with the wider commerical system of commodity exchange. The officals' major miscalculation was that they were unable to control these loyal forces sufficiently, and they underestimated the resistance they would face.

As a result, Zululand suffered a decade of violence in which thousands died, a good portion of their land was taken over by the Transvaal, and the officials themselves were discredited. Their advice had quite clearly not created the peace and prosperity they predicted but quite the opposite. At one level this is true. The Zululand of 1890 was a desperate and unhappy country, its manpower depleted by war, its people cowed and mistrustful. And yet we must not be misled by surface appearances, An examination of conditions in Zululand at the beginning of the 1890s indicates the essential strength of the Shepstone system as a means of incorporating a pre-capitalist system into a developing capitalist system by gradually diverting the surplus created in the former to the latter.

Firstly, it is useful to examine what happened to the leading chiefs during the ten years between 1879 and 1889. Of 44 chiefs who represented the most powerful men in the land in 1879,[29] 17 died violently during the decade. Five others were dead, and in some cases their demise was hastened by the civil war. Four were imprisoned or banished and five lived in the Transvaal. Thirteen survived, although a number of these had been driven from their original territories, and some were fined or imprisoned. Nearly all these survivors were included in the 54 chiefs officially recognised by 1889. The other recognised chiefs were drawn from leading chiefdoms, but few of these chiefdoms were now under one head, and most of them were divided between the sons and brothers of the original chief. Nearly every district had amongst its chiefs a man who had been an *induna* of one of the officials. Thus, the representatives of the old chiefly class had undergone considerable changes: by violence, the fragmentation of the leadership by official decree, and by the introduction of Natal Africans who had been 'raised up' by the authorities.

Essential to the working of British Zululand was the income derived from the hut tax, which formed the substantial part of Zululand's revenues. By 1890 the revenue from Zululand was £42 000, some £8 000 in excess of expenditure. The chiefs were responsible for the collection of the hut tax, passing the demand to their headmen, and assembling them on the day appointed for payment. Although in 1883 a proportion of the hut tax was paid in cattle (with a 15% reduction on the 'fair price' estimated by the magistrate), it appears as if it was soon paid almost entirely in cash.

To a considerable degree the hut tax appears to have been made up from wages earned by the sale of labour. While the civil war had been taking place in Zululand, an event had occurred which was to affect profoundly the course of southern African history — the discovery of gold on the Witwatersrand. By the end of the decade the goldfields were drawing an enormous supply of labour from neighbouring territories, causing shortages in Natal and driving up the price of labour. The Natal Government Railway was advancing in northern Natal towards the Transvaal at the greatest possible speed and in 1888 the Colonial Engineer and the Secretary for Native Affairs applied to the Resident Commissioner in Zululand for labour for the railway works. Although the country was suffering a 'rebellion', this was the first year of the hut tax in British Zululand and the magistrates were able to send out large contingents. The cost of their recruitment was borne by the Natal Government.[30]

In 1889 the magistrates were finding it more difficult to supply labour, and one of them, at least, forced out men by using the Zululand Police.[31] It was reported that districts were 'denuded' of able-bodied men, and that the workers preferred seeking work on the goldfields, the diamond fields, the railways and harbour works on their own. Large numbers were recruited by Labour Agents and perhaps one of the most important reasons why the magistrates were no longer able to recruit was that the Labour Agents paid the chief a fee for each man he recruited.[32]

But it is not only the chief's role as labour recruiter which is interesting. It is common in the records for the workers to be referred to as 'young men.' In 1889 some chiefs received permission to delay paying the hut tax until the young men had returned from their six month contracts.[33] In another case, it was asserted that all able-bodied men had left the district, except for those responsible for the safety of the homesteads.[34] This sort of evidence does suggest the ultimate success of the attempt to impose the Shepstone system in Zululand. The young men, who in the older system would be leaving the homestead to serve the king, were now leaving the country to labour for wages, thereby creating a surplus which allowed the continued existence of the homestead, covered the cost of the colonial administration which forced them out to work, and created profits for the developing southern African capitalist system.

On 22 December 1888 Msilana, the son of the chief Somopo appeared before the Acting Magistrate of the Lower Mfolozi district where he was charged with 'Using threatening language to uKombizwe, a court policeman, & a party of natives . . . when on their way to Eshowe to join a working party of the Natal Government Railway.' It was alleged that he refused to house the court policeman and threatened the 'gang of natives as aliens to the uSutu cause as they had gone over to the side of [the] Government by allowing themselves to be press-ganged.'[35] Msilana's awareness of the nature of the fundamental changes which had taken place in Zululand in the 1880s did not save him from being found guilty and fined £5 or two months imprisonment with hard labour.

NOTES

1   Originally in 'A Note on Firearms in the Zulu Kingdom with Special Reference to the Anglo-Zulu War, 1879', in *Journal of African History*, XII, 4, (1971), pp.567–9.

2   Much of the empirical evidence upon which this paper is based can be found in my Ph.D. thesis 'The Destruction of the Zulu Kingdom: the Civil War in Zululand, 1879–1884' (London, 1975), published by Longmans in 1979.

3   The following discussion is based on my article 'Production and Exchange in the Zulu Kingdom', in *Mohlomi, Journal of Southern African Historical Studies*, II (1978).

4   It would be wrong to consider the Zulu social structure as just a three-tier pyramid – the horizontal strata were penetrated vertically because every mature man in Zululand was a homestead-head.

5   C.W. de Kiewiet, *The Imperial Factor in South Africa: a Study in Politics and Economics* (Cambridge, 1937), quoting a letter by Shepstone to Carnarvon, 30 November 1874.

6   These Memoranda were dated 23 August 1879 and 14 October 1879 and were printed by the Colonial Office as Confidential Print, 204, No.168.

7   CO 179/132, 16424, Minutes.

8   Confidential Print, 204, No. 221: Wolseley to Hicks Beach, 9 October 1879.

9   There does seem to be continuity in Shepstone's thought from his earliest years in Natal through to the 1890s. The extent to which Shepstone was able to put his theory into practice is a question that still has to be answered. I have made use here of David Welsh, *The Roots of Segregation: Native Policy in Colonial Natal, 1845–1910* (Cape Town, 1971), especially chapter 2 'The Annexation of Natal and the Creation of the Shepstonian System' and also Shepstone's fascinating letter, written at the end of his life to the *Natal Mercury* and reprinted in *Natalia*, 2 (1972). The Memoranda and letters he wrote in the 1880s have of course been the focus of my research.
       Those who have read Shula Marks's article 'Natal, the Zulu Royal Family and the Ideology of Segregation' in *Journal of Southern African Studies*, IV, 2 (1978), will know the extent to which I have drawn on the ideas she put forward there.

10   A. Preston (ed.), *The South African Journal of Sir Garnet Wolseley 1879–1880* (Cape Town, 1973), p.270.

11 Natal Archives, Sir T. Shepstone collection: Osborn to T. Shepstone, 6 January 1883.

12 The Sir T. Shepstone collection in the Natal Archives has letters from both Colley and Havelock which show they were depending heavily on his advice, and Bulwer wrote long and detailed letters about Zulu policy when he left Pietermaritzburg to interview the Zulu chiefs at the end of 1882, and when Shepstone travelled to Zululand to install the king in 1883.

13 Natal Archives, Sir T. Shepstone collection: Osborn to T. Shepstone, 22 May 1880.

14 For evidence to support this see 'The Destruction of the Zulu Kingdom', pp.147–157, 165–181.

15 CO 179/138, 19985, Minutes.

16 BPP, C.2695, No.30, Enc. 2: Memorandum by T. Shepstone, 4 June 1880.

17 CO 179/140, 1848: Memorandum by T. Shepstone, December 1881.

18 British Parliamentary Papers, C.3466, No. 106: Bulwer to Kimberley, 3 October 1882. Hereinafter cited as BPP.

19 Natal Archives, J.W. Shepstone collection: Bulwer to J.W. Shepstone, 24 January 1883.

20 BPP, C.3615, No. 31, Enc: T. Shepstone to Bulwer, 27 February 1883.

21 'The Destruction of the Zulu Kingdom', p.325.

22 BPP, C.5413, No.10, Enc.1: Osborn to Havelock, 8 February 1887.

23 Natal Archives, GH, vol. 703: Osborn to Havelock, 8 February 1887, conf.

24 BPP, C.5413, No.8, Enc. 3: Memorandum by Sir T. Shepstone, 17 February 1887.

25 BPP, C.5331, No. 2, Enc.3: Memorandum by Sir T. Shepstone, 23 April 1887.

26 BPP, C.5331, No.2, Enc.4: Memorandum by Sir T. Shepstone, 31 July 1887.

27 CO 427/2, 683, Minute.

28 BPP, C.5331, No.13, Enc.: Memorandum by Sir T. Shepstone, 12 August 1887.

29 This list was prepared for a study of the political structure of the Zulu kingdom as it existed before the war and will appear in schematic form in *The Destruction of the Zulu Kingdom*. It is difficult to be sure exactly who were chiefs in British Zululand. The official lists I have seen are frequently contradicted by information in the court records, or hut tax registers. The information must exist but my research on this question is not complete. (*The Destruction of the Zulu Kingdom* was published in 1979. Ed.)

30 SNA 1/1/108, 705/88.

31 Natal Archives, Resident Magistrate, Melmoth, 5/1/4: Knight to Osborn, 294/89.

32 GH(Z), Z749/89: Minute by Osborn, 28 October 1889.

33 Natal Archives, Resident Magistrate, Melmoth, 5/1/4: Knight to Osborn, 1 June 1889.

34 Op.cit., 27 March 1889.

35 Natal Archives, Resident Magistrate, Lower Mfolozi, Criminal Record Book, 2/7/1, case 27.

Qulusi

SEKETWAYO

Mvunyane

Ncome

Telezini

Nquthu Hill

Isandlwana

Nondweni

Rorke's Drift   Sobexe

SIHAYO

Isipezi

MATSHANA KA SITSHA-KUZA

Mzinyathi

MATSHANA KA MONDISA

Mangeni

Sketch map of the Nquthu District c.1878
showing the areas of the Major Rulers

The Nquthu district, c. 1878

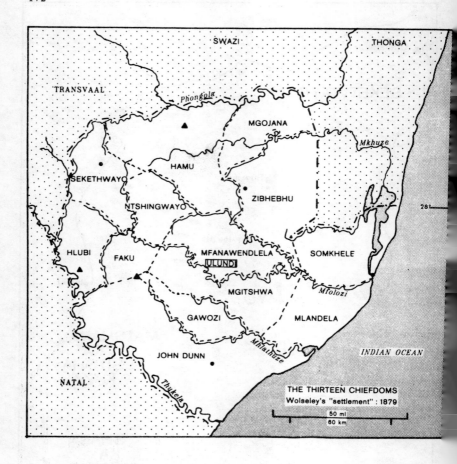

Wolseley's 'settlement', 1879

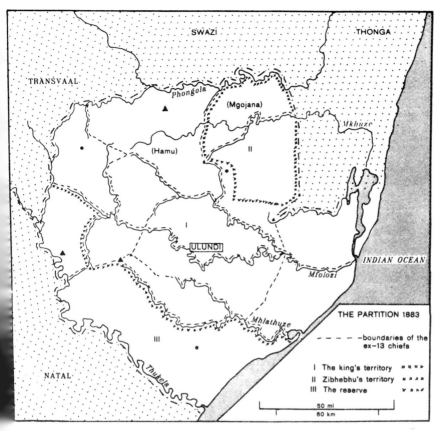

The partition of Zululand, 1883

Index